The World Less Travelled

To Paddy,

All the best in your onward travels!

Nick & Debs Procter

Nick Procter

First published 2019

Copyright © Nick Procter 2019

Nick Procter has asserted his right to be identified as the author of this Work in accordance with the Copyright, Designs and Patents Act 1988. So there.

Wanderlust Press

ISBN: 978-1-0914867-8-2

theworldlesstravelled.net

To Debs, Daniel and Amy

Acknowledgements:

Thanks to Debs, Daniel and Amy for affording me time to write this. Thanks to Jonathan Sargant and Helen Holmberg for proofreading and bringing the whole thing up to your high standards. Thanks to Simon Duke for publishing his first book in 2014 and making me realise such a thing was possible (he's written three: Out of Bounds, The Perfectionist and Suspect No. 1 and they're all excellent). Thanks to Debs again for challenging me to have a crack at a book and ushering me towards the subject matter. Thanks to my parents for giving me the travel bug as a child and sending me a copy of Bill Bryson's 'Neither Here Nor There' to read in that lonely flat in the middle of winter in deepest provincial France to cheer me up; it evidently had a stronger effect on me than you could have imagined. Thanks to everyone I travelled with for coming along with me and not minding me turning our escapades into a book, even though I didn't know I was going to at the time. Thanks to you for being here to read this.

Foreword:

I didn't mean to write this book. I didn't even mean to travel to most of the destinations. Between 2013 and 2017, life accidented me to Gibraltar, Finland, The Isle of Wight, Seattle, Denmark, The Vatican, Monaco and Wales. Some because of a change in job, some through obligation, some because it was time for a holiday and I couldn't think of anywhere better to go. It was only when all the travelling was pretty much done that I thought it might make an interesting book. I hope you enjoy reading it as much as I enjoyed the journey of writing it. May you go and write something yourself; everyone's got a book in them.

All internet links were present and correct at time of publication.

Two roads diverged in a wood, and I –

I took the one less travelled by,

And that has made all the difference.

- The Road Not Taken, Robert Frost

CONTENTS

1.	Luxembourg	8
2.	Gibraltar	32
3.	Finland	56
4.	Poole Harbour and the Isle of Wight	91
5.	Seattle	118
6.	Denmark	148
7.	The Vatican	185
8.	Monaco	210
9.	Wales	241
10.	Mystery Destination	277

1. Luxembourg

"Peculiar travel suggestions are dancing lessons from God."

Kurt Vonnegut

It was 1999. I was half the age I am now. Cocooned in an inglorious student house in a gritty part of a grimy city, I had applied to spend the third year of my French degree teaching in France and was now sitting on a chintzy junkshop sofa, holding the envelope which contained the letter that was to tell me where in France I would be spending the next year. I was nervous. Much to the disbelief of all my peers, I had acquired a girlfriend, and a serious one at that. But it was deeply inconvenient for us to fall in love at university; academic demands would separate us for a year: me to France and her to Germany.

In my application form to indicate where in France I fancied being posted to, I ignored the tropical sunshine of the French Caribbean and the glamour of the Côte d'Azur – both tickable options – and selected three counties in north-eastern France so I could be close to the France/Germany border for romantic getaways.

I opened the letter and discovered I was to become a resident of the 'Lorraine' region. More specifically, I was also informed that I was to live in a town called Hayange. I stared at the woodchip walls and wondered what a town called Hayange might be like. Possibly a farming community with a touch of the angelic about it. I had no idea. Remember, this was all happening in 1999; the internet didn't exist in student houses yet. I made a cup of tea and drank it until my housemate, coursemate and best friend Jon came home so he could open his identical envelope. Jon is one of these big-brained, preternaturally self-assured people who doesn't panic about anything because his natural calmness ensures that everything will be ok, which it of course then is. Jon had had no qualms about which part of France he would be dispatched to and we had both only realised that, in our self-absorbed teenagery kind of way, neither of us had consulted the other about which locations in France we both might tick on our application forms until we had put them in the post. Jon had selected the same three counties as me in north-eastern France, similarly in order to have easy access to as many countries as possible for mini-break purposes.

Jon ripped his envelope and announced that he would also be spending the year in the 'Lorraine' region, specifically in a town called Hagondange. This sounded very encouraging indeed. I told Jon my news, we smiled at each other in disbelief, and prepared for a year on the continent.

Jon and I both wanted to know more about Lorraine, Hayange and Hagondange as soon as possible, so I did the only thing I could do in the information vacuum that we now call pre-year-2000 life; I called my mum to tell her the news and ask what she knew about Lorraine that wasn't quiche-related. Naturally, my mother was pleased with the news that her one and only son would enjoy companionship with a close friend while marooned on a diffcrent landmass to her, but unsurprisingly she hadn't heard of either

Hayange or Hagondange and promised that afternoon to take a trip into the Kingston upon Thames branch of WH Smith where she enquired if they perchance had any Ordnance Survey maps in stock that covered eastern France. Unlikely as it seems, they did, and the following day the map was to be found trussed up in an envelope and lying where my doormat would have been if Jon's and my student budget could have stretched that far.

Jon and I spread the map across the patchy veneer of the perennially sticky dining table that lived at the side of our lounge and feasted our eyes on all the information available to us on Hayange and Hagondange prior to our arrival. We learned that Hayange and Hagondange lay between a decent-sized town called Thionville to the north and a city called Metz to the south – where all the fun was to be had, judging by its size, the fact it ended in a z and that Metz was also the name of a popular alcopop at the time. But to the north of Thionville was what intrigued me the most: Luxembourg. I let the concept roll around my mind a few times: Luxembourg. I was going to go and live on the edge of Luxembourg. I immediately and immensely looked forward to living on the edge of Luxembourg, more than any other aspect of my posting, for it was not just another country but a quirky little country – one of those tiny ones where no one ever goes and where I surely would not have gone had life not sent me there now. A country that, despite a recently acquired A Level in Geography, I had no mental image of; its exact size and shape I had no idea about. But I was hooked, I was gripped, I was ready to go, I was – and I don't think this is a sentence that has ever appeared in print before – drunk on Luxembourg.

**

Six months later, I had taken a Eurostar to Lille and changed trains for Hayange. As I approached the town, nose pressed against the glass, my eyes scanned the horizon to the north, hoping to catch a glimpse of Luxembourg as I made to pass the Duchy on the left hand side[1], but all the land looked the same to the horizon and I couldn't be sure I could tick Luxembourg off yet as a country I'd seen. Finally, the train slowed to a halt in Hayange, where half the town seemed to have come out to witness the event. I climbed the footbridge off the platform, a rucksack the size of a dustbin on my back and took in a view over the rooftops that made my heart sink.

Dominating the skyline was the doom-laden shape of what I dimly remembered from chemistry lessons at school to be not just one, but three blast furnaces: giant industrial towers, each the height of Big Ben, used for converting iron ore, limestone and coke into iron by way of heating it all up to volcanic temperatures until the molten iron ran off, ready for making into steel. One of the towers' chimneys was expelling an impressive amount of sulphurous smoke into the local atmosphere which I had made plans to breathe for much of the next year. I had effectively been posted to France's industrial heartland, a sort of gallic Middlesbrough. Was this what I had let myself in for? The guard blew his whistle and train doors slammed. For half a second I considered vaulting the parapet in the manner of a cowboy and riding the train's roof to somewhere more pretty, but the rucksack weighed me down and the crackling pantograph beneath put me off the idea. I trudged on,

---

[1] I fully intend for you to have that tune in your head all day now.

determined to make the best of what life was about to put in my way. I left the station, rounded a corner and saw my second arrestingly depressing sight of the day. Hayange was in a valley and over this valley ran a concrete motorway flyover some 100 metres high. I slapped my forehead. What was this place? How had the town planners let both iron furnaces and a motorway flyover loom over the same town? I carried on for no other reason than it was my only option, remembering to look left when crossing the street (to be run over when looking the wrong way crossing a foreign street is surely the dumbest way to die) and soon enough was in the town centre. There wasn't much that would be of use to me: A pet shop, a women's shoe boutique, a large Catholic church that played Beethoven's *Ode To Joy* on the hour but had one bell-note missing, a small shopping mall made out of concrete, a men's clothes shop that sold suits without collars but with stencils of Chinese dragons where the lapels were meant to be, a shop for old people to buy cushioned chairs in and a bus stop on which someone had scrawled a threateningly tribal "CETTE VILLE EST A NOUS – UCKANGE" and someone else had encouragingly – for the only Englishman in town - scratched "VIVE BECKHAM". I took a taxi to the school where I would be teaching and, as the driver hurled the car around blind bends on the wrong side of the road in the way the French are wont to do, asked the driver about the town. He explained with Gallic shrugs how the town was on its knees as the entire local economy depended on the steel factory which was barely profitable nowadays and if they shut down then the town would lose its soul. I gave him the tip I felt he needed and disembarked ready to see the place and perhaps a few places nearby too.

But first, I had a job to do. I was required to teach English to French schoolchildren; a duty that sounds vanilla enough until I discovered that this was no ordinary school; this was a harsh, blue-collar technical college, educating children up to the age of 23, which was notably older than I was. Not only that, but this school was on the border of four countries - France, Belgium, Germany and Luxembourg - none of which spoke English. Somehow, I divined that learning English was not going to be high on the list of academic priorities of these schoolchildren – that is assuming anything academic had made it onto their list of priorities at all.

I gulped going into my first lesson, in which the teacher, the suspiciously Italian-sounding Monsieur Maggi, introduced me to the class (who spent the rest of the year calling me "Andrew" because that's what the previous two English teaching assistants had both been named) explaining somewhat unconvincingly that I spoke no French at all (an assertion that was certain either to fail the test of time or significantly reduce my ability to control a classroom) but that I knew everything about English that there was to know on account of my actually being English, such as knowing that "used to" was always followed by an infinitive (I had never thought about it like that). He asked the class to ask me questions and, once I had confirmed that I indeed did not know David Beckham, the Queen, or one student's penfriend in Bristol, Monsieur Maggi asked me in front of all the students what the English call one of those indoor cranes found in engineering workshops that consists of a high, horizontal girder that can be wheeled the length of a shop floor and has a chain hanging from it on a pulley. I had absolutely no idea. "A rolling crane?" I offered, as though guessing in a pub quiz. "A rolling crane, everyone, write it down! He's English remember, he knows,"[2] shouted Monsieur Maggi with authority. I faked a smile and nodded with the illusion of authority that all teachers have learned to develop.

**

It was a few weeks before Jon and I made it to Luxembourg. Remember, this was the 1990s; neither of us had mobile phones, and armed only with each other's addresses, our correspondence had had to be by letter initially – a laughably archaic way of communicating even a couple of years later. After a few 'Dear Jon' letters and bus rides to the *France Telecom* shop in Metz, we had both managed to acquire wall-mounted telephones, successfully plug their curly wires into activated phone lines, and write to each other to inform the other one of our new phone number; there was no other way to make the first phonecall happen. In our first conversation, we made a plan for Jon to climb aboard the second carriage of the 11.02 to Luxembourg at Hagondange on Saturday morning; I'd board the same carriage at Thionville at 11.17, thus enabling the two of us to cross the border together and step off onto foreign soil for the adventure to begin. But it didn't quite work out like that.

I presented myself at Thionville station as planned to observe the arrival of a small train with LUXEMBOURG written on it (a sight few are privileged to see), but when I climbed aboard the second car, Jon wasn't there. I walked

---

[2] I'd only find out the answer 18 years later, happily whilst in one of the destinations in the second half of this book, so keep reading and I'll tell you the answer there.

the length of the carriage, checking every face in every seat to confirm his absence. What to do? Should I stay on or get off? I thought quickly: if Jon was late, he'd be on the next train an hour later. If he was ill or worse, he wouldn't be coming at all. If I got off, I would spend a cold November hour shuffling my feet on a windswept platform in a small town in provincial northern France. If I stayed on, I'd spend that hour strolling through the busy streets of a European capital city. I took a seat, the doors closed, and I was off, irrevocably bound for Luxembourg.

The excitement turned to ennui as I settled into my journey, before some low-level tension entered the carriage in the form of a ticket inspector. They always seem to get into a bit of drama with someone in the carriage during their walkthrough and I opened half an ear and half an eye to see who it would be. He proceeded along the aisle with repetitive efficiency and minimal courtesy until it was my turn. I offered my ticket with a nonchalant confidence, but the length of time he took to study my ticket put me on edge.

"Monsieur, vous n'avez pas composté votre billet, et nous sommes dans une période bleue."

My brain translated each word as they came. "You haven't composted your ticket and you are in a blue period." I repeated the words to myself under his glare, understanding every word but not the sentence. Was there an allotment on the train? Was I going through a Picasso-like experimental phase? I asked my judge, jury and executioner to explain more clearly what he meant and it was outlined to me that before boarding a train in France, I was required to insert my ticket into an orange punching machine on the platform which stamps an inky smudge onto the corner of the ticket, illegibly denoting the date and time I was using it, therefore rendering it unusable for any other trips. The verb for doing this was 'composter', and I hadn't composté-d it, because I didn't know I needed to. Not only that, but French train timetables are separated into semi-randomly assigned peak and off-peak periods (blue period and white period) and if you tried to use an off-peak ticket in peak period, you'd be in trouble, which I now was. Double trouble. Foolishly, I decided to not to act like a dumb tourist who didn't know how any of this worked, but – having got an A in my French oral at A Level – chose instead to engage in a debate in a foreign language, something I have never tried to do since and I urge you never to have a go at, no matter how proficient your language skills are. Even if you don't speak French, I think you can get the gist of the following conversation:

"Mais c'est toi[3] qui compostes mon billet?"

"Non, monsieur. Vous compostez le billet à la gare, je vérifie que vous avez bien composté le billet."

"Mais peux-tu compostes le billet maintenant? J'utilise le billet maintenant, c'est évident."

"Vous êtes obligé de me payer une pénalité de 200 Francs monsieur pour ne pas avoir composté le billet, et une pénalité de 300 Francs pour avoir utilisé votre billet de période blanche dans une période bleue."

A fine of 500 Francs. That was £50. I was being paid £500 per month. 10% of my monthly income for accidentally buying the wrong train ticket on my first ever train journey in a foreign country seemed a touch unjust to me. I travelled the rest of the journey under a black cloud.

---

[3] I know, I should have used 'vous' here. It didn't help my plea.

But on arriving, I bounded from the train with a spring in my step, and lifted my spirits by the act of planting my foot on a new country's soil. I stopped for a moment and took a deep breath of the Luxembourgish air and then immediately wondered what to do next about Jon. Should I jettison him and have the day out I'd planned? Should I sit on the platform and wait for him to arrive? Neither felt like the right answer, so I decided I'd give myself an hour to wander the streets of Luxembourg and see what I could see but without clapping eyes on anything too remarkable, before returning for the next train in the hope that Jon would disembark it. I didn't know what I'd do if he didn't.

There was plenty to see, there is in any new foreign city. There is something intoxicating about that first hour upon arrival anywhere abroad, and I walked along with my head up, taking in the architecture, the advertising, the street furniture, the car number-plate formats, the chit-chat of fellow pedestrians, the headlines on the newsstands, the road markings, the vegetation, the Luxembourgish version of the walk/don't walk signs – everything there was to be seen. The poles to which the traffic signs were attached were hooped in orange and white, like handball goalposts. I didn't know why but I deeply adored that in particular – such a wacky improvement on the dismal grey I'd seen everywhere else. I turned round and admired Luxembourg's train station; it's a shame if you've never seen it because whilst not large (nothing in Luxembourg is) it was one of the most handsome train stations I'd ever seen; it could have passed itself off as a miniature cathedral if it tried. Constructed in light grey stone, a tall stained glass window overlooked the plaza in front, next to which was a slim and pointy clock tower with an elegantly detailed turret in that pale green roofing material that Parisian garret flats are bedecked with. There was even a little balcony and a lookout arch. I haven't the foggiest why it was built that way, but if it was for aesthetic purposes only then that was good enough for me because I happily wondered at it for several minutes. The station's main roof was pitched at that slightly steeper angle that Germanic roofs are, punctured every ten feet or so by a little round dormer window with its own roof jutting out from the main slope. It must have been fiendishly complicated to construct, but I was pleased that the Luxembourgish, modest as they were in the world's pecking order, had allowed for beauty in this way. It wasn't the biggest train station in the world, but it was theirs and they were proud of it.

After about thirty minutes of idling, I felt that there really wasn't much worth seeing in Luxembourg when deliberately trying to avoid seeing any sights. I repaired to a café and scanned the menu for something unusual, ordering a mango juice for the simple reason that it was the only time (before or since) that I'd seen mango juice on a café's menu and even 20 years later, I hold the view that that the mellifluous mango is the best-tasting fruit by some distance. When I approached the station, Jon was there, sheepishly beaming at me from afar. We both endured a brief awkward silence, maintaining eye contact until we were near enough to be in earshot for each other. He cascaded apologies in the manner of any well brought up young man from deepest Surrey. "So sorry about that, I really am. I've been taking the train the other way to Metz in weekday evenings a lot and I thought I'd got the walk to the station down to a fine art at exactly 11 minutes. So I left 15 minutes before the departure time, but didn't account for the increased Saturday morning footfall so it took me 13 minutes today and then there was a queue at the ticket booth and then I had to cross the tracks to the other platform which means I missed the train and I'm late and I'm frightfully sorry. Is there anything left of Luxembourg to see, or is 60 minutes all you need?"

Jon and I stretched our legs in the general direction of the city centre and after ten minutes along the main drag from the station, we happened upon something quite unexpected. Luxembourg must be the only city in the world, certainly the only capital city, to contain a deep ravine. Who knew this was there? We stood on the south side and looked to the northern edge, where the twin spires of the Notre-Dame cathedral stood to attention, with the kind of valley you might find in England's Lake District separating us from it. This was a significant geographical feature – not a groove in the landscape that required a dip in the road, but a serious drop of surely 150 feet or more to the ant-like people milling about at the bottom. To traverse the valley, we were required to cross the Pont Adolphe, one of the world's great single stone arch bridges. The central span at 85 metres was an audacious endeavour for the time – upon completion it was the largest stone arch bridge in existence. It was built in 1900 but pleasingly let buses and lorries and other such heavy vehicles that could not have been envisaged 100 years ago cross it without so much as a thought. Little did we know as we strolled across it that earlier in the decade the Luxembourgish government had discovered extensive signs of damage to both the steel and stonework, necessitating significant repairs, and three years after our visit, had installed 258 steel bars to reinforce the superstructure. I have no doubt that the bridge was as safe as anywhere to be on that day but it is hard not to be disconcerted now to discover it was near the end of its natural life when it took my load all that way up from the ground. But this is not to take anything away from it; if you like your bridges, the Pont Adolphe is about as impressive as you can get without venturing into the territory of massive world-famous Golden Gate-esque bridges. I'd twin it with the Clifton Suspension Bridge in Bristol if I could.

Jon and I had a curious debate about this bridge. I inadvertently opened the discussion by venturing that giant bridges like this, and similarly challenging engineering projects such as aeroplanes and skyscrapers, represented the pinnacle of human achievement to a point where it frankly bordered on the miraculous. How could any group of humans design a bridge out of rock to span a deep and wide ravine with enough confidence to allow royalty and plebs like us to pass over it without as much as a second thought? Was this bridge not as close to a miracle as man can create?

Jon is a genius. And that isn't a term I use lightly, for Jon is certainly the most intelligent person I've ever had a conversation with. In his A-Levels, he took English, French, and (of course) Maths, and Further Maths too, just for fun. Having obtained a string of As, he chose to shun the Oxbridge life he could have cruised through and selected instead a more grounded university where he could study an absurdly niche course: English with European Literature. I don't think that in the four years I spent in his presence I ever really saw him academically break sweat and it was no surprise to see him be awarded a First class degree and he never really expected anything less. When Jon speaks up with an argument that goes against intuition, I listen. "This bridge is all very well, but why are we crossing it?" I didn't know where Jon was going with this but felt sure he had a counterpoint lined up to whatever answer I gave. I did a politician's trick and dodged the question "It doesn't matter. The fact is that we're hanging in mid-air about 150 feet up and someone's built an arch out of stone that's 85 metres across and it's taking our weight and the weight of all this shuddering traffic. It doesn't matter what's over there, what matters is that we're here." I was quite pleased with my answer. "But what does this bridge matter if there's nothing on the other side? Where is this a bridge to? Science can get us to the other side, but we only want to get to the other side because art is there. Look at the architecture, look at the theatre and the art gallery we're hypothetically going to. What about the ideas you're going to be exposed to on the other side of the bridge? You're going to hear different perspectives, you're going to see a different way of doing things. That's why you wanted to come to Luxembourg, isn't it? And that's what gives this bridge its value."

It's taken me nearly two decades to realise it, but Jon's right.

After crossing the Pont Adolphe, we spent about an hour popping into the cathedral and pacing around Luxembourg city centre, which is no larger than you'd expect a city centre one-tenth the size of Birmingham to be. It had a few shops selling bling to rich bankers and a string of clothes shops. I had a strange impulse there and then to go into a shop and buy a jumper because more than anything I wanted to meet people back in England and have them say to me "That's a nice jumper, where did you get it from?" And I could twinkle my eyes and reply with enigmatic honesty "Luxembourg." I found a green woolly v-neck in H&M and bought it and wore it with pride for a few years, until I realised that H&M basically stock exactly the same thing in all of their stores all around the world. I was in New York on Fifth Avenue nine years later and noticed that half the merchandise was identical to the contents of my local H&M back in the UK where I'd been a few days previously buying a few last minute bits and pieces. A couple of years after that I was in an H&M in Germany with a friend where he saw a shirt he quite liked and so, with his birthday coming up, sent a photo message of it to his wife, comfortable in the knowledge that she'd be able to pick it up in their local town centre H&M in provincial England before he got home. She could and she did.

We stopped for lunch and suffered the agonising students' choice when eating out, which was to eat somewhere that wasn't expensive but also wasn't grotty. The thought of making our first Luxembourgish meal a McDonald's was too much to bear, but we didn't want cutlery, tablecloths, waiter service and a meal that cost the same as the penalty fare I'd just given the ticket inspector on the train, so we found a compromise, which of course means a solution that made neither of us happy. We dined in a *Quick*. *Quick* is BeNeFraLux's attempt at McDonald's and this suited our desire for local cuisine on a budget. But it didn't satisfy. Firstly, we were confronted by a menu that tried to sound like its writers had tried to translate the spirit of a McDonald's menu into French. Burgers were thus monikered: 'Le Géant, Le Long Chicken, Le Suprême Cheese, Le Quick'n Toast' (yes, that apostrophe before the n is where Quick put it, not me). I forget now what I ordered, but I do remember that the burger in question was square-shaped, for reasons not explained at the time or since. Jon and I worked our way through our little scuttles of fries and wondered what to do next on the grounds that we had, in essence, already ticked Luxembourg's sights off. Jon quite liked the idea of descending into the valley below the Pont Adolphe, but that somehow didn't seem to have the entertainment factor, nor would it divert us for more than about ten minutes. Then there was a sudden epiphany when I suggested we go to the Tourist Office and ask them what we could do. This is what Tourist Offices are for, after all.

Having established that we were day-trippers without a car who had already noticed the cathedral and Pont Adolphe, the gentleman in the tourist office furrowed his brow and provided us with a little map displaying a highlighted walking route which would take in everywhere worth seeing and quite a lot of other places that weren't. Devoid of other options, this didn't sound like such a bad way to spend the next couple of hours, even if it was the only thing to do in urban Luxembourg out of season.

I think this walk was perhaps the first routed walk I had ever done in my adult life for no reason other than the pleasure of walking. I have done many walks since, but without doubt the Luxembourg walk is one of *the* most rewarding and refreshing walks I've ever undertaken, and I'd like to take you there now.

For a start, the beginning of the walk is accessed by descending by a lift whose shaft is bored through the bedrock in the valley-side. That one fact alone made the adventurous part of my brain prick up. This lift we would ride in had been liberated from its customary indoor setting and shown the world. Its doors gave onto the street and after burrowing down 50 or so metres through the hillside to the valley floor, the rear doors surprised us by parting, revealing a peaceful new world into which we emerged, city centre bustle replaced with birdsong as we blinked and rotated our maps, trying to work out where we were. We were in Grund, which we supposed might just mean 'ground', on the floor of a deep valley fortified with a wall the height of a decent skyscraper, whose presence immediately next to and above us startled us both. We took a right out of the lift to proceed to the confluence of the canalised, almost industrial Pétrusse river and the broad and meandering Alzette, completing its lazy loop through the secret subterranean world of Europe's most unassuming capital. Disappointingly, the route didn't continue to hug the water (for the best bit of any walk is always the bit by the river) but jerked to the right, as though something had jogged the routeplanner's elbow, and we found ourselves in the belly of the valley making our way towards the Pont Adolphe. There is something inexpressibly wonderful about strolling along a valley floor with both sides stretching up above a great many metres either side of you. And this valley was a pleasing contrast to all the other valleys I had seen – most valleys have the town in the valley floor with the rural life on the hilltops. This one had the greenery at the base and was crowned with bustling civilisation. I liked the fact that it was the wrong way round.

We passed underneath the Pont Adolphe, which piqued Jon's interest to the point that he spent a good five minutes craning his neck and considering load-bearing calculations, or whatever it is people with an A in A-Level Further Maths do for fun. Meanwhile I consulted the map and reasoned that following the route religiously would take us back into the city centre and right past the Quick we'd just eaten in, which frankly didn't sound adventurous at all, so I resolved that, rather than retrace our steps, cross to the southern side of the valley in the hope of seeing something different before making our way back along the Pétrusse to do a loop at the end of the walk that would, the map suggested, present us with a spiky church, a passage called the March-aux-Poissons[4], a rail bridge consisting of many tall stone arches in a row like an aqueduct and what looked to be an adventurously steep climb to some grand-looking buildings in the heart of the city. I communicated this idea to Jon by way of walking off in the direction I proposed to take and waiting for the realisation to dawn on him that he was suddenly alone and gazing, trance-like, at the underside of a large bridge in a foreign country.

It was on the way back to the Alzette that we noticed a small brass plaque on the door of a cottage which informed us that this building was Luxembourg's Ministry of Culture. I don't mean to belittle the place; Luxembourg punches above its weight in many ways, but the idea that a developed country's entire cultural representation could be housed in, well, a house, struck us as fetchingly comic. Maybe the Minister of Culture's office was in what was once the master bedroom, with perhaps a tiny call centre set up around the dining table and a little lounge where the handful of employees usually broke for coffee, biscuits, and in spring, prayer that they would not be lumbered with the burden of organising next year's Eurovision Song Contest?

The Alzette's path through Grund is one of the most endearing northern-European vistas I think possible. A tidy patchwork of little multicoloured homes – yellow, salmon, duck-egg blue, each with steep slate roofs and balanced on the edge of the riverbank with Velux windows that gazed across the river. Upstaging the homes was the backdrop of the city's fortifications. Here mighty stone walls, there a ruined abbey. The Alzette dropped a level by way of one of those pleasing weirs that run diagonally across the river,

---

[4] A fish market/walk? In landlocked Luxembourg?

dispensing the water into its next section with the consequent benefit of increased babble volume, something I think we could all do with a little more of in life. It was a perfect scene and was of course all over far too quickly as we climbed sharply back to the top of the valley where we found ourselves wandering around in an old part of the town where more dinky government buildings announced themselves as charming little Ministries of Whatever to us. An information board told me that where I was standing now was the Bock Promontory and was chosen by Luxembourg's first ruler to be the location of his first fortress and therefore the cradle of the city. The imposing ramparts did their job until 1443 when the Burgundians took the city by surprise, making Luxembourg strategically important on the European chessboard. Over the next 400 years, the best military engineers of the Burgundians, the French, the Spanish, the Austrians and the Germanic Confederation all worked together (the board did not tell me why or how) to transform the city into "one of the mightiest encampments in the world, the 'Gibraltar of the North'". Gibraltar, as militarily strategic a high point as the world can offer, was well known for its might. I wondered what sort of army Luxembourg was equipped with.

I was to get my answer seconds later as Jon and I stumbled upon a square where a crowd had arranged itself around a young brunette in her twenties wearing fatigues, jackboots, a white sash, an asymmetric beret and, most saliently, a machine gun strapped across her chest. She was statuesque next to her charcoal pillbox in the drizzle and we deduced that this was the Changing of the Guard. And she was the guard. Singular. The Guard of Luxembourg. This was the country's ceremonial show of military strength and somehow I was a little under-awed. If her machine gun weren't loaded and I were the combative type, I reckon I could have overthrown the country and proclaimed myself Duke by nightfall. As it was, I rather liked to pretend that behind all that uniform her name was Shazzer and whenever she wasn't on duty she'd don giant hooped earrings and lie tummy-down on her bunk, smoking and reading a trashy magazine while idly gossiping on the phone to her best friend and waiting for it to be her turn again to come outside and be on duty. Anyway, with very little ceremony, Shazzer proceeded to stomp around in the ridiculous tradition of European ceremonial marching, raising one foot high and on the other turning through 90 degrees on the spot in a manner not seen since the heyday of John Cleese. We stared while Shazzer patrolled up and down, snapped her heels together, grabbed her rifle butt, let it go, then grabbed it again, stamped on the pavement, turned round three-quarters of a turn, marched on the spot, flicked a crisp salute – it was as though she were a computer game soldier under the command of a toddler randomly hammering at the buttons. The two of us mused how benign a nation must be for it to be guarded by just one soldier, and – and this was last century, remember – a female soldier at that.

Well, after a long walk culminating in an arduous climb up a great height, there is only one thing students can do to refresh themselves and that is find a bar. Jon found a typically continental beer dispensary - a newsagent with large glass window in a steel frame, behind which was a counter selling stamps and postcards at the front and cigarettes and beer at the back, where we sat down and ordered goblets of something blond, foamy and Belgian. A TV screen in the corner doled out some local news and Jon – never a man to breach etiquette – was totally distracted from my gripping conversation by the screen. I hauled Jon back into the conversation by pausing and staring at the same time, at which point Jon apologised for his inattention and revealed a fact about Luxembourg that even now I still struggle to believe. Jon explained that the TV screen was showing the news (what daily national news is there in Luxembourg?) and that curiously, the newsreaders were presenting in Luxembourgish, but the interviewees in the studio and on reports quite happily talked in French or German, and there was no dubbing or subtitling at all. We know that in many small western European countries children are brought up to be bilingual in English as well as their mother tongue, but trilingual? And none of those languages being English? So Jon decided to crack out his schoolboy German when it was time to get the next round of drinks, resulting in him ordering fizzy water instead of beer for me and Fanta for himself when what he actually wanted was Appletise, which he gallantly admitted was a poor show. I sipped my drink nonetheless and decided I liked what I had seen that day.

**

Well, that was my first trip to Luxembourg. But the second trip gave me the opportunity to see Luxembourg the country. It was a couple of months later - Jon's parents had come to check on him and, I was thrilled to find out, invited me to spend the day out with them, exploring rural Luxembourg. I hadn't had "visit rural Luxembourg" on my bucket list and so wasn't sure of my desire to do so, but you can never judge a nation by its capital, so I was happy to climb into their car and spend the day gazing out of the window.

The day's destination was a town near the northern border named Esch-sur-Sûre which boasted a castle and a population of just 314, which draws into question a) the legitimacy of the endeavour of constructing a castle in the first place and b) why we were bothering going to visit the village. Luxembourg abounds in castles; it has well over 100, which is a hilariously high number when you think how many castles there are within a 30-minute drive of wherever you are sitting now. Holidaying in Luxembourg is often described as ABC tourism, with A standing for 'another' and C for 'castle'. Esch-sur-Sûre's castle is not much more than an abandoned upright cuboid with tufts of wild grass sprouting from its neglected orifices. I discovered there that the river Sûre is dammed just above the village, creating a snaking reservoir which was built in the 1960s to provide drinking water for everyone in the land. So if you didn't want to overthrow the nation by engaging in hand-to-hand combat with Shazzer, you could easily access the country's water supply and poison it, which probably explains why a castle was built where just 314 people lived. Anyway, next to the castle was a car park containing a Talbot Tagora (a rare find that made Jon give it a walkaround and take a photo) and a gift shop where I purchased a teddy bear for the sole reason that I wanted to name him Benny Lux. Jon's parents acquired a bottle of cherry brandy that Jon tells me to this day still sits in their drinks cabinet unopened. Maybe I'll reunite Benny Lux with it one day so he can have a sip.

Unable to find anything else to do in Esch-sur-Sûre, we piled back into the car and headed east to Schengen, a place you might have heard of, but you're not sure why. Schengen is an anonymous village in the South-easternmost point of Luxembourg on the banks of the River Moselle that shot to fame in 1985 when various political bigwigs from Belgium, France, Luxembourg, Netherlands and West Germany gathered to sign an agreement to gradually loosen border controls within the European Union, which in 1990 was stealthily supplemented by the Schengen Convention that enabled the complete abolition of border controls altogether. So it's thanks to Schengen that you have (at the time of writing!) a blue channel at Heathrow airport that you can wheel your drugs through without fear of reproach. Schengen was strategically chosen as the location for the signing of the agreement because it's a tripoint; an interesting if ubiquitous geographical feature in that three countries (France, Luxembourg and Germany) meet here and it was perhaps symbolic to pick a place where big and little countries connect. The European Union has been good to Luxembourg. The 21st century has meant that Luxembourg has become a reputable tax haven, with companies like Vodafone and Amazon setting up offices there and channelling as much international business as possible through what is, in a technical sense, a piece of paper in somebody's drawer, at the expense of tax receipts in the countries where the physical trade is actually taking place. This has made Luxembourg an appealing place for multinationals to do business and consequently net migration has skyrocketed, something that couldn't have happened if the Schengen Agreement hadn't been signed. Looking at the figures from the United Nations Population Division (the things I do for you, dear reader), Luxembourg gained an extra 14 people per 1000 in the period from 2000 to 2015, which may not sound like much, but compared to the UK's figure of 3 per 1000 in the period containing the influx of eastern European nationals following the European

Union enlargement of 2004, it is enormous. Luxembourg's size is such that plenty of Luxembourg's workers commute in from surrounding countries: a report from STATEC published in *Luxemburger Wort* (March 15th, 2013) that I have just been reading for your pleasure, informs me that cross-border workers account for 44% of Luxembourg's labour, making it second only to (yes you've guessed it) Qatar in the International Monetary Fund's 2015 measurement of GDP per capita, so these 44% contribute to Luxembourg's GDP without Luxembourg having to spend any of it in the form of healthcare or education or a larger Ministry of Culture building. Luxembourg has approximately three times as many people in it on a Tuesday lunchtime as it does on a Saturday morning. The country is a success, but its success does seem to have a fair bit of hot air in it, to say the least.

Speaking of hot air, a footnote on Hayange's blast furnaces: They gave up the ghost in 2012. The plant (technically in neighbouring Florange, if you're googling it) was a political hot potato for a while, attracting international headlines after being mothballed in the aftermath of the 2008 recession as they symbolised France's industrial decline in an increasingly competitive world. The site was closed in 2013.

And it's 2013 where we'll start our next chapter. After my year on the Luxembourg border ended, my girlfriend and I had successfully managed to remain together throughout our year in separate countries and when we got back, I proposed. We married shortly after graduating and Jon was the best man. By 2013, we had two children.

2. Gibraltar

"How do you make God laugh? Tell Him your plans."

Anon

I'm sorry for such a long gap between chapters 1 and 2, I really am. I can only offer the explanation that there actually was a 13-year gap in real life, and if you are giving up what little spare time you have to read this, then the least I can do is be honest with you. I did lots of travelling in that time – as far away as Australia and as exciting as New York, but none of those trips quite had the small and quirky, pray-why-did-you-go-there factor of Luxembourg, Gibraltar, or indeed any of the other places you will read about in the oncoming pages. Like Luxembourg, I didn't mean to travel to Gibraltar either. And the trip didn't turn out to be quite what I was expecting. Indulge me in a little context.

On New Year's Eve 2012, Mrs Procter (or Debs, to give her her proper title) and I were reflecting over a glass of wine how the year had been marked both by the cost of my working a great many more hours than normal in the office, and also the financial benefit of a small promotion that the fruits of all that overtime had given rise to. Living in a country where it is accepted as immutable fact that monthly childcare costs are higher than the average mortgage, the holidays of the previous few years had been thin affairs: We'd driven an hour down a motorway and camped in the rain for a week with a toddler (while my dear wife was six months pregnant to boot), we'd taken budget flights that had cost less than the clothes we were flying in to visit friends who had emigrated to conveniently sunny locations and had spare bedrooms, and one year, we'd simply not taken a holiday at all. As 2013 dawned, we decided that we were going to do a 'proper' holiday, finally, and having never done the southern Spain holiday that pretty much everyone else in Europe had, this was all the justification we needed to go. It wasn't the cheapest holiday we'd ever taken, but after a year spent working hard and a promotion earned, the holiday had been earned and paid for.

Well, that was in January. In May, my employer's customer decided they no longer wished to use our service which had worked so well for them for so long, and consequently jobs servicing this particular customer could no longer be guaranteed. The contract was up in the autumn. The second half of summer was clearly going to be an uncertain time; interviews for my next job in the company would happen then and August would be crunch time with regards to finding out whether I'd still got a job or not. But the holiday had been booked and paid for and would go ahead in August, regardless.

**

It was only a week or so before setting off for the Costa del Sol that Debs and I became aware of how close to Gibraltar we would be staying. We weren't in any sense aware of its proximity to our chosen destination and as time sped up in the immediate days before departure, the idea of a trip to Gibraltar took on an almost romantic notion and it became impossible to think that we could spend a week so close to Gibraltar and not see it.

One of my favourite moments in travel is when you suddenly clap eyes on a desired landmark. Be it the Sydney Harbour Bridge, the Empire State Building or the Eiffel Tower – there is something immensely pleasant about a world-famous sight suddenly and unmistakeably filling your field of vision with such triumph that you can almost hear it. The approach to the Rock of Gibraltar is perhaps the most gradual version of this I have ever had the pleasure of encountering. As we cruised along the coastal motorway, the Rock appeared at first like a witch's hat on the horizon before gradually filling the windscreen over the next hour until it dominated the towns at its base, practically throwing the car into shade. Gibraltar is a mountain in the sea, connected to the mainland by a narrow strip of sand. It's almost impossible to articulate how incongruous the Rock of Gibraltar is until you see it. If you try to imagine standing on your favourite beach and visualizing a range of world-famous skyscrapers standing in the sea half a mile out then you have an idea of what an unusual sight you have.

Crossing the border at its base wasn't necessarily going to be as straightforward as we'd hoped. You may remember that in the summer of 2013, Gibraltar's tensions with Spain suddenly hit the headlines. Gibraltar had deposited 200 tons of concrete onto a patch of sea floor that Spanish scallop fishermen liked to dredge in, turning into action the highly politically-charged assertion that it would one day create an artificial marine reef for the benefit of Gibraltarian fishermen, with the doubtless intended consequence that it would kill all the scallops on the sea bed that the Spanish were planning to dredge. The Spanish government responded by running a go-slow at border checks, obliging Gibraltar's tourists and residents to wait for six hours in 40° heat for no other reason than it pleased Spain to make them do this. Our children were aged five and one and we didn't think they'd really enjoy this as a day out. So we followed the tourist guidebook's advice to ransom our car for €40 for the day in one of the capacious underground multi-storey carparks in border town La Linea and crossed on foot.

We walked to the border with a degree of trepidation, unsure how we would entertain the children and ourselves if oversized queues presented themselves at the barriers, signalling that Gibraltar was, in effect, closed. The approach to the border was through a sheltered parade of multicultural streetfood restaurants, one of which was memorably named "Last Sausage Before Africa" and staffed by Moroccans, which was the most Moorish thing about their food, judging by the backlit photos on display[5]. For 750 years, Gibraltar actually was Moorish (original name "Jebel Tariq", meaning Mount Tariq), then for the next 240 years, Spanish. Then one day in 1700, the heirless King Charles II of Spain died, which triggered a devilishly complicated series of interlocking diplomatic disputes, culminating in the War of Spanish Succession which would determine which of France, the Netherlands, Austria, and Great Britain would own which bits of Spain. Madrid ceded Gibraltar to Britain through the 1713 Utrecht Treaty (according to Britain at least, but I'm sure Spanish

---

[5] Moorish/moreish. No?

historians would have a different view, please contact me if you fully understand how all this worked).

Anyway, under Gibraltar's 1964 constitution, its residents get to decide which country has sovereignty over them, and in two referenda since then have both times voted to remain British, most recently in 2002 when, asked whether they wanted to accept shared sovereignty with Spain, the 'No' vote sneaked home with a 99% to 1% margin. Gibraltar is Britain's smallest Overseas Territory; as much a part of Britain as central London but with much less cloud and rain and a much lower chance of bumping into Piers Morgan too. Its residents have British passports and can vote in European elections as a constituency in South West England, though they have their own healthcare system and parliament, but decisions on foreign policy and defence are left to Westminster which is good because Gibraltar wouldn't stand a chance in a fistfight with Spain.

Upon reaching the border, Debs and I were pleased to discover that there were no pedestrian queues at the border that day, but also strangely disappointed as we weren't to have a front seat on the major news story of the week. Our passports were glanced at by a guard in a booth who was more bored-er than border and stepping out of the passport control booth, suddenly we were back in Britain; we were immediately greeted by a Waitrose, which I like to think outbid Marks & Spencer for such a high profile spot that needed to scream Britishness.

Buses ran from the border to the town centre and as our bus drew up (it was a number 1 bus; there are only nine bus routes, numbered 1-9) we were quietly pleased to find it was an open-topped bus. This was how we wanted to travel, and the children who were at that sweet preschool age where top-deck bus travel is the most fantastic thing in the world, bounced excitedly at not only being on the top deck, but outside too – I'm not sure their tiny little soft heads could cope with the concept of being upstairs *and* outside at the same time. The bus set off, and – in a sentence you have never read before and will never read again - our double-decker bus crossed the runway. Yes, the runway. Gibraltar has an airport, and not just a light-aircraft strip of tarmac for tiny pleasure planes, but a properly large commercial operation, taking fully-fledged jet-powered Boeings and Airbuses from Heathrow and Gatwick on the isthmus linking the foot of the mountain to mainland Spain.

Gibraltar's airport is the most dangerous airport in the world to fly into. You may recall that back in the 1990s, Hong Kong's airport had a famously scary approach. If I'm remembering everything correctly (and I appreciate my memory on this topic has been mainly fed by watching episodes of *The Krypton Factor*), pilots were required to at one point twist their aircraft's wings into a vertical position to pass between tower blocks before limboing under a washing line strung between two apartment blocks until the plane was low enough to see a giant sign in the middle of a park saying TURN RIGHT NOW, at which point the captain would yank his control column with all his might to line the aircraft up with the runway, on which he would touch down six seconds later, blood leaking from all the passengers' ears. That airport is now closed for being too scary and Gibraltar is now the most feared place to land a jet plane. On this narrow north-south sand strip, the runway has been built east-west onto a ribbon of reclaimed land that juts out into the busy, working harbour. The runway measures just 1,700 metres long (Heathrow's main runway is 4,000 metres), and if that isn't enough of a challenge, the runway has a level-crossing on it too (surely the only one in the world), with flimsy barriers being the only thing preventing a van driver with an agenda crashing through or an off-course Airbus ploughing into an open-topped bus full of tourists. There are densely populated towns to either side and a 400 metre tall wall of rock immediately next to the runway's apron, which funnels a bracing crosswind across the touchdown point. When the wind's not blowing across the rock but onto it, the gusting updraft creates sudden thick fog known as the Levanter which has a knack of completely ruining visibility at a moment's notice. This happened to a Monarch pilot in 2002; upon aborting the landing and swinging the plane around for another go, he in his shock, neglected to remember the need to regain altitude and so passed over Gibraltar at a squeamishly low 600 metres, which was perplexing for those on board because the Rock is 400 metres high and pilots aren't meant to miss mountains by a distance that the plane can cover in a quarter of a second. The Captain had a lot of paperwork to fill in that evening.

Our bus meandered its way through the hot middle of the day and we gazed at the Gibraltarian way of life. Apartment blocks gleamed in the bright sunshine, their shared swimming pools in full and happy use. Giant succulent plants in tubs dotted the pavements, palm trees grew everywhere we looked as if a positive example of an invasive species (is there any tree that lifts the spirits higher than a palm tree?). Then we passed the football stadium. Gibraltar's team had had an interesting few years: They'd spent the 1990s enviously eyeing the likes of minnows such as San Marino and the Faroe Islands who every couple of years played in high-profile World Cup qualifying football matches against the likes of Germany and

Italy, and so in 1999 the Gibraltarian Football Association, which can't have been much more than a few blokes meeting above a pub, decided to apply for membership of the European Football governing body, UEFA. Spain objected, but Gibraltar didn't let the matter go away, and tried again, taking the matter to the Court of Arbitration for Sport in 2011, where it was ruled that there was no grounds to refuse Gibraltar UEFA membership. So, in 2013, Gibraltar suddenly had a legitimate international football team. Now the only problem was that their stadium didn't comply with international safety regulations and with Spain gleefully not allowing Gibraltar to use any of their stadiums as a home, the Gibraltar players and fans had to make a 12 hour, 600 mile round-trip to Portugal for their 'home' ties. In their qualification league for the Euro 2016 tournament they lost all ten games, scoring twice, but crucially conceding 56 in the process, which rather left their World Cup hopes dashed on the rocks, if you'll pardon the pun.

Moments later, our bus reached its terminus and deposited us at Gibraltar's centre, Casemates Square, where we poured down the steps and onto the cobbles, in search of a restaurant for lunch.

Choosing where to eat in Gibraltar was difficult. Casemates Square has plenty of restaurants around its edge, but most were the sort of egg, chips, beans and lager places that unaccountably abound in southern Spain and the restaurants that didn't serve chips with everything and advertise lager prominently were slightly nicer but were guaranteed to burn through a £50 note on a holiday when I didn't know if I was going to be in a job or not at the end of it. We selected Burger King.

I made full use of the free WiFi and took a moment to download emails to see if there was any news on the only job I'd been able to interview for in the company I was working in. The interview had gone well, but the job was with a customer who hadn't yet signed the deal to come on board. If I got the job, the crisis would be averted and my family would still have a livelihood. If I didn't, I would become unemployed. There was an email from Matt, the company's HR manager, informing me that whilst he was hoping I was having a lovely holiday, a decision had been made on whether I'd got the job or not and that he would call me today at about 4pm to tell me my fate, which changed the complexion of the day entirely. I felt like a pensioner awaiting important test results from the doctor. How are you meant to think about anything else with that impending? And when you're on the big day out of your holiday, too? Suddenly Burger King food lost its appeal, which wasn't much to begin with. I watched my family compress their foam patties and slot them into their mouths. Pigeons hovered nearby, waiting for our chips to become theirs. I wondered whether the pigeons were introduced to Gibraltar to make it feel more British, I certainly hadn't seen any in Spain. Eventually, our potato matchsticks met their fate and we set off up the main street, Main Street, to take in the sights.

And the sights we took in were discounted booze and fags shops, mainly. One of Gibraltar's unique selling points is that it's a Duty Free location. You may remember many years ago that you could buy plenty of cigarettes and alcohol in UK airports at cut prices because you'd technically left the UK so no tax was payable in what was suddenly a strip of retail space that didn't answer to the usual laws. Then something in the law twitched one day and the concept of Duty Free became defunct, but the shops still continued to ply Johnny Walker and Marlboro at what was now high-street prices on people who hadn't kept up to speed with changes in international trading tax laws which was and is, everyone. But in Gibraltar, the concept of Duty Free lives on and many shops exist only to provide as many legal drugs to the rock's population as is physically possible. The shops all had the downbeat feel of those general purpose homeware stores you get on mainland British high streets that have plastic boxes stacked up on the pavement in front and the window filled with all sorts of mundane objects like tall pull-along trolleys, ladders and washing baskets. These shops shouted their whisky prices in large black and white text, they evangelised how many cigarettes it was possible to buy with so little money. They screamed at me to cross their threshold so as not to miss out on a bargain that was not fiscally possible on my native landmass. But I walked by and entered a branch of Next, for no other reason than it was my ambition to continue my Luxembourg-born tradition of purchasing everyday clothing in odd destinations and was mildly surprised to find that the price of my desired t-shirt was quoted in Sterling. I asked the cashier if I would incur any fees for paying with my British bank card and to my delight I received a reply in English from an English-speaking lady with a Mancunian twang that I wouldn't incur any bank charges for paying with my British bank card whilst in Britain at any point today.

We walked along a little further and noticed that as well as the continued availability of cheap drink and cigarettes, there was an increasing number of opportunities to gamble. At the dawn of the internet in the late 1990s, Gibraltar, like Luxembourg, saw the birth of a lucrative industry and worked hard to attract online companies with low tax rates. Gambling companies were courted and businessmen with a penchant for dissolute lifestyles begged to set up offices in a place that offered sun, sea, sand, all the cheap drink and cigarettes you can manage and had English as a mother tongue to boot. Gibraltar's bet paid off spectacularly as the industry soared and its economy (in 2014) had the fastest economic growth in Europe and an unemployment rate of just 6%. Gibraltar's online gambling business is estimated to constitute as much as 25% of Gibraltar's entire GDP, as well as millions in corporation tax, gambling duty and income tax from the thousands of people employed in the industry, most of whom are highly-paid software geeks who keep the websites alive and whose algorithms quite literally ensure that these automated games mean that house always wins. So Gibraltar's making money, and plenty of it too. But along with swish cars and shiny bling, the cash Gibraltar has brought tensions across the border. Gibraltar abuts Andalucía, a poor, Cornwall-like tourism-dependent part of Spain whose residents aren't strangers to poverty in the winter months. La Linea, which you'll recall is the town on the Spanish side of the border, is a collection of high rise apartment blocks, built by General Franco in the 1960s when he closed the border, with the intent that Gibraltarians could look north at La Linea's rapid development and develop a deep jealousy of life under Spanish rule. But the plot didn't work, the tower blocks aged badly, and now La Linea has one of the highest unemployment rates in the most deprived province in Spain. One in five hasn't worked in over three years, and more than half of all women are jobless. All of this makes Gibraltar's hugely visible money factory less than half a mile away understandably galling for La Linea's unemployed youth, the majority of whom pay their rent by hawking smuggled VAT-free Gibraltarian cigarettes on the cheap in Spain. In the year of my visit, Gibraltar imported a staggering 134 million packets of cigarettes (that's 4,151 per resident, or 11 a day for every man woman and child), 86% of which are thought to have made it into Gibraltar illegally. According to a private report by the tobacco consortium KPRG, more than half of all illegal tobacco in the whole of Spain is smuggled in through Gibraltar, with an estimated cost of more than €700 billion in lost tax revenue to Spain. It's a serious problem, and now Spanish customs limits the number of cigarettes local residents can import to 80 per month. If their border control guards on the way out are as inattentive as ours was on the way in, we can assume this measure is not working.

Before long, we were approaching the second half of Main Street and noticing the way ahead contained a continuation of familiar British high-street brands interspersed with boozy newsagents, we sought refuge in the only place we could: Marks and Spencer. We didn't really need anything from Marks and Spencer, of course, but it had air conditioning and it was just nice to be in a Marks and Spencer, just as it's nice on holiday to read your favourite British newspaper or watch BBC News. Taking advantage of the fee-free transaction, we bought a little food to see us through what – if the phonecall at 4pm went badly – would become a restaurant-free holiday, and went to pay where the cashier was again English and (unusually for me) called me "pet" when asking me to insert my bank card. While waiting for the machine to slowly ready itself for my PIN, I asked her what her story was.

"Oh, my husband was in the army. He came out of service and I was working in a shop and we just wondered what to do next. We'd lived all our life in Manchester and just wanted a change of scene. A posting became available for him in Gibraltar, so he took it and I came to work here." I asked if there was anything she missed about living in England. "Not really no. Our friends are still in Manchester, but they come and visit often and we're happy to visit them from time to time and of course, we make new friends here." I couldn't fault her logic in any of this, her life sounded perfect.

I looked at my watch back on Main Street; we still had three hours to pass before I had my life or death phonecall. Having got the feel of the centre of the town (and you can't get any more central than outside the Marks and Spencer) we resolved to do what all good tourists to Gibraltar should do: Go up The Rock.

The top of any mountain isn't easy to get to under your own steam. We were, remember, trying to ascend this mountain with a five year-old and a one year-old, which I promise you is harder than doing it with a pair of babies, who can be carried, or ten year olds, who can walk it. We resolved to take a cable car, which brought a frisson of excitement (it isn't very often you travel by cable car after all) and so we walked to the base station, passing a red telephone box – glowing like lava in the sun - along a cobbled, sun-drenched lane signed 'BAKER'S PASSAGE' in raised 1960s capital letters, and a set of traffic lights that could have been lifted straight out of Piccadilly Circus, before arriving at the cable car's base station. We joined a queue that wasn't as hideously long as we had feared, in which minibus operators begged us to climb aboard to so we could get to the summit in less time than the cable car, and at half the price as well. The portly German tourists ahead of us discussed this in animated fashion before loping away towards the waiting vehicle. It was tempting; we'd save time, we'd save money; we'd get to the top anyway, what were we waiting for? Something didn't seem quite perfect about the whole arrangement. We saw our German friends heave themselves and their bags into the sort of 15-seater that your school would take you to the swimming pool in when you were ten years old, then place their bags between their feet and hunch their shoulders over their knees and start to wait in the heat for their driver to round up another half dozen passengers to make the operation worthwhile. The idea of climbing aboard to share their limited space with a small child and a toddler slowly lost traction with us. Did we want to press our sweaty shoulders against theirs and strain to steal a sight of the sea a long way below us as the bus rounded hairpin incline after hairpin incline for twenty minutes, unable to maintain conversation over the screaming engine? It may have been the cheaper option, but it surely had its cost. We stepped inside the station and bought tickets.

There is surely no more frightening way to travel than by cable car. There is something uncomfortable about being hung in a Portakabin from a steel rope and dangled across what is guaranteed - by the very existence of the cable car - to be a foreboding and impassable landscape that fills me with dread much more than any other statistically safe activity that I can think of right now. Gibraltar's cable car surely takes you closer to a feeling of death than any other cable car in the world. It ascends 412 metres in six minutes, passing over three support towers as it does so, each of which is stapled to the rock face at an unreassuringly steep angle, calling into question the physical strain placed on the stanchion as the car passes over the top. One thing I've never been able to understand about cable cars (and frankly I still don't) is precisely how the hook, which normally grips the cable, manages to hang on when it passes over the concave guide wheels that the cable runs through at the top of a support tower. I'd always supposed that the hook completely wraps around the cable as though gripping on for dear life in a failsafe kind of way. But when the cable passes over the groove in the wheels, the car would surely then be at risk of derailing, which is not a risk you want to embrace at 300 metres up an almost vertical cliff with crashing waves at its base. So does the car's hook sit on top of the cable like a cushion? In which case, what happens when there's a gust of wind and the whole thing wants to slide from side to side? It doesn't bear thinking about. There are some mysteries I'm resigned to simply never fully understanding. Cable cars, Soda Streams, mirrors, and the continuation of Mrs Brown's Boys on BBC One.

But I'm pleased to report that the cable car dispatched us to the peak without incident (as you'd probably already worked out by now) and I was delighted but suddenly shocked to find that we were greeted at the top by a grinning monkey sitting on the railings and idly playing with his penis as we rose into view. This caused mirth and embarrassment in equal measure in the cabin as we swung to a halt and stepped with relief onto the viewing platform.

I used the word monkey in the previous paragraph for brevity, but monkey is too casual a term for my liking. If you care to swim with me in the pool of biological classification for a moment, monkeys are separated into two clades: New World Monkeys (found in central and South America) and Old World Monkeys (Africa and Asia). There are many species of New World Monkeys, identified by some of the most exotic and Scrabble-friendly animal names ever invented: talapoin, vervet, guenon, mangabey, colobus, surili, douc, baboon, and then the macaque. There are 22 species of macaque, the first of which (alphabetically, anyway) is the Barbary macaque. And it is these little fellas that abound on the Rock of Gibraltar. Native to the Atlas Mountains of Morocco and Algeria, a small population was introduced into Gibraltar in the 10th century, making them the only free-living ape in Europe. An interesting quirk of the Barbary macaque is that it seems accepted that the males have unlimited 'access' to any and all the females they desire, which leads to none of them knowing who their offspring are and a curious but naturally occurring coping mechanism called alloparental care, where the male monkeys act as parents to all the young whether they are theirs or not. There are currently 200-250 of these primates on the Rock of Gibraltar and if they leave then Gibraltar will fall to Spain, according to Winston Churchill at least, although perhaps a greater truth is that if the monkeys leave then the tourists will too. A couple of days before leaving the UK for the holiday, I stumbled across a mildly entertaining fly-on-the-wall documentary on Channel 5 called 'Gibraltar: Britain in The Sun'. It profiled a long haired middle-aged man with a Mancunian accent named Dr Eric Shaw, who holds the uniquely grand title of Officer In Charge Of Apes and whose job it was and presumably still is to ensure the difficult balance of stopping the apes from running riot whilst also ensuring there are enough of them for the tourists. I wasn't taking notes on this programme as I watched it, but I do recall Dr Shaw explaining the importance of the monkeys being given food to forage for, as is in their nature to want to do. Failure to do this would mean the animals would descend to the town in search of food, where presumably they'd get up to no good hanging out in bars all day stealing the complimentary peanuts or being commercially farmed for supermarket salami.

The signs at the cable car terminus at the Top of The Rock that this is indeed the Top of The Rock are as hard to miss as they are numerous. There was literally no way you could not be aware that you weren't meant to feed the monkeys, yet everywhere I looked I saw some oversized berk in Birkenstocks tossing a crisp towards a tiny pair of pinky-brown hands and watching with glee as the greasy potato was popped in before the cheeky scamp would lollop off for a lollipop from a similarly-shaped human who could repeat the trick.

After about 20 minutes of wandering aimlessly around on this patio in the sky, the urge took us to explore a little further; there are paths that run the length of The Rock with low fences on the downhill side providing excellent views, but if ever you've been walking with a child under five on a clifftop, riverbank, or even pavement, you'll know how utterly terrifying every step is. It's not that we felt a sense of any danger, but when you are on top of a 400 metre high mountain in the middle of the sea and you have a steep and irreversible drop inches away from your giddy, carefree, staggering child who has absolutely no sense of danger, you find that you do not make your way very far along the path before experiencing a strong desire to turn around and retreat to the coffee shop to observe the view through a window instead. Thereafter, coffees drained, we had run out of things to do with toddlers on top of an arid and precipitous mountain and so headed back to the cable car to descend back to the real world, where my big phonecall was edging ever closer. We piled back into the cabin and made small talk with the operators who made note of our home counties accents and pledged to make the thing drop off its wire if Wayne Rooney was lured away from their native north west to Chelsea, as was looking likely. Then suddenly,

I had a Eureka moment. Mancunians! Gibraltar wasn't crawling with macaques, it was crawling with Mancunians! The cashiers in Next and Marks & Spencer, our cable car operator, the Officer In Charge Of Apes Dr Eric Shaw – so many people had clearly emigrated from Manchester to come to this part of Britain, and suddenly it all made sense. I have been to Manchester on several occasions and each time had a perfectly good time there, but Manchester is not noted for its sunny climes and – and I hope this does not sound too leafy south east England – there are some parts of northern England that don't have a high quality of life index. Perhaps Gibraltar was populated by Britons who'd had enough of grey skies and a drizzly lifestyle and had made the choice to sell their redbrick terrace on Coronation Street and live in an apartment where the temperatures were guaranteed to be hot, where the transparent sea would forever glitter, where they could still buy a loaf of Hovis and a pint of Carling, where they could have paella in Spain for dinner, hop to Portugal on the Saturday and Morocco on the Sunday, where they could actually be in an environment that lifted their spirits. And why not? Good on them for having a go and not passively accepting a half-measure from life.

**

What do you do when you're on holiday with the family in a sun-soaked paradise and have to fill an hour before taking the phonecall to find out whether you're losing your job or not? It's not a puzzle many of us are often faced with in life, but I will confirm that it is a peculiar feeling trying to relax and enjoy yourself when you can see your fingers shaking and feel your scalp tingling where your bald spot will be. Having just sat down for a drink at the Top of the Rock, it didn't seem right to come down the mountain and immediately sit down and have another and certainly if you are under five, then two sit-downs in half an hour is no fun at all. Instead we decided to climb aboard the number 2 bus and visit Europa Point.

Europa Point is at the very southern tip of Gibraltar. It would be Europe's most southernmost point were there not a much less famous headland five miles west of Gibraltar that narrowly claimed the crown instead. Noting that the bus was going to travel mainly south along the western side of The Rock, we reasoned that sitting on the right hand side of the bus would give us a sea view and were pleased to see that the bus company hadn't gone all capitalist and decide to charge more for what were clearly the premium seats. The elevated view over the dark blue Bay of Algeciras was excellent and you really must ride the number 2 bus if you make it to Gibraltar.

We hadn't exactly researched what to do at Europa Point and so travelled there without a plan – indeed, a visit to Tripadvisor after returning home informed us of the many things we could have done: There is St Michael's Cave, a spooky cavern with all the expected stalagmites & tites; The Great Siege tunnels that run through The Rock, which is your dream if you're the kind of person who prefers battle re-enactments to real life; dolphin-watching excursions on little yellow-hulled boats; even Julian Lennon's Beatles Exhibition (John and Yoko married here), but we only had time for one more attraction in the day, and both Debs and I wanted to see something that we'd never seen before: Africa.

It is only nine miles across the sea. It looks swimmable – and it has indeed been swum many times by many people who see it as a training run for a channel swim. But it is a perilous stretch of water for even the most experienced navigator; the Mediterranean - a larger body of water than the Gulf of Mexico - has no other natural inlet or outlet. Water flows more or less continuously both eastwards and westwards at the same time, making it a bit tricky if you are trying to get across it. The westward outflow is saltier and therefore denser and deeper, while the inflow from the Atlantic tends to form the surface waters. These general flow tendencies are sometimes interrupted by brief periods of contraflow, depending on the position of the moon, the sun, the seasonal changes in the temperatures of both the Mediterranean and Atlantic and various other factors that basically makes the whole thing such a confusing endeavor to cross that many mariners do little more than tie on their lifejacket, grip the wheel and pray to Neptune. The sea bed is littered with shipwrecks, but I was unable to catch a new one being created as I watched cargo ships chug imperceptibly west away from all the great Mediterranean ports of Barcelona, Marseilles, Athens, Istanbul and Beirut, to literally everywhere else in the world whilst their sister ships made the return journey.

And out of the sea rose Africa. Morocco, to be specific, looking not greatly dissimilar to Andalucía but very definitely Africa. It was protected by a haze of evaporating sea that shrouded ground level, leaving only a low range of craggy peaks on view. But they were African peaks, and comfortably the most African thing I'd ever laid eyes upon. Not far behind them was the Sahara Desert, and behind that the deep and poisonous jungles of the Congo, then the Equator, and the Serengeti. After that, South Africa –

Pretoria, Johannesburg, Cape Town. The greatest living human, Nelson Mandela, was moving about on the landmass I was looking at right now. It is one of the most remarkable parts of planet Earth, Gibraltar; The Rock of Gibraltar is one of the great – and one of the most underrated - wonders of the natural world; there are few places in the world where you can stand on one continent and look across water to another. Europa Point in Gibraltar is that place and I now add it to your bucket list of places to see.

Europa Point was also interestingly undeveloped. Were this in any large country in the world, the place would be teeming with restaurants and bars with expansive decking, restaurants serving African cuisine, coffee dispensaries and souvenir shops selling monkey teddy bears, binoculars and sticks of Gibraltarian rock (never saw those for sale anywhere, they missed a trick there). But Europa Point had none of this. It had a cricket pitch (!), a church, a lighthouse, a couple of ornamental cannons, a Union Jack on a flagpole halfway through the process of being worn to a nubbin by the winnowing wind and a much-larger-than-expected children's playground. Debs and I agreed that the best plan of action was for her to take the children into the playground and I would go where they would be out of earshot and wait for my phonecall. Debs gave me a hug and assured me that everything would be ok. I tried to smile then turned and walked away from my wife and my children to face this one alone.

I sat on a bench and waited, as tense as a snare drum. I passed the time looking over the edge into the sea below. It was filled with an uncountable number of large fish which were doing nothing more than just bask in the warm water near the surface without a care in the world. They looked like they were enjoying themselves more than I was.

It was about fifteen minutes before the phone rang. An eternity when you are waiting for big news. But I didn't know how many of those fifteen minutes were left as those minutes elapsed, I just increasingly thought Matt had probably forgotten to call. It was almost a shock when the phone did ring; but as it did, my heart sank; this moment was clearly going to happen. There was no good news to be had on this phonecall whatever happened – there would either be neutral news, continuing with my job, or bad news, joblessness.

"Hello, Nick speaking."

"Hello, Nick Speaking, this is Matt Speaking!" Hilarious.

"Hello Matt, how's things back in Britain?"

"They're good thanks – probably not the hot temperatures you're having. Is it hot in Spain?"

"It's 35 degrees. I've actually left Spain for the day, I'm in Gibraltar at the moment, trying to enjoy myself!"

"Oh Gibraltar! They've got those monkeys there, haven't they? I went a couple of years ago, I ended up feeding one an entire packet of crisps! Did you see any of them?"

"Yes, I was concerned for the welfare of my children at one point!" Children, Matt, I am concerned for the welfare of my children.

"Classic. Can you see Africa from there?"

"I'm looking at it right now." Now Matt, tell me now.

"Oh, is it…what…it must be Tunisia you can see?"

"Morocco." I left an awkward silence in the conversation so Matt could fill it.

"Anyway, you must be wondering about the outcome of the discussions about customer alignments."

"Yes, it had crossed my mind…"

"Yuh, so…I've had news…and…" And? And? That was surely good news; they say 'but' when it's bad news, and 'and' when it's good news, don't they?

…and I'm sorry to say that the customer's not signed the deal, so there isn't a job to offer you. I'm sorry."

This was like a thunderclap.

"I haven't really got anything to say, Matt, it sounds pretty terminal. What do we do next?"

"I'm sorry Nick, I don't have anything on what next at the moment. I'll have some more detail on your exit from the company when you get back to the UK. The thing now is to forget all about it, enjoy your holiday, and try and relax."

I considered this to be the least-likely-to-be-followed advice ever given. I said goodbye as politely as I could and hung up.

I remained on the bench for a moment, not quite knowing what to do, where to look or what to think. My life had lacked bad news phonecalls up to this point and I didn't know how to react. After a minute of total physical and mental inactivity and with nothing else to do, I stood up and took a few steps forward to the railing at the top of the cliff, leaned forward onto it and stared down at the basking fish a hundred feet below, they still blissfully unaware of what had just happened to me up here. I watched the waves crash onto the rocks and let my gaze linger on the impact and its unfolding chaos before my eyes. Then I looked up to the sky and let out a deep sigh, then across the horizon towards Africa, the most desolate, bleak and impoverished place in the world. Then it hit me:

I had lost my job.

In the hunt for a new one, I'd have to go somewhere I never thought I would.

3. Finland

"So sadly neglected and often ignored; a poor second to Belgium when going abroad."

Monty Python

In the purgatory that followed the Gibraltar phonecall, a frantic few months ensued of putting my CV in the inbox of anyone who wished to see it and travelling wherever I was asked to go to meet anyone who wished to interview me.

After what felt like a dozen of these interviews – always the same questions, always a different interviewer – I was offered a job. Not the best job in the world, but *a* job – one that would keep the bank manager happy. In relief, I took a day to myself to poke about in a local attractive town – an activity that we so seldom have time to do. I was in the street when my phone rang and I was given feedback from one of the many interviews I'd attended.

"Nick, I'm pleased to say it's good news. We thought you gave a very strong first interview and we'd like to take you through to the final round. The company's headquartered in Finland and everyone who needs to interview you is there. Rather than fly them all over to London, can we fly you to Helsinki? We'd like to suggest that you take a red-eye out of Heathrow, we do the interviews at 1pm to 4pm, then you can fly back in the evening or I'm sure our budget can stretch to a hotel if you wanted to stay overnight and travel back the following day."

I took stock of the situation. Here I was, unemployed yet with a job offer on the table, and being asked if I wanted to have an all-expenses-paid minibreak to a European capital on the condition that I spend a few hours of it sitting in a room having stimulating conversation with some intelligent people. I'd booked the flight and hotel before the end of the working day. Then a thought popped up in my brain. Why not take the flight home in the evening of the following day? Why not have a day seeing the sights in Helsinki? I wasn't working, so I booked the return flight for 7pm and packed for Finland, still surprised that I was going. A couple of days later I was queuing for Heathrow security at 6am in my suit.

"Business or pleasure?" enquired the woman in a trouser suit with a clipboard.

"Excuse me?"

"I'm from the Office For National Statistics. Can I ask if you're travelling for business or pleasure today sir?"

"I'm not sure."

"You've been selected as the 15th passenger in the queue to be surveyed. Is the purpose of your visit business or pleasure?"

"Both."

**

I boarded the plane without incident – not something I'm able to write in every chapter of this book as you will see – and, as Finnair conveyed me north-eastwards over the North Sea, I tried to recall everything Finland-related my memory held. For such a physically large country (in western Europe, only Germany, Spain and Sweden are larger). There wasn't much:

Helsinki is the capital.

It's called Suomi in its native language.

Motor racing driver Mika Hakkinen and the country's inexplicable dominance of motorsports.

Footballers Jaari Litmanen and Sami Hyppia. Wasn't there a goalkeeper too? Antti Niemi? He played for Southampton or something?

I didn't have much more to go on. Wait....Pingu? Wasn't he Finnish? He certainly sounded like it.

Beyond that, I had nothing. I wasn't sure of Finland's currency[6], I didn't know who the Prime Minister was. I couldn't name anywhere in Finland apart from its capital. I was going to feel alien here and began to wonder how I would make business small-talk with Finns – something I had never contemplated that I would ever have to do.

The flight to Helsinki is three hours and when the plane finally circled around Helsinki airport – thus setting me a new personal best in northern latitude - I consulted the in-cabin screens, and was surprised to learn how far east I was. On the map, I appeared to be only a few centimetres from Estonia - or Russia, as I had called it growing up. I could practically see it from my window. I was level with

---

[6] The Euro.

far-flung sounding Belarus and Ukraine, east of Sofia and Athens. I was more northern than Moscow, St Petersburg and Oslo. I really was on the northern reaches of the civilised world; Reykjavik is the world's only more northern capital[7].

I hailed a taxi outside the airport, climbed in, and immediately realised that I didn't speak a word of Finnish – I couldn't even say "Do you speak English?". Is there anything more dispiriting in normal life than being unable to express your basic thoughts? On a couple of occasions in life, I've gleefully booked a holiday in Portugal or Greece, then stepped off the plane to find myself in a shop on the first afternoon all too quickly realising that I've failed to learn how to say hello or even thank you. And exacerbating this sense of verbal impotence is that I've actually gone to the trouble of learning a foreign language as well – put me anywhere in France and I can happily pass myself off as a native. But I wasn't going to be able to do that in Finland.

Much to my relief, the taxi driver spoke English (everyone in Finland speaks English) and I asked how much it would cost to go the centre of Helsinki and was told a sum of money roughly equivalent to what I spend on all my children's Christmas presents. Helsinki's airport is about as far away from its host city as it is possible to be without getting into dodgy Ryanair-esque definitions of airport/city proximity. Let me put it this way – the population of Helsinki is about 1 million, that's roughly the same size as Birmingham. Birmingham's airport is 6 miles from its city centre. But Helsinki's airport – and its only airport at that – is 11 miles away from the action. I don't wish to sound all urbane and precocious here, but does a one city country out

---
[7] Apart from Leeds of course, capital of Yorkshire.

on the very edge of the of the map perhaps want to make itself slightly more accessible to international trade and tourism than this? Maybe the Finnish government just wanted to give the taxi drivers some easy money and therefore themselves some extra tax. It was certainly working.

Resigned to the fare and doing well for time, I stared out of the window at the pewter skies and asked the driver to take me on a scenic route through the city centre when we got there and point out an interesting sight or two en route. I couldn't have hoped for a better tour if I were on an open-topped bus; I didn't just have a taxi driver, I had a guide. Once we'd passed the endless grubby pine forests that lined the underused two-lane motorway, I was able to examine the city close up, and what a marvellous sight I was treated to. Along a broad boulevard of imposingly sturdy granite buildings, my savant pointed out of the window and informed me that that over there was the Olympic Stadium from the 1952 Olympics. It seems that every purpose-built Olympic stadium has to have some sort of design feature to distinguish it from all the others: As such, London built a crown, Beijing a bird's nest, Athens a spaceship, Sydney a giant levitating Pringle and Atlanta a giant car park when the stadium was bulldozed a decade or so after the games finished and the newly-resident baseball team decided to relocate to an even newer stadium on the other side of town. I was pleased to see that the Helsinki games' organisers had not constructed an anonymous concrete bowl (despite this being the 1950s and very close to the Soviet Union), for the Finns have a knack for bold, simplistic design and this stadium's notable architectural feature was a simple tower at the finish line, 72.21 metres in height (the length of the winning Finnish javelin throw from the

Olympics 20 years previously), and it was at the top of this tower that the Olympic Cauldron was placed. Over the years we have become accustomed to seeing the Olympic flame being lit in all manner of creative and complicated ways involving flaming arrows and whooshing fire, but Helsinki's moment of the lighting of the Olympic flame was quite simply its famous endurance althete Paavo Nurmi running all the way up the staircase to the top with a flaming torch in hand. It must have been exhausting, but it's quite literally the most fitting way an Olympics has ever been opened. But even though Finland may not be known for its Olympic prowess, there is one thing it is recognised the world over for.

In 1865, an engineer called Fredrik Idestam noticed a pleasingly fast-flowing stretch of river in a forest near Tampere, 100 miles north of Helsinki. With nothing but an agitated river and acres of pine forest for miles around, Idestam decided the conditions were ideal to set up a paper mill. Through success or just plain boredom, Ideastam expanded to open a second mill in 1868 on the neighbouring Nokianvirta river. For the next 54 years, the mills successfully pulped the forest and as the Industrial Revolution quietly gave rise to the electrical era, Idestam's mills' output gradually changed from paper to electricity. Then in 1922, Idestam formed partnerships with a cable company and a rubber company and soon the mill wasn't just generating electricity, it was transporting it to surrounding towns via insulated cables. And so the business continued until 1970, making nothing but electricity and cables, quite happily, with no other news to report.

But times change, good business leaders move with them and it was realised that if all these rubber cables that started at the mill plugged into a range of electrical devices, then the business could not only make money from selling electrical devices, but also more money from the increased demand for electricity. So the corporation turned its attention to the growing market of radios and telephones.

In 1977, a gentleman named Kari Kairamo became CEO. Part of the legendary Kihlman family of artists, Kairamo worked with energy and efficiency and had the vision to build the business into one of the large multinationals that were becoming all the rage at the time. The planets aligned for Kairamo in the late 1980s to be able to do this; Russia – Finland's main importer - was breaking up and the European Union was on the rise. Kairamo was now CEO of the largest company in Finland and he focussed the firm's attention not east to Mother Russia, but west and south to the up and coming European Economic Community, of which Finland was a part. With Kairamo's help, the company would become internationally renowned. Sadly for him, this was caused by his suicide in 1992 – the flipside of the bipolarity that gave him so much energy and vision to build the business in the first place. The company promoted one of his direct reports, Jorma Ollia, from Head of Mobile Phones to CEO, and to describe Ollia's tenure as a success would be like saying that the invention of the wheel improved human productivity. Mobile phones were now front and centre of the company's product portfolio and within a decade, they had one of the most famous brands in the world: Nokia.

Venerated management consultant Charles Handy writes about a business phenomenon known as 'The Second Curve': Once a company finds success, it then has to innovate – to start on a second curve - b*efore* it has finished the first one if it is to continue to thrive and its initial product set has ceased to be relevant. In the late 2000s, with mobile phones' First Curve beginning to flatten out, Nokia got caught out.

On January 9th 2007, Steve Jobs, CEO of Apple – famous for making portable music players and also computers that were far too expensive for the mass market to consider buying in great numbers - stood on a stage in California and decried the 'baby software' running on Nokia phones and showed the world a rectangle with a touchscreen on the front. Behind it was software that was smarter and more powerful than anyone had ever seen before. But Apple had made some pretty interesting tradeoffs to do this: We now think nothing of the fact that our phone batteries are pretty much dead come the evening. We know that if we drop our phone the screen will probably crack. But in 2007 these features were thought to be absolutely unacceptable; it was firmly believed in Finland that the iPhone had inherent frailties and what customers really wanted was a stockier Nokia. Then Nokia bought a shipment of iPhones and one of the execs took his home and gave it to his five year old daughter to play with[8]. She could work it instantly and a few nights later asked her daddy if she was allowed to sleep with the "magic phone" under her pillow. Instantly the exec knew Nokia was in serious trouble – in effect, they only had one product and now a competitor was making a far superior one. Heads had turned, and one by one, mobile phone customers traded in their trusty Nokia for an iPhone. The burst of Nokia's bubble was as spectacular as anything in corporate history. On 31st December 2007, Nokia's share price was €38. On 31st June 2012 – just three of your mobile phone contracts later, it was €2. And this was disastrous for Finland, for Nokia's collapse accounted for

---

[8] Anecdote from The Rise and Fall of Nokia, BBC Four, broadcast July 10th 2018.

one third of the 8% decline in Finland's GDP in 2009 and one fifth of all increased Finnish unemployment between 2008 and 2014.[9]

But I had my own unemployment to worry about – for it was a good job I was interviewing for and I wanted to get it. I tried to make all the right noises in the interview and after handshakes and exchanges of best wishes at the end, a taxi was summoned to whisk me to my hastily-selected hotel in central Helsinki – a cathedral-like granite pile called the Glo Art in a district called Kaampi, which sounded like a company that made educational playsets for toddlers. The main entrance door was quite simply the most beautiful aspect of any architecture I had ever seen in my life, ever. It was like something out of the Natural History Museum in London and I was agog. It had a gothic point at the top and was lovingly crafted in one of those stoically hard woods that every European country north of Scotland specialises in. The door was surrounded from hinge to handle by intricate stone carvings of fossils, and for good measure a black iron footplate and push panel had been attached across the width of the door with rivets the size of a baby's fist. The centre of the door displayed a carved tableau of a bird in flight against a fantastical backdrop. I stood in the street, mouth open, as the taxi sped off. Then I realised something: The door was shut. Was this door for display only? What level of business did a semi-suburban hotel do midweek in one of the coldest cities on earth out of season? Was the hotel closed for winter? Was I going to have to spend the night on the semi-Arctic streets? I stood for a few moments in a lather of indecision then, not wanting to admit defeat by resting my suitcase on the slushy pavement, noticed an arch embedded in the building's façade out of

---

[9] https://tinyurl.com/yd84khx9, if you're wanting to read more.

which a car was emerging. I walked to it then through it to find myself in a small courtyard car park, through which I tiptoed, the only person in the place, wondering if this really was the way into the hotel when, unannounced, a sliding door in an exterior wall opened to reveal another sliding door to me, placing me in some kind of airlock, clearly to keep the heat in. Suddenly, I twigged: the hotel's main door was shut to keep the cold out; this is Finland, stupid. Little by little, I followed my nose to reception and came to the check-in desk from behind. But this was no ordinary hotel lobby.

A few years previously, I'd been to Barcelona. I found the place pretty disappointing, truth be told – the Sagrada Familia was a building site, the Ramblas was a pedestrianised high-street not too dissimilar from most I had walked down over the previous decade, and this famous Gaudi architecture I'd been promised by all the guidebooks appeared to exist only in a handful of buildings. But I booked in a tour of one of Gaudi's works – Casa Battlo – and *what* a building it was: spiralling ceilings whirled inwards to decorative light fittings, whalebone arches propped the roof up in the eaves, multicoloured roof tiles adorned the outside, shadowy corners on the inside had been deliberately set in bright white plaster. In the Glo Art's lobby, it was as though Gaudi's Scandinavian half-brother had been briefed to do Casa Battlo's sister building in Helsinki, replacing the Mediterranean light in Casa Battlo with Nordic shadows here. I could have stood there for an hour just gazing at the arched interior space, the snug library replete with log fire and local ale on tap and the wide staircase leading up to the conference rooms. But I had a city to see.

**

A few years ago, when I'd just moved house, I one day opened the post to find a letter – totally out of the blue - from the electricity company that had supplied my old house, which read: "Dear Mr Procter, as discussed, here is a cheque for £563.62 for your overpaid electricity bill payments from your previous property." Open-mouthed, I slid my finger into the next envelope, encouragingly similar in design to the first and again discovered I was also the beneficiary of £709.68 for overpaid gas. I raise this now because if you can emote with me on the thrill of unexpectedly receiving a cheque for £1,273.30 when I had just moved house then you can begin to understand a little of the pleasure I felt at finding myself very suddenly milling around a large and pleasant city that I would never in my life have visited and had had no plans to visit as little as 48 hours previously. It felt that good.

I bounced along the sleety pavement and, consulting the freesheet tourist map reception had given me, turned left to head for the city centre, clocking an interesting looking bar called Boothill. I peeked through the window to see if it might qualify as my dinner venue. After less than one second, I had made the decision that I would never cross the threshold of this place through the whole of the rest of my life, let along tonight, no matter how hungry I got. Boothill was a Rock Bar, and by that, I don't mean an imitation of a Hard Rock Café where they promise HARD ROCK and then once you're inside and it's all burgers and chips and a catsuit on the wall that Cher once wore – this was a *real* rock bar, for real Harley-Davidson-riding, tattooed on the knuckles, dangerous goatee greybeards. The bottom half of its windows was blacked out (always a bad sign) and this blackness was covered with stick-on plastic flames. Peering into the gloom, I could see the bar had been decorated to create a frighteningly realistic depiction of hell. I've been in all sorts of dive bars but this one actually managed to make me feel uneasy in my skin. I was repelled by the place, feeling like there really was something dodgy about it on a spiritual level. There probably was.

But bars like this are not unusual in Finland, for Finland is the global epicentre for heavy metal. And by global epicentre, I mean that if you were to look at a global heat map of how many heavy metal bands there were per 100,000 of population (and you can here: http://tinyurl.com/zmqkste or more up to date but slightly different numbers here http://tinyurl.com/zlmhwlw), you'd see that whilst Great Britain (Iron Maiden, Def Leppard, Judas Priest) has given the world 11.96 metal bands per 100,000 and the USA (Slayer, Marilyn Manson, Slipknot) 6.44, Finland tops the charts with an unthinkably dense 53.2. That's nine times as many per person as the country that gave us Kiss – and we thought God gave rock and roll to *them*!

Yet here's the thing – although I could probably reel off five to ten heavy metal bands off the top of my head right now, I could only name one Finnish one: Lordi.

If you have an extremely good memory and a passion for musical kitsch[10], you may remember the Eurovision Song Contest from 2006. Amidst all the glittering cheese that year, four monsters took to the stage – literally, dressed head to toe in terrifying horror movie monster outfits – with horned faces, skull masks, clawed hands, and filled the

---

[10] Jon, my Best Man from Luxembourg, I'm looking at you here.

auditorium in the ancient city of Athens with the most apocalyptic sound that anybody with the desire to purchase a Eurovision Song Contest ticket had ever heard. They won by a huge margin, of course and I wondered whether they were in Boothill right there and then, playing poker and drinking vampire bats' blood from the skulls of dead nuns. I couldn't be sure. I'm certain they'd been in for a pint or a gig at some point though.

I walked on a few more blocks and then found myself in the centre, where I was confronted with the actual Hard Rock Café. Call me picky, but I've never been comfortable with the idea of travelling the world and choosing to dine in the same restaurant and café brands as you can get at home. Also, I've always found the phenomenon of Hard Rock Café t-shirts to be an intriguing one; I've never been able to buy into the idea of the Hard Rock brand trying to claim ownership of diverse foreign cities. And yet, whilst they're not as ubiquitous as they were before the dawn of the 21st century, when you see someone wearing one in the street, despite the fact that it is the most pointless piece of knowledge you will acquire that day, you still have to look to see which city, don't you?

And so, I walked on past the 'Hard' Rock Café, looking for somewhere to dine. I passed Italian restaurants, Spanish restaurants, Indian restaurants, Chinese restaurants, even a Czech restaurant (can anyone outside the Czech Republic name three classically Czech dishes?), but I couldn't shake off the feeling that if this (if the job interview turned out badly) was to be the only meal I ever ate in Finland, I was determined to make it an authentically Finnish one. After maybe three quarters of an hour of appetite-building roaming, I found what I was looking for in a courtyard off a main square opposite Helsinki Cathedral.

It was called Savotta, and was the epitome of that memorable sidestreet restaurant you hope to find when you travel and as soon as I put my head inside, I knew it was not only where I would eat tonight, but a place I would remember for the rest of my life. The menu outside informed me that I could feast on an entrée of reindeer salami, followed by bear steak, to be washed down with several Finnish beers which I had never heard of before but could taste already. It had been dark for about four hours now and I was experiencing the notorious Finnish cold and was ready for a cushioned snug with a drippy candle and a brown ale served to me in a tankard, perhaps by a cheerful waitress with smiling blue eyes and perfect teeth. I descended the spiral staircase in hope and expectation – it was a Tuesday evening, about 8.30pm, out of tourist season.

"Excuse me, do you have space for one?" I asked, suddenly confident that people who wait tables in foreign countries would reply in perfect English. The reply was spoken by the man who I think was employed to do the voiceover for Pingu, but was traditionally dressed in a rough white workshirt, lederhosen style shorts, brown braces and knee-high socks with garters.

"Uuuuuh no, sorry, we very full tonight."

In my head, I reasoned that some diners might be finishing soon.

"Oh. You see this is the only meal I'm ever going to eat in Finland and I was hoping to put some of your wonderful country's food inside me. Can I buy and drink beer from you until a table comes free?"

"I'm not sure. Just wait one minute." Pingu shuffled away from me down the stairs, reappearing a minute later, smiling and gesturing me to follow him back down the staircase, at the bottom of which he picked up a small but sturdy square table, raised it upside down over his head and led me through the crowded dining room. We stopped towards the back and Pingu set the table jutting out halfway into the walkway that led to the toilets. I was grateful to have been fitted in at short notice like this, but there was clearly now no getting out of the fact that I was going to be sharing my evening with a steady stream of customers who would be give their hands a little shake as they walked past. But I was hungry and sat down as Pingu laid up.

"What can I get you to drink?"

"A large glass of the most Finnish beer you have please."

Suddenly Pingu came alive as though a switch had been thrown, transforming from dowdy waiter into born salesman.

"OK, I'm going to give you a Lapin Kulta – the most popular beer in Finland, you'll love it, I guarantee. And I'm going to give you a special deal: a set menu that gives you all the tastes of Finland, OK?"

"How much is the set menu?"

"65 Euros, not including your Lapin Kulta."

I baulked but didn't show it – fifty quid for a meal for one! He surely knew this was a bit steep and that tourists were there for ripping off and this restaurant was in a prime tourist spot. This meal was going to be paid for by the company which had just interviewed me and whether I got the job or not, I didn't want to be submitting an expense claim for a €70 meal before I'd even been offered the job.

"Bring me the Lapin Kulta. I'll see how good it is, then I'll decide what I order."

"You got it – you're going to love all the food I bring you."

Pingu returned with my beer and a blini with a slice of salami on it.

"Here's a taste of bear, to get you in the mood. Real bear, from the forests of northern Finland."

I'd never eaten bear before and popped it in with alacrity. It tasted just like beef, but this didn't change the fact it was part of a bear until quite recently. I took a sip of the Lapin Kulta. Time slowed down. For several lingering minutes, I just sat and supped, looking around me and making friends with the room. The place was a cavern with an arched ceiling and had been decked out as a logger's hut – clearly for the tourists – but they'd made a really good job of it and it *felt* real. Here was actual, tough, rough Finnish wood, real Finnish atoms surrounding me - not a fake veneer shipped in from a factory in south-east Asia to make the place feel like every other chain restaurant in the world. The tablecloths were checked red and white, the menu was in Finnish, the waiters were clearly told to dress the part. It was like being in Mr Tumnus's home in Narnia. I loved it. And then, the most curious thing happened. In those hanging moments in which I sat and did nothing but take in the atmosphere between gulps of beer, I thought to myself. "This is really good. I could take more of this in my life. I hope I get offered the job so I can come back to Finland. If they offer me the job, I'm going to take it." It was a bold decision and quite out of character for me to make such a big call on factors irrelevant to the major consequences of my choice; but you are what you eat and I'd just eaten bear and was feeling like I could take on the world. I was ready for this. My dam burst, and I ordered the special menu and selected every Finnish delicacy my waiter could offer me over the next hour, filling my body with pickled herring, shredded reindeer stew, roasted root vegetables that had been grown not just on but in Finnish soil, cloudberries, liquorice ice cream and plenty more Lapin Kulta. I slept well that night.

**

Helsinki's centre is as compact as it is charming. The city basically consists of two shopping streets crossing a major boulevard and that's about it as far as the city centre goes. But look at a map of Greater Helsinki and you will see it as a splat at the end of a peninsula, like a jagged frying pan being held out over the sea. It was tantalisingly too large to explore in a day on foot. Shortly before my hastily arranged trip, I'd asked my Facebook friends if any of them knew Helsinki and what they would do if they only had six hours there. My friend Di insisted I do one thing: Temppeliaukio.

Something I've never fully understood about travel guides is why they insist I spend most of my time at my destination indoors. The general drift of guidebooks seems to be that you should be in hotels, bars and restaurants at night and museums, art galleries and cathedrals in your days. Now, I don't mean to talk any of that down if you can think of nothing better than a day in a foreign city that includes all six, but my point is that I can do almost exactly that in my home town. I could easily travel to Bristol or Leicester and stare at paintings, pottery, pews, then hit the town for steak and Malbec, so I'm not sure why when having made the effort to go to Helsinki / Budapest / Lisbon I should do exactly the same thing. Wandering around a new city is by far the best way to get to know it – I can think of no more satisfactory pastime than ambling past shops and cafés looking for Munich's snuggest Konditorei or Stockholm's most gingerbread-house-like restaurant. The pressure on a tourist to visit any city's church or cathedral is almost unbearable to the point where you go in anyway just so you can report to friends that you did it. Cathedrals, like football stadia, are at their best when they are full and something is happening that fulfils their purpose.

But I trusted Di, and made for Temppeliaukio.

Temppeliaukio is a church like no other in the world, for its architect was God Himself. Of course, that's not 100% true, but in the 1930s a plot of land near Helsinki's centre was selected for a church to be sited and a competition held to design the building. Famous-in-Finland architect Johan Siegfried Siren, fresh from designing the Parliament building, won the competition but work on the church was inconveniently postponed by the outbreak of the Second World War and by the time the building of the church was a high enough priority again, it had become 1961. Siren had ruled himself out of helping further, so the competition was rerun and won by another architect called Tuomo Suomalainen who, pleasingly, had been born in 1931 and so was as old as the project itself. Tuomo (and his brother, who was called Timo - I assure you I'm not making this up), found that in the thirty years it had taken for nothing to happen regarding the building of the church, all the money funding it had been siphoned off in other directions and the church was only now to be one quarter the size of the original. It was hardly the project Timo and Tuomo had signed up for. To make matters worse, residents of newly constructed post-war adjacent buildings were beginning to grumble about the actuality of suddenly having a large edifice exist over their back fence after three decades of planning prevarications, so as well as needing to do the job on the cheap, Timo and Tuomo had to make sure this church wasn't too tall either. Necessity being the mother of invention, the brothers struck upon the capital idea of just blasting a giant crater in the bedrock and fitting a dome over the top, thereby satisfying both the accountants and the locals. It was a stroke of genius, but like most radical ideas, the public was initially against it. Timo and Tuomo feared the craggy interior walls would be far too weird for the competition jury and so decided to plaster them over until acoustic engineers and orchestral musicians begged the brothers to reconsider, petitioning that acoustically, there was little better for their art than a bare rock face. The church was built as the 1960s progressed and newspapers – aware of and doubtless fanning the flames of public sentiment to create a 'gift-that-keeps-on-giving' news story, nicknamed the church the "rock mosque" and the "devil's bunker"- printing photos of the construction whenever there was little news in Finland, which I presume was quite often. The Finnish Universities Christian Union felt that constructing a new church building was a gigantic waste of money as the world licked its wounds from World War Two and daubed the word "Biafra" - a war-torn state in Nigeria suffering mass famine at that time - on multiple locations at the building site, suggesting, not unreasonably, that it was more Christian to resolve famine than to construct a new church building in an already Christian city.

But the church was consecrated in 1969 and all the controversy was quickly forgotten – the church received 100,000 visitors in its first year (that's 275 a day – approximately the church's seated capacity), and half a million the year after. It was drawing tourists to the city who wouldn't otherwise have visited and it quickly became the symbol of 1970s Helsinki and a smash hit for a country with a subdued tourist industry.

And I was heading for it now – except that I wasn't, because I couldn't find the blasted thing. I stared at the creases in the now dog-eared map I'd been given at the hotel the night before and rotated the map through 360 degrees in both directions as I turned around on the spot but no joy. As sleet began to fall and the shops started to be replaced by residential buildings as I left the city centre, I sought help in some passers-by. They didn't speak any English, which surprised me, especially as they were in their seventies and I assumed were wise owls. Grunts and gesticulations followed, from which I deduced that I needed to go uphill a bit and that I was round the back of it at the moment and that needed to be corrected. I headed off and knew I when I was nearly there because I saw a tourist shop, which I entered on a whim.

I don't think you can ever fully prepare your mind for what the contents of a Finnish tourist shop will be. What do you think of as inherently Finnish that you could buy in a good department store? I'm not one for souvenir tat, but realised that this could well be the only time in my life I could acquire any Finnish objects.

I could hardly move in the place, it was so crowded with knick-knacks. The products could broadly be defined into two categories, inauthentic (baseball caps, mugs, t-shirts etc all in white saying FINLAND in an outdated font) and authentic, and it was the authentic items that interested me the more. Wooden homewares and furry blankets were stacked everywhere. Delicate trinkets hung off wire racks that covered all the walls. There were little wooden mugs for hot chocolate, butter knives, cushions in the shape of a reindeer, Russian dolls[11], pine trivets, pine backscratchers, pine bath brushes, sauna flannels; I have never wanted to acquire so much from a shop of such a modest size. In the end I chose some Christmas tree decorations, a cushion in the shape of a reindeer and a blue t-shirt with the word SUOMI emblazoned across the front so I could leave passers-by wondering what the word meant.

But my time in Finland was up. I longed to stay and hang around a bit more; I hadn't anticipated being in Finland, and I wasn't ready to leave just yet. I trudged back to the hotel to collect my things, hailed a cab and headed for the airport, hoping to return one day.

And I did: I got the job.

**

On my next visit, the travel schedule offered me the gift of a free afternoon and evening in central Helsinki. The sky offered me just the seven oktas of cloud cover today and the locals were clearly going to enjoy what little sun they had while they had it. I strolled down Helsinki's pedestrianised boulevard Esplanadi to the seafront, where couples canoodled on benches, children were passed ice creams down from lofty serving hatches by aproned adults, and everything was generally pretty swell. I was engaged again in the happy task of selecting a seafront restaurant when I noticed an LED sign next to a shelter at a docking point on the harbourside saying:

SUOMENLINNA 4 mins

---

[11] I can't stand Russian dolls, they're so full of themselves.

SUOMENLINNA 20 mins

SUOMENLINNA 36 mins

I didn't know what Suomenlinna was, but it was clearly a short boat ride away and if the ferry services were that regular, then it must be a popular destination. And if it must be popular, there must be things to do there, and I didn't think it out of the question that one of those things might be a restaurant. I consulted a timetable on a poster – the last ferry back was 11pm – well after dark. Suddenly, my evening had a plan and I stepped aboard.

Standing on the back of a ferry, chugging away from a capital city towards a leisure island, I will say this – the view of the Helsinki seafront was a bit of alright. Go to any internet image search engine now and type in 'Helsinki' and the most ubiquitous waterfront image you will be presented with was the very view I had. It was a palette of every possible shade of blue: The leaden sea in front and Helsinki's stately buildings capped by the dome of the Cathedral in the middle of my field of vision, all framed by a bright blue sky; I just stood there for a couple of minutes, hands on hips, drinking it in. Life is too short on these moments.

Suomenlinna, it turns out, is a family of islands in the Gulf of Finland a mile off the mainland. There are eight islands in total but four main ones, all linked by bridges and fortified as a strategic defence point. In a charmingly modest, cold-country sort of way, Helsinki fits the cliché of East meets West, with Estonia being about as far across the sea as Calais is from Dover. I was to learn after my trip that when Finland was under Swedish rule, the Swedish army had predictably lost many of its battles with Russia and decided that fortifying each island was the best way to prevent the

Russians from obtaining a beach-head from which to stage attacks on Helsinki. Construction of the fortifications started in 1750, but plans were scaled back by something called the Pomeranian War in 1756 and only the southern tip of the southernmost island was fortified in the end, which I'm not sure really helped. Whether or not this was a good idea is not up for debate; it is a fact of history that in the Russian-Swedish war of 1808, the islands were besieged by Russian forces and the ever-sensible Swedes surrendered quickly.

The Russians had big plans for their new asset, but in 1809 Finland became a Grand Duchy of Russia and as the 1800s passed, the military importance of the islands declined, budgets were cut and they fell into decay, which was catalysed in August 1855 when Suomenlinna was heavily bombarded by an Anglo-French fleet during the Crimean War. The Russians made repairs, but Suomenlinna was just one Russian fortress amongst many and was therefore left to not do very much for half a century until 1906, when, inspired by revolutionary unrest in Russia – and possibly bored by the long cold winters on this rocky plateau off the coast of a city that was becoming less and less strategically important - there was mutiny, and the Finnish islanders had a good go at the Russians, trying to take over the islands for themselves. But the phrase "you and whose army?" was invented for this type of situation and the mutiny was over in a few days as the Russians replied.

In 1918, Finland gained independence from Russia and gave the islands their current name, meaning 'Castle of Finland'. Finland sagely placed Defence Forces units there so Suomenlinna became a garrison, but it also opened itself to picnics for daytripping families, which I think is just great. Clearly, the picnics were not allowed from 1939 to 1945, but in the 1960s, the Finnish Department of Defence announced that they were vacating Suomenlinna completely, and whilst there's still a naval academy there today, 800 people call it their home and it's also a UNESCO World Heritage Site and the number 1 thing to do in Helsinki on Tripadvisor. So things turned out rather well.

I stepped off the ferry and noticed that, cunningly, a restaurant had been placed immediately next to the ferry terminus and, tempted as I was to go in there immediately and eat parsnip soup or whatever it was they'd laid on for the evening, the temptation to explore was far greater. What a waste it would have been to disembark the ferry, immediately make for the restaurant and emerge from it an hour later, only to take the ferry straight back home again? Far better to explore the island in the evening light and then step into the restaurant when dark, I reasoned.

It must have been 8pm when I set off on my self-guided tour. I clutched a tourist map and it was immediately obvious that Suomenlinna was crammed with much more to do than I could fit into a couple of hours. The islands covered less than a square kilometre but the map listed 46 pleasingly diverse things to do: Vesikko Submarine, Hytti Glass Studio, the Toy Museum, Prison, Café Samovar Bar, Summer Theatre, Beach (a beach, in Finland!?). I set off at a brisk pace, threading my way between wooden barracks, past granite war memorials and brightly coloured children's playgrounds, just following my senses and keeping going, trying to take it all in as I went. This being a Wednesday evening in a week when the children were in school I admit most things were closed, but then how much did I want to be the only visitor to a toy museum? How long did I want to stare at a boat in a dry dock on my own? I walked and walked, past a submarine on props - sadly closed to interior inspection – past the rainbow window of the glass studio, past the Japanese Tea Room and then past an open air swimming pool which in the crisp air and surrounded by soggy turf managed to be simultaneously the most inviting and least inviting swimming pool I'd ever seen. Its walls were constructed from granite blocks the size of loaves of bread which were housed in cages of chicken wire, and the water was the same shade of grey as the granite. However, to dive in and use it – there was no-one stopping me - looked as rich an experience as, say, plunging into the Caribbean Sea in Jamaica[12], yet the overriding sensation here was one of it looking unappealingly cold. Towel-less, I continued.

I slowly understood that I needed to start to find the second half of a circular path to take me home and realised that there was only one path to be had and it took me all the way around the fortifications at the southern tip of the island and past the distant Valhalle restaurant. Much to my frustration, Valhalle was closed and I set off back to the restaurant next to the jetty, where the hunger pangs started to hit.

I entered the restaurant at about half past nine and the party was in full swing – the place was about three-quarters full and happy people were sipping white wine around candles, liberating clouds of steam from their potatoes, breaking the glistening berry glazes on top of their cheesecakes and generally having about as good a time as it is possible to have in a restaurant. Waitresses in white blouses and black skirts busily criss-crossed the floor and I had to wait at the entrance desk flashing my eyebrows and

---

[12] No, she went of her own accord!

teeth at any and every member of staff for a few minutes before I was attended to.

"Do you have table for one? Just me..."

"No sorry, we are finishing now."

"But...the place is half full! Everyone's having such a good time!"

"Sorry, we don't serve food any more."

"Can you put a fish on a plate and I'll be gone in twenty minutes? I've just walked round the whole island and I'm really hungry."

"No, sorry, you must go."

I was tempted to press the issue further, but remembered one of the golden rules of travel: never be rude to someone preparing food for you behind a partition. But I was hungry! I stepped back outside and saw that mercifully it was only six minutes until my boat to a landmass with active restaurants on it. I wandered to the only shop on the island and impulsively bought a bag of sweets by the name of Dumle and insist you do the same if ever you're in Finland[13]; they were, and still are outstanding little blobs of confection – like soft centred Daim nuggets, which I think the world needs.

Back in Helsinki, I walked the streets for another ten minutes, praying I'd find Nordic cuisine so I didn't have to eat in a globally ubiquitous Italian or Chinese or Indian and I suddenly hit the jackpot. Zeteor was its name and in the unlikely event that TGI Fridays ever decide to open a Finland-themed restaurant then this is as good a job as they can do. Sure it was fake Finland, without the more

---

[13] Or even Ikea, nowadays; I'm eating one now.

authentic woody charm of Savotta before, but the place had been done up like a barn, with all sorts of Finnish accoutrements hanging from the ceiling - double-handled woodsaws, wooden sledges, tin buckets, local newspaper cuttings in Finnish about goodness-knows-what, stuffed beavers, and best of all in the centre, an actual tractor with a breakfast bar wrapped around its bonnet which was clearly the most popular seat in the house and consequently was full. So I slid into one of the dining booths, delighted to see reindeer on the menu again, and asked one of the pearl-toothed and aqua-eyed waitresses at which Finland excels for a Lapin Kulta and reindeer steak on mashed potato served with a side of another Lapin Kulta. Suddenly, my hunger was satiated, and everything was alright with the world again.

**

I was pleased to find out the following day that my new Finnish colleagues had arranged for me to experience one of the bastions of Finnish culture that I had, to their disbelief, not yet encountered: the Sauna[14]. I was looking forward to it, but the imbroglio of that evening would be something that I'd remember for the rest of my life.

After a day holed up in a hotel conference room, we repaired to a tiled room on an upper floor where a glass-topped table had been surrounded by wicker chairs and a beer fridge promisingly placed within reach of the chairs. The sauna in Finland is basically a pub with nudity and I was pleased to see that we were going to have our beers

---

[14] Rhymes with browner, not corner.

before going into the sauna, mainly because the niggling fear was playing on my mind that I might have to socialise naked in front of some very important colleagues in my new job and that – heaven forfend - it might be a mixed sauna. Happily, the ladies in the group turned left upon entering and placed their handbags down by a steamy glass door on one side of the room and seeing a similar door at the other side, I deduced that this was not going to be a mixed sauna.

And so, the beers were cracked open and as I tried to make conversation with the nation's famously introverted citizens. I asked how saunas came to be in Finland and why they had caught on north of the Baltic in such a way.

I was told by way of reply that as well as being an important heat source when it's -32°C outside and also something to do indoors to take the edge off winter, saunas also served an important hygienic function. Saunas are proven to help cure the common cold, rheumatic pain, chronic fatigue syndrome, fibromyalgia, rheumatoid arthritis, glaucoma and lung disease; so feel free to book a spa day at some point saying it's doctor's orders. In the days before fast, motorised transport, many babies were born in saunas when hospitals were out of range after the onset of labour as it was quite simply the most bacteria-free room in the house.

All this was very interesting, but it still hadn't escaped my mind that I shortly had to take my clothes off in front of my new colleagues.

We chatted some more. The beers were drained. As we all rose from the table, I downed mine, sensing the need for courage at this point in proceedings and willing to avail myself of any that was on offer. We walked across the room, my bonhomie becoming a little more forced. I was chatting to a senior manager, Jarkko, who I would in this job frequently have to have Skype meetings with, in which I would have to look him in the eye and beg for approval to do something risky. Trust was going to be important in our relationship and I needed to make a good impression. Jarkko led me over to a corner of the room intended for changing; it was lined with benches, above which were hooks about half a metre apart. From each hook hung, thankfully, a towelling bathrobe, with a small towel draped across its neck. Jarkko continued to engage me in conversation as he started unbuttoning his shirt in front of me. I tried to mute the stripping music in my head and mirrored him, suddenly sensing something in me markedly stronger than mild discomfort as I revealed my torso, but was thankfully able to take a step back as Jarkko leaned forward into my personal space to ease down his trousers, oblivious to my inherently British awkwardness. Then the dreaded moment was upon me: I had to do the bottom half, and Jarkko was going to be watching it all. I turned and sat on the bench as I slid the waistband of my trousers down to avoid the dreaded full frontal. Then it happened. Jarkko – ignoring my subliminal request to mirror me, whipped his underpants off in front of my very eyes. It was exactly at eye level.

Now what do you do when the polite thing to do is rude and the rude thing to do is polite? I was on the horns of a dilemma. I could strip naked in front of this very powerful colleague and everything would be fine, or I could slink away in my clothes and forever be referred to as the feeble English guy who was too stiff[15] to join in on the naked sauna. Still seated, I leaned forward again and slowly, as if to buy time while coming up with a cunning plan, removed

---

[15] Leave it

my socks in a manner not unlike that of Mr Bean. I have never been in a situation so absurdly desperate. Jarkko was at the sauna's door now and, with one hand on the knob (stop it) and his buttocks glistening in the steam, he looked coquettishly back at me over his shoulder and flashed me an expectant 'come-hither' smile, in the way a famous actress might on a red carpet. Leaning fully forward now, with fingertips on the floor, I slid my hands up to the waistband of my underpants and in one quick movement, removed them. For a nanosecond, I sat there, naked as the day I was born with Jarkko looking straight at me. Only then did the brainwave come. I'd done it! I had fulfilled the non-verbal contract to get naked with my new colleague and had therefore done justice to the situation and to myself – I had found a 'third way' and passed the test! The robe was clearly not for wearing in the sauna, but there was nothing to stop me taking the towel in with me, was there? Quick as a flash, I placed the towel on my lap and stood up, nonchalantly grasping it in front of my navel as I boldly went where I had never been before; into a room full of naked sweating men.

**

Generally unheralded as it is, Finland is the best country in the world at some remarkable things: It drinks the most coffee per person: Each Finn consumes an average of 12 kilos of coffee a year: that's 48 of those bag-of-sugar sized ground coffee you get in supermarkets, the equivalent of one per person per week – including children in that calculation. The cappuccino-loving Italians can only cope with five kilos.

More importantly, Finland also has the lowest infant mortality rate in the world and there's an intriguing and happy story behind this:

In the 1930s, Finnish infant mortality was 88 out of 1,000 (a similar figure to much of central Africa today) and as Finland set up its welfare state, it was universally agreed that something had to be done about this. And so it was decided that expectant mothers, provided they visited the doctor before the fourth month of their pregnancy, would be given a cardboard box, paid for by the government, in which all the basics would be contained – initially fabric and sewing patterns for baby clothes but as time passed the contents became more substantial and elaborate: bodysuits, blankets, toys, muslins, a bath towel, nappies, nappy cream, a sleeping bag, bra pads, and at the bottom of all this, a proper mattress. So the cardboard box became – either intentionally or unintentionally - the baby's first bed. Better than that, because every baby born that year is given the same sets of clothes, barriers are broken down between new parents as their babies meet and there becomes a sense that they're all in this parenting thing together.

Did it work? Outstandingly. A decade after the introduction of the scheme, the mortality rate had more than halved from 88 to 39 and a decade later nearly halved again to 21. Today, it's five per 1000, which is still five too many, but statistically about as low as you can get. But here's the lovely thing: Mothers don't have to take the box; they can choose a cash option instead - €140 at present. But 95% choose the box, which warms my heart so much that I'm going to go and pour myself a glass of wine now and toast the Finnish welfare state.

**

There, I enjoyed that – Malbec, since you ask. Anyway, where were we? That's right, Finland as world leaders in something. My first ever whiff of Finland was one year previously – I'd been asked to drive to the Nokia offices in Farnborough for work purposes, and during the journey, I drove at one point down a wide straight road where the speed limit was 30 mph but I didn't know that as I cruised past a speed camera at 35. The fine, £100, was dressed up as a speed awareness course, with the money going to the private company which ran the course rather than Police funds, which I still think is wrong. Of course, it felt pretty unjust at the time, but in October 2001 in Helsinki, a man named Anssi Vanjoki was out for a ride on his motorbike, enjoying the crisp autumn air before the onset of a predictably cold winter and all the black ice it would bring. Vanjoki was clearly enjoying the thrill of his last ride for months and crept over the speed limit by 15 mph – about the speed that you or I jog. Vanjoki's fine for doing this was €116,000 - the highest speeding penalty ever awarded; and the Police were laughing all the way to the bank because in Finland, speeding fines aren't a fixed penalty, but are set at 14 days of the speeder's annual income. Whilst this isn't a trivial amount for anyone (could you afford two weeks' pay every time you got a speeding ticket?) Vanjoki was unfortunately on the board of Nokia and received generous share options, which he had cashed in shortly before the dotcom crash one year previously, making himself a fortune and outsizing his annual salary for the year. If Vanjoki had been on his bike one week later, his's income would have registered as the significantly lower amount of the following financial year, resulting in a much smaller fine. Vanjoki appealed and – and I'm not suggesting wealthy business leaders in any way have the lawmakers in their pocket here – received a 95% reduction in his fine, proving that you're not innocent till proven guilty any more, you're guilty until you're proven rich.

**

But all good things must come to an end, and my time in this country had to finish.

I took a taxi to the airport and the driver inadvertently treated me to one final sight on the way out of the city. A drive past Linnanmäki, Finland's main amusement park. Gratifying as it was to see the tangled spaghetti of roller coaster tracks, what really pleased me was its location, on a clifftop, overlooking the city centre and the sea beyond. I am sure that in many cities in the world, a location this prime would have been snapped up early by some real estate speculator or owned by the aristocracy, and on it would be built either a suite of 'luxury' apartments or a stately pile that would either stay in the family for generations or be used by the President as weekend retreat, from where he could overlook his minions. But in Finland, they installed big dippers and ferris wheels and I think that's how the world should be. I felt a pang of sadness to be leaving the country behind and before I could stop myself, I was telling the taxi driver this.

"Of course, we are a happy country," he explained to me. "We do not have a good economy now Nokia has suffered, it is cold in the winter but our quality of life is as good as anywhere in the world. And only Finland has Father Christmas."

Suddenly, the country clicked into place. Finland was never going to be an important global country – it was too unpopulated, too chilly, too remote. It didn't have a strategically important port, it would never boast of golden beaches or bustling metropolises. But the Finns are happy with all this. Rather than expend their effort on pushing Finland perpetually onwards and upwards in the pointlessly glittering global race of international prominence that Dubai and Qatar seem to be winning at the moment, the Finns prefer to reserve their energy for the important task of just bursting with national pride for successfully overcoming nature and managing to *keep going* in spite of the disadvantageous climate and location. Finland's winter is a joyous season – Finns don't wish away the cold in the way that my temperate Britain does, they embrace it with saunas. Looking closer, it was possible to see this attitude everywhere: Striking designs of bold colour and bright patterns on their snow-proof clothing and scarves and luggage, revelry in the form of heavy beers, brown meats and volcanically hot and lava-coloured root vegetables, an insistence on good design – Finnish products *had* to be good to survive multiple deep winters. The Finns have a word for this: 'Sisu' – the ability to keep going in the face of adversity without weakening the spirit. I didn't want to go back to England's drizzly dusk, I wanted to stay and stare at the onset of Finland's space-black sky. As a treat, it was starting to snow as the taxi reached the airport. I spent the journey drinking in the views of the snow settling on pine forests, knowing there would be a day I left Finland and never came back and fearing that this was it.

By the time I had checked in and made it to the departure lounge, a carpet of snow had covered the airfield. I passed time in the airport shops, picking up a pack of reindeer salami (with the sole purpose of serving it on blinis on Christmas morning for amusement purposes) then enquired at the gate as to whether my plane might be delayed. "No, we are used to snow here in Finland, your plane will depart on time." And it did, though the consternation of boarding a snow-covered plane in the dark whose window still has not cleared of snow as it raced along the slushy runway is a feeling I would prefer not to experience again. We were airborne without fuss – always a miracle – and I pushed the button in my armrest to lean back and unwind. The map on the in-cabin screens showed I had crossed the coast. It was official: I had left Finland; a country I had never intended to visit, but a country I had fallen in love with. Monty Python had got the lyric right; Finland was the country for me. I was missing the place already as I cradled my wine, gazed out of the window, and watched the sun rise in the west.

4. Poole Harbour and the Isle of Wight

"The sea was blue and covered in dancing spangles, the sky was full of drifting clouds white as bedsheets, and the houses and hotels of Sandbanks behind me looked radiant, almost Mediterranean, in the clear air."

Bill Bryson – Notes from a Small Island

When you have a baby, the world is positively teeming with advice for you. Bookshops' shelves groan under the weight of pastel-covered A4 coffee table hardbacks exalting the virtues of baby-led weaning, sleep patterns, double-babbles, wonder weeks, and just about every other jumble of words baby psychologists use on a daily basis. Everyone dotes on you. Your friends deposit a cumulative acre of lasagne on your doorstep every day after the birth and generally a big thing is made of how hard this sudden change in life is for you. I felt as prepared as anyone could be for all the mental and physical challenges of having a baby, but as the baby started to walk and talk, there seemed a curious void of information on how to make the transition from having a baby to having a toddler, and that was a transition that was – for me – much harder to make.

My firstborn decided he was going to announce he'd become a toddler at 8pm on Sunday 11 July 2010. I remember the date very clearly, because that was when I was settling down to watch the World Cup Final, and that evening, for the first time in his little life, he had decided he wasn't going to go to bed in the calm, docile way he had for all for the 700+ consecutive evenings until now. I tried everything; gentle chiding, stern words, using every metaphorical carrot and stick I could think of, but nothing worked. He just didn't want to go to bed and for the first time in his life, he realised that he didn't have to. Remember, this was 2010, just before the hitherto magical ability to pause live TV had become a widely adopted technology. I coaxed, cajoled, promised chocolate and ice cream, threatened the removal of teddy bears and shut doors while the commentator howled like a hyena from the television below as the Spain team – the greatest international football team of all time – scored to deservedly win their maiden World Cup. The moment the goal was announced, I knew the game was up: I had a toddler.

None of this is the fault of my firstborn, of course – he had no idea about international football fixtures as his little brain expanded that day, it's just what toddlers do. One of the ways that the turbulent nature of a life with a toddler isn't really thought about compared to life with a baby is the holiday experience. With a baby, the airport make a fuss of you and whisk you through the terminal on a red carpet of fast-track lanes. White-gloved staff pick you out in a queue and wave you to the front. The baby gets his ticket for free and receives a luggage allowance too which you can fill with wine for the journey home. You're boarded first and have lots of lovely legroom at the bulkhead and the stewardesses slip you contraband alcohol with a knowing wink because they know you need to be calmed as much as the baby. All this time, the baby's asleep and the journey's frankly a cakewalk for you as a parent. But with a toddler, there's none of that. You have to keep them entertained for the duration of a 40-minute check-in queue lest they run off with a stranger to some distant corner of the globe, then immediately repeat the process through security. Once on the plane, you find that there is literally nothing to entertain your fidgety toddler with for the three and a half hours they are in their seat, except a set of crayons which they then use to decorate the traytable and window shade. Then, once the holiday has ended, the entire charade must be completed again in reverse in a successful attempt to reacquire all the stress you have just spent the last week getting out of your system, at the cost of the annual bonus you have just spent 12 months striving to achieve.

For this reason, I asserted to Debs after the Gibraltar trip that my preference was to holiday in the UK next year. Debs was opposed to this opinion and so we embarked on ten months of negotiation, compromise and deal making which would put some international trade agreements into the shade. About eight months into the discussion, we had established that whilst I wanted to holiday anywhere driveable and not too far from home, Debs had three non-negotiable demands.

1) To go south.
2) To go overseas.
3) To be near a beach.

And so we went to the Isle of Wight.

But first rather than smash and grab our way in and out of the island, we were going to make a meal of this holiday – a lengthy, delicious banquet taking in a magical place we wanted to visit along the way. Everyone has a special place they go to get away from it all. For some it is Cornwall, or Cape Cod, or the Isle of Skye. For us, it is Poole Harbour.

If you've never been to Poole Harbour then you'll be surprised to know that it is, after Sydney's, the second largest natural harbour in the world. It's 14 square miles, and therefore forms what is essentially an inside out city – with the rural joy in the centre and the urban miasma of commercial and industrial activity relegated to the fringe of existence, where it should be.

To get to our desired beach, we had to cross the mouth of Poole Harbour, which meant driving through Sandbanks, which is – and this is a fact as incontrovertible as it is surprising – a parcel of land as expensive to live on as can be found anywhere in the world – including such urban hotspots as Manhattan, Tokyo and central London. It measures just 0.4 sq miles, but has come to hold a cachet in the twenty-first century as a place where rich people simply *should* be living – or at least holding property until they can think of something more profitable to do with their cash. Relatively elegant homes that fall some way short of being palatial change hands for comfortably more than £5 million. View-restricting pine trees mysteriously tumble down in the dead of night to make way for new developments that commercially exploit every inch of the prime real estate that these plots occupy. Heritage is in some cases not even given a second thought; in 2008, a Russian buyer pulled down a smart New England-style clapboard house that had been constructed by its previous owner just five years earlier to build something even more up to date. In September 2013, Tom Doyle of Lloyds Property Group was quoted in the Daily Mail as saying "we've just had our best month ever, exchanging on £24 million worth of property." An inordinate amount of business for any estate agent. Sandbanks is a perfectly nice tract of seaside land and I could live there quite happily, but it has simply become famous for being famous and is now attractive to the wealthy because wealthy people are there. In 2017, a weed-strewn plot of land was on the market for £13.5 million. It would cost another £4 million to then build a house. But you and I can access this land for free and observe its wealthy houses closeup by queueing for the chain ferry across the harbour mouth from Sandbanks to the sandy headland on the western side: Studland.

Studland is one of my favourite places in the world. The mouth of Poole Harbour is the very point where the bustle and hubbub of South East England is left behind and the gentler South West starts; the South West Coast Path begins the moment you step off the ferry and continues all the way to Land's End. Its beach is as exquisite as any England has to offer – certainly as high quality as any beach that this temperate zone will give you anywhere in the world. From Sandbanks, Studland Beach actually looks as if it is made from gold powder. It is accessed by a boardwalk (always a rare treat) across a nature reserve. The end of the boardwalk submerges under sand, and what sand it is; as fine as you will find, comparable to the Caribbean (I may have secreted a few litres of it back to my garden in Tupperware boxes over the years) – underfoot, it feels finer than caster sugar and is nearly as white, too. Debs and I took a large group of friends there a couple of years previously and a friend who had been raised in Poland helplessly exclaimed as she climbed the first dune, to be hit by the sea view for the first time: "Oh, wow, this is like Spain!" She's right too. It *is* like Spain. Everything about it is perfect: The distance from the dunes to the sea, the temperature of the sea itself, the play of the light through the decorative clouds, the shallowness of the paddling water – no deeper than waist-height for a good 50 metres out – the warmth and clarity of the water, the microclimate; you could set a film there pretending it was the Algarve or the Costa Del Sol and no-one would complain. Monty Python and Harry Enfield[16] have both used it as a tropical island location for their sketches. Debs and I spent a happy day there with the children, alternating between splashing in its Volvic-like surf, spending an hour horizontal and reading inferior fiction. At the end of the day, we decided to make use of a hardbacked folder we had on our bookcase at home produced by the Automobile Association entitled "1001 Walks in Britain" and took a circuitous route through another part of the nature reserve back to the car. Draping a little map in a plastic pouch on red string around my neck, we set off for a stroll in the sun, fully expecting to see things we hadn't seen before. And we did.

The walk along wet sand was as pleasing as any coastal walk, but after half a mile the map then told us to turn right at 90 degrees and head inland. Here is where it got interesting. The idea was that we were meant to turn inland at an indeterminate point on the coast, un-notated by any landmarks, then find a footpath through a nature reserve back to the Studland Road. Of course, there was no way to know when to leave the sea and head for the dunes so we made our best guess, reasoning that at the dunes we would at least be high up and could to see where the path inland was. What actually happened was that we hit the dunes and promptly lost all track of where the path was and happened instead to come across – in clutches and taking

---

[16] http://bit.ly/1xcs2qh

cover amongst the sandy knolls – nudists. With two small children in tow we were at almost every turn surprised by pairs of geriatrics supine and pallid in the altogether – like upturned tortoises without their shells. The children took it in turns to pronounce "euurgh!" and "look at that one!" for a period of time that took too long for our liking before we finally found the path back to the road and the safety of our car, in which we could speed to Swanage.

**

Swanage is a paradoxical place. It exists for the benefit of tourists yet is about as inaccessible a seaside town as you will find along the coast from Sussex to Devon. As a place to daytrip from Poole, it's perfect, but it isn't on the way to anywhere; upon reaching the town, the road around Poole harbour juts to the right by ninety degrees to head inland to rejoin…er…the harbour road it had deviated from. So you pretty much have to get there by car and we did, which made finding a car park the first activity of the day. We intended to park up and have a leisurely poke about in the town for a few hours but all the car parks we came to were the dreaded pay and displays. I don't know why pay and display car parks have been allowed to exist for so long, particularly in leisurely locations, as here. It's absurd that car park operators think that, upon arriving at a place where we're to be at leisure, we want firstly to make a decision on how long we intend to stay for before we've even seen the place – resulting in either having to hurry back and curtail our fun because we fear a traffic warden or wasting cash. Once we've succumbed to this way of doing things, we then find that parking there for our estimated amount of time needed for pleasure costs £4.50 but the machine doesn't accept £5 notes or £2 coins or anything smaller than 10p and you only have £3.80 in the remaining coinage. So you take a little walk to find a cash machine then visit the beleaguered newsagent to pay for a chocolate bar with a £20 note.

But in Swanage, it was worse than that. We were faced with a horrible pricing structure intentionally designed to gratuitously extort money from us. We could pay for one hour's car parking, or two hours, or four hours, or any amount above four, but the three hours (and its price) were mysteriously absent. I know local councils don't run on thin air, but why won't they realise that they exist for the good of the people and not the other way round? Does it not just take a little edge off the pleasure of your day out to find you're being rinsed like that? It did mine. I headed for the large Co-Op supermarket on the edge of the town centre where free parking was to be had provided we spent £5 in the shop.

But I digress. Swanage is a nice enough place in a chocolate box kind of way with buildings in local Purbeck stone nestled in between rising headlands either side and a sparkling sea out front. It has all the amenities that a town needs to live decently in – estate agents, banks, cafés, a post office, some clothes shops, as well as a miniature fairground for the tourists (whose café tables displayed a sign saying (word for word) "THESE TABLES ARE FOR THE CONSUMPTION OF FOOD AND DRINK PURCHASED FROM THE KIOSK NO NAPPY CHANGING THANK YOU", some fine chalky cliffs, a clean and tidy sand beach right at the end of the high street, some fish and chip shops and a little flat-roofed theatre whose café had a poster in the window announcing that the "SEASALT RESTAURANT AND CAFÉ

ARE NOW CLOSED FOR THE WINTER" (it was July). Swanage is a more interesting place to do nothing much in than to write about, so I'll smashcut to the supermarket car park at the end of the day, where I'd dipped in to the shop to spend £5 while Debs spent the same amount of time dusting the sand off the children and buckling them into their seats. Thinking on what costs little more than £5 in a supermarket, I of course made straight for the wine aisle and selected a bottle, but was surprised to be told at the till that the alcohol wasn't a valid purchase for car park ticket redemption, a policy I didn't understand then and still don't now. I bought flowers for Debs.

**

One of the things I was keen to do in Poole was visit Brownsea Island. It is the largest in Poole Harbour – 1½ miles long and ¾ of a mile wide – consisting of 500 acres of glorious semi-tropical English pine and oak woodland and salt-marsh on the northern side which had been converted into a bird-filled nature reserve. The entire island is owned by the National Trust. A small portion to the south-east of the island, along with Brownsea Castle, is leased to the John Lewis Partnership an is where their staff - in that wonderful mix of capitalism and socialism in which the John Lewis Partnership and Waitrose specialise – take holidays in a company-owned hotel. It is not open to the public. The island is one of the few places in the country where you can see a red squirrel. Quite a feat as, according to The Forestry Commission, there are estimated to be only 140,000 red squirrels left in Britain, compared to over 2.5 million greys.

Many people I trust say it is well worth a visit. 100,000 travel to Brownsea every year, most aware of the red squirrel and enough seeing one to give me confidence that I'd have the same experience. But getting there is not an easy task. You may have noticed already that travelling to an island necessitates a boat, and, not having a boat in our possession, this meant making our way to the departure point for the pleasure boats, which was in the centre of Poole. This meant driving to the centre of Poole and parking the car in a multi-storey car park in the full knowledge that it would be the best part of a day before we returned to it on a tariff that we came to recognise in Swanage as having been designed exclusively for the use of tourists. Upon arriving at Poole Harbourside we presented ourselves at a tiny yellow hexagonal wooden kiosk with a pointed roof and a window giving onto the pavement and enquired of the lady as to how much the aquatic locomotion to and from Brownsea Island would cost us. We were presented with a sum of money that managed to be both expensive and reasonably-priced at the same time - £28 for a family of four – and so I offered my debit card as payment but was met with the surprise response that a debit card issued by one of the big 4 banks for a transaction of £28 wasn't acceptable as a form of payment and we would need to find cash instead. Taken aback, I asked where we might procure cash in the handful of minutes before the boat departed and was assured that if we crossed the threshold of a Wetherspoons pub along the seafront, then there, in the dingy back-quarters of the pub, there would be a cash machine that would supply us with the required combination of banking papers to get us waterborne. We asked if the boat would wait for us and followed directions to our goal, where we were disappointed to find out that this cash machine was one of those horrible semi-portable units that charged us £1.50 to access the money that we had worked hard to earn, but, faced with little choice, we procured ourselves £30 and returned to the quayside just in time to watch our boat moving away from the harbour – what a lot of fun we were having! It was 40 minutes until the next departure and so we decided to entertain the children by leading them away from the harbour wall with its unguarded 20 foot drop into the deep sea and into a café where we paid for four baguette sandwiches with a debit card and hurriedly consumed most of them before dashing to a blue hexagonal wooden hut adjacent to the yellow one we had just been disappointed by to make enquiries with a separate ferry operator. Disappointingly, this boat charged £32 (cash only, naturally) and also told us that this £32 would only get us to the island; we would have to pay to actually set foot on it, just as we would any National Trust property.

After another trip to Wetherspoons, we were finally on the boat and the journey could now begin. It was one of those pleasure crafts with an open top deck with wooden benches arranged in rows facing the front, and a slightly dingy carpeted room underneath with large windows either side and a bar at the back that wasn't serving any drinks. We sat out up top to take in the view and, having the whole deck to ourselves, were just beginning to unwind from the stresses of the morning when a little voice next to my elbow exclaimed "Look Daddy, pirates!" And indeed there were, for on our port side was a middleweight wooden ship all jazzed up to look as pirate-like as possible to amuse the children and it was having the desired effect. Local out-of-work actors dressed as pirates were theatrically strutting around on deck, aaharrrrghing and yo-ho-ho-ing as their jolly roger ploughed through the surf. The mood began to lighten. One pirate with an impressively ugly face and teeth that may or may not have been naturally that yellow/brown when he woke up that morning squirted a super soaker high into the air; the wind whipping across the bay brought the spray down unpleasantly close to my left shoulder. Then immediately after that, an unexpected and unnecessarily large quantity of water bombs were launched not just in our general direction, but directly at us. They burst against the side of our boat below the level of our deck, but these were just sighters. Higher and faster they came, causing us to pay urgent attention to their flight before we could consider any exit route (sitting on a bench, there was none that wasn't along the trajectory of the missile). We dodged projectile after projectile as they whizzed past our shoulders and met their rubbery demise on the deck beside us with a mixture of mirth and consternation from onlookers. Then, like a test match delivery, one came in low with the element of surprise. In slow motion I tried to flick my hips out of the way, but my feet were rooted to the floor; hemmed in by rucksacks and benches and tiny feet. But it was impossible to avoid. The balloon snuck over the rail – a real waistcutter – and, with a moment of incredulity that still smarts, it slapped onto the inside of my thigh and instantly exploded, depositing a pint of cold water over my groin and dribbling down. Now, I'm not easily given to anger, but if you really want to make me see red, you couldn't do much better than take £50 off me then pelt me with water balloons while I'm dressed in the only set of clothes I have at the start of a day out. I reacted instinctively, for nothing can prepare you for an assault of this nature. I stood up and in a fit of unplanned yelling, hurled what I was holding at the pirate. Unfortunately, what I was holding was the last bit of my baguette sandwich. This was not one of those torpedo-like skinny mini-baguettes so popular in sandwich bars, this was a light, foamy affair that made me suspect either a Asda had been involved or the proprietor had recently insulated her loft. I launched it with the most anger I've ever thrown anything in my life, with the kind of sidespin you'd put on an American football to improve accuracy, but my technique dismally failed to translate into any sort of bullet-like speed once it had left my hand. It floated through the air with all the impotence of a beach ball, little circles of cucumber and hard-boiled egg losing interest in their vocation as ammunition and parachuting out of the mission milliseconds into the flight, which was becoming increasingly sheared as the wind got hold of it. The dough reached the halfway point of the twenty foot gap between boats before completely losing all momentum and catching the wind to start its journey back towards me and down into the water like a seagull diving in for lunch. But this was my lunch, and worst of all, it floated – the ends curling out making the thing grin at me. Well, honestly. I sat back down, sunk my neck into my shoulders, and with a leg coated in wet denim, we finally departed for Brownsea Island. Harrumph.

**

Brownsea Island has a claim to fame. From 1884 to 1901, a young officer in the British Army found that his love for all things military overflowed into a series of books he couldn't help himself but write regarding either military techniques or write-ups of his campaigns. The titles wouldn't exactly cause you to gravely inspect a copy in Waterstones – to name three: *Cavalry Instruction, Pigsticking or Hoghunting*, *The Downfall of Prempeh* - but on returning from service in Africa in 1903 he was amazed to find that the unsnappily-titled *Aids to Scouting for N.-C.Os and Men* had become an unlikely national bestseller, with teachers and youth organisations particularly inspired by the volume. Thus it was decided that the book should be rewritten to suit a youth readership and, in August 1907, he held a camp on Brownsea to test his ideas. He organised various outdoor activities around camping, woodcraft, lifesaving, plus a few more odd pastimes that haven't stood the test of time: observation, patriotism, and chivalry. In case you haven't worked it out yet, the officer was Robert Baden-Powell, the title of the book he rewrote was *Scouting for Boys*, and Brownsea Island was where the Boy Scout movement was born. The Scouting area forms around 50 acres of the island's 500 and I inspected it respectfully as I passed by, but nothing was going on that day so there was little to see except a collection of vintage canvas tents, the like of which I sincerely hope I never have to sleep in. And so we passed by, on a mission to do nothing much on Brownsea Island except see it, deciding that a lap of the island would be the best way to do that - we figured we'd have that done in a couple of hours at most. And we were right, because about a quarter of the way round, having left behind the tourist concentration around the quay, we realised there was nothing especially special about Brownsea Island; it was just a parcel of land too small to be totally independent of the world around it, but too big not to have tourist pull. The island was more or less empty – there was little more to do in the middle of it than have a picnic or go for a walk, neither of which was an activity that required a journey across water. The walk became a trudge of little note, though about halfway round we did venture onto a beach along which a peacock was strolling. It remains the only time in my life that I have seen a peacock on a beach and I can't think of when I will see another one. What a pointless achievement. I thought of Suomenlinna off the coast of Helsinki and how it was filled with quaint little attractions that respected the personality and history of the island and wished that the National Trust had let a little of that joy happen here. After too long working our way around the perimeter, we finally came to the patch of woodland next to the nature reserve and after a miserable morning of travel and something of an anticlimactic circumnavigation, I craned my neck up to the tall canopy, hoping to see a red squirrel darting about. I stared until my neck told me to stop, but there wasn't one to be seen. I forget how long the walk through the woodland lasted – it was more than ten minutes, it was less than half an hour, but there was absolutely no sight of any red squirrel anywhere. Then we were back at the quay to take the boat home. After my eagerness to 'do' Brownsea Island, nothing of note had happened there. And now there was nothing to do but sit and wait for the boat to turn up to take us off the island. I pulled out my copy of *A Kingdom By The Sea* by Paul Theroux and read a few pages to pass the time. In it – a journey around Britain's coast – Theroux stops at one point to ask a local if a particular landmark was worth seeing. "Oh, it is," replies the local, "it's worth seeing, but it's not worth going to see." It summed things up.

**

Southampton is where the Titanic sailed from. I had never been to Southampton before, an oversight surely, considering it's a little more than an hour from home and surely has much to commend it to the 850,000 people that live in that built up area of South Hampshire, making it more populous than higher-profile urban areas such as Tyneside, Sheffield and Bristol. But that is how we travel nowadays; I'm prepared to bet that you have set foot in more of Paris, Barcelona, Prague, Rome and Budapest than Southampton, Leeds, Lincoln, Worcester and Sunderland. Still, the memory of the Titanic's doomed departure at the forefront of my mind, I drove my most financially valuable possession (containing my most non-financially valuable possessions) onto an Isle of Wight ferry[17]. I was sure the crossing would be safer than 102 years previously, though a trip across the Solent is not without peril. Shortly after leaving the harbour an enormous rusty iron shell stood proudly in the sea with MONROVIA stencilled on its stern. I didn't know anything about Liberian shipping regulations, but looking at this rusty hulk in front of me, I fancied they were a little looser than the ones that the ferry I was on was adhering to. I wasn't sure if it was stranded or had just dropped anchor there, but it wasn't a great advert for the joys of boating in this part of the world. Many captains come a cropper in The Solent. It did for the Mary Rose, and – with a touch of irony no doubt noticed at the time – HMS Invincible in 1747. But neither of these succumbed to the Solent's greatest danger: Bramble Bank.

Bramble Bank is a sandbar in the centre of the Solent which at low water spring tides (ie one hour per year) reveals itself to the world just enough for two dozen English eccentrics from local sailing clubs to descend on it in and have the annual Bramble Bank cricket match.[18] The other

---

[17] One of only two things in the world which can be truthfully described as being brown, steaming, and coming out of Cow(e)s backwards.

8,759 hours per year, however, it is obscured, but lurks dangerously close to the surface, snagging amateur boaters who should know better. However, it is certainly no threat to large modern vessels such as the QE2. Except for the occasion when the QE2 was making her final approach to Southampton prior to her retirement in November 2008 and managed to run aground there for 90 agonising minutes until tides rose and things carried on as normal. Or in January 2015 when the Hoegh Osaka, a 180-metre car carrier which was turning out of Southampton on her way to Germany, developed a list and her rudder and propeller made a rare appearance above the waterline. At this point, the captain, intentionally (apparently) decided to ground the ship off Bramble Bank at an unusually jaunty angle of 52°, which is as we all know more than halfway to the horizontal. This caused a problem for its operator as its cargo was 1400 expensively painted Range Rovers and buses, all of which slid sideways. The investigation into the causes of the incident makes for much more interesting reading than it has any right to, with the parts of it posted on Wikipedia containing such juicy phrases as:

"No calculation of the vessel's stability had been made, [...] the weight of cargo on board was [...] 265 tonnes greater than [...] calculated. [...] Cargo had shifted as a result of the ship listing; [...] the ship's ballast water system was not fully serviceable, [...] a situation that had existed since at least July 2014.[...} Some of the straps used to secure the cargo to the deck were found not to meet regulations in force at the time, only being half as strong as they should have been."

---

[18] http://tinyurl.com/9t2dxk4

I waved at Bramble Bank as we passed where I had expected it to be and nodded respectfully, hoping that my Vauxhall Zafira was going to come out of a the encounter better that all those Range Rovers did. Then, shortly after that, we were docking in the Isle of Wight itself.

There are a great many falsehoods about the Isle of Wight. The first is that it nothing great has ever come out of the Isle of Wight, an argument I will dismember now when I tell you that fine actors Jeremy Irons and Sheila Hancock, A-list comedian Phill Jupitus, greatest bass-guitar player in the world Mark King from the band Level 42, celebrated journalist Polly Toynbee and Oscar-winning film director Anthony Minghella all hail from a patch of land less than 150 square miles in size, with a smaller population than Dundee. The second falsehood is that you could fit the world's population upon it. I discovered this this morning when, with no knowledge of the fact that I was writing a chapter on the Isle of Wight, a book based on the TV panel show QI (I think it was a Christmas present from my brother in law Jonathan - thank you Jonathan, I don't think I ever sent a letter) presented me with the information that this had become untrue some time ago, with the island being only (assuming one square foot per person) able to accommodate 2.5 billion people - the world's population in 1950.

Anyway, The Isle of Wight was very much there as we disembarked, and we pointed the car at the town that we'd decided to stay in. Every other postcard on the island will tell you that there are many pun-rich resorts to choose from: Ryde (where you walk), Cowes (where there are sheep), Freshwater (which you cannot drink), Newtown (which is very old) and so on and so on – we picked Shanklin mainly because it didn't pun, but a very fine pick it was. It proved to be an assortment of charmingly British houses with thatched roofs, tea rooms (in one of which we discovered the hard way still only accepted cash), a medieval pub with a pillory in the garden, pleasingly upmarket Victorian typefaces on shop signs and attractively manicured parks. We set about exploring this little corner of the island and discovered at that point that Shanklin is separated from the sea by some towering cliffs, and the only access to the waterfront seemed to be by one road or via a pretty walk through a short gorge called Shanklin Chine where a small stream ran underneath a large wooden gate, next to which was a man in a hut demanding that we as a family pay £13 to walk through this piece of nature – which seemed a touch pricey for a whimsical decision to take the scenic route to the beach, even if there was the promise of a waterfall somewhere in there. There seemed something inherently wrong to me that a private company could simply fence off a naturally beautiful landscape feature and charge people to see it, so I stood there at the entrance and watched a Youtube video of it on my phone before stepping away from the steep entrance fee and towards a steep set of cliff-front steps which provided an acceptable level of entertainment for the descent.

The Shanklin seafront managed to be smart whilst at the same time offering that ever so slightly tacky British seaside experience that we've come to expect and even hope for by now. Now, one thing that you're forewarned about by everyone when you announce that you'll be going to the Isle of Wight is that you need to be wary of the hospitality, which hasn't gone to the trouble of updating itself since about 1956. If you think of the kind of in-decline British seaside leisure that inhabits the set of *Fawlty Towers*, then you're getting the idea – faded tearoom-style restaurants with thin carpets patterned with the kind of design you see when you rub your eyes too hard and worse food than you cook at home, served with a certain well-practiced flourish. I was pleased to report that our accommodation for the week had by a good distance vaulted these expectations, and here we were on our first morning now in a café, experiencing Wightian[19] hospitality for the very first time.

I'm not sure how you can really get a cup of black coffee wrong if you work in a coffee shop, but inexplicably, this place managed to. I ordered Debs a tea, and a 'black coffee' for myself, but as we took our first sips, we compared experiences: Debs's tea was perfectly vanilla, as it were, but my black coffee had been made with instant granules. I failed to drink it and instead spent the time looking left and right to take the seafront in. In front of the small parade of café-shop restaurants I was seated in was a hardly-used road running above a gently sloping sandy beach. Next to the café-shop restaurants was a mutedly-cacophonous games arcade and not one but two excellent crazy golf courses – the type with a green baize to putt on, colour-matched bunkers and an extravagant pirate theme. Past this little strip was a dinky but permanent fairground with a twisty roller-coaster that was clearly king of its jungle and various smaller rides for the under fives. If was a good little find and if you're in Shanklin now you must go there before you leave; Britain's seaside pleasures may be a little more solitary in an era of £25 flights to the Mediterranean, but there is still pleasure to be had.

**

---

[19] Yes, that's the adjective: http://tinyurl.com/n5nmv52

But Shanklin wasn't the only place in the Isle of Wight we wanted to see, so the following day we took a trip to neighbouring costal town Sandown. It's about three miles along the coast from Shanklin and it's fair to say that if Shanklin is a Ye Olde England place for tourists, then Sandown is a place where local people actually live. Its high-street wasn't Shanklin's row of thatched tea-rooms and gift-shops, it was a succession of dreary shopfronts that seemed relatively unchanged since about 1986. They all seemed to consist of a large recessed window in a wooden frame and a hinged door you had to push open to get in, that is if it was your wish to part with your cash to buy an old train set or clothes for your grandmother or to refill your printer cartridge or acquire a fancy dress outfit for a party you were attending before Amazon had been invented. Sandown didn't have the nookish charm of Shanklin, but it did have a pier. There were signs on the beach warning us to beware of wash from container ships passing in the English Channel, which put an innovatively industrial slant on a way to be put off your holiday dip. We decided it was time for lunch.

Sandown didn't abound in seafront places to eat, so we climbed a steep pavement inland to a pub that overlooked the pier whose name I regret I failed to record, but Google Streetview tells me it might have been Flanagan's. It was a prime site, right in the middle of the beachfront, the nearest pub to the pier, with an elevation that gave a pleasingly improved view of the sea. If you were looking to run a successful seaside pub somewhere in the South of England and had Sandown on your list as a possible town then you really couldn't do better than this location. The food hit the spot, the beer was cold, the leather sofas comfy, the little box of plastic toys provided for the children was welcome, but here's the thing: the place was virtually empty. This was, let me remind you, a Saturday lunchtime in August – surely one of the busiest hours of the year for an urban British pub with a sea view. We had the place virtually to ourselves. I overtipped.

Refuelled by the trinity of a hot burger, salty chips and a cylinder of lager, we made our way back down to the beach where we hung out for a couple of hours while the children buried each other in sand and the locals walked their dogs. Three years previously, one of those locals would have been Michael McNiff. McNiff had lived in a small flat in the centre of town, during which he was for his final two years there on the 'Most Wanted' section of the Crimewatch website. McNiff was an unremarkable figure who was to be found dressed in everyday clothes as he took his dog along the beach twice a day, but when not doing that, he was overseeing the import of £4 million of heroin. No wonder he had the time to walk his dog twice a day. It does make me wonder why a man should take so much time to care for an animal whilst at the same time having total disregard for the many thousands of human lives, families and loving relationships which he was destroying with his enterprise. And it all happened right here in plain sight on this very beach where I was now. He'd probably sat in the pub I'd taken my family to lunch in. Maybe he'd had meetings with some of his associates there. Maybe that's why the pub was so quiet.

**

In the ferry terminal at Southampton, I'd rifled through the tourist leaflet rack for ideas and by far the least convincing of all prospective destinations was one with the words BUS MUSEUM printed on the front and photographs of many aged buses sitting almost derelict in what was described as an 'open air experience' but looked remarkably like a parking lot. There was nothing about it that appealed, irrespective of how many bus carcasses I could inspect from the inside. Next to it was a swish black leaflet with THE GARLIC FARM in artful white lettering which sounded like it would deliver far less than it was promising, which wasn't much. But something flickered in the back of my brain and I remembered a former colleague who was from the Isle of Wight had listed it as one of the top five things to do, as intractably dull as it sounded. So, as an act of faith, I went.

Well, I don't think I've ever had a better day out on holiday anywhere ever. It was much, much better than it should be and still significantly better than any travel writer can make it sound. But I'll try.

Garlic really is the most fascinating foodstuff and The Garlic Farm was about to give me a lifetime of information on this mysterious plant. It's easily grown, and the simple act of planting it will keep moles away, so you're winning before you've even harvested any. And when you do, the size of the bulb will be dependent on a number of factors, one of which is the latitude where it was grown – interestingly, large cloves grow in colder climates and small in hot ones. 80% of the world's garlic is produced in China, which made me wonder why the owners had bothered to make a British tourist attraction based around garlic, but as I experienced the attraction, I found out why; the place was a living museum, an active monument to all things garlic and each installation was more interesting than the last. As well as a working farm, there were cookery workshops, an education centre (into which surely every school on the island had emptied a busload at some point) llama trekking, a fully-functioning restaurant, a casual café for when you wanted a break from the restaurant, tractor tours, a frisbee golf course, a shop that literally had every kind of foodstuff that garlic could be contorted into, and assurances that red squirrels could be seen. I still wanted to see a red squirrel.

We started in the education centre on the grounds that we thought the children might make friends with the place amidst the colouring tables and tabletop mini-gardens, but I was stopped in my tracks by a poster depicting a full-size skeleton and a headline telling me that during World War I, the British Army ordered 100 tonnes of garlic to be dispatched to the front line – its antibacterial properties made it the penicillin of its day. Around the skeleton, arrows zinged in on every part of his body and a brief descriptor at the edge of the poster explained how amazingly good garlic was for every part of you: Thiamine is vital for maintaining neurological health. Garlic's strong antibiotic properties will protect your teeth by disinfecting abscesses. It will help prevent heart disease and your pancreas will be grateful that it lowers your blood sugar. Your digestive system will benefit from garlic's proclaimed ability to reduce the risk of intestinal parasites and colon cancer. Manganese in garlic will fight osteoporosis. You blood will be thinned and your blood pressure reduced. Your liver's toxins will be neutralised and your lungs will tell you that garlic is used to treat respiratory diseases such as asthma and whooping cough. It's also antifungal so can fight fungal infections found in your feet. I was impressed. Garlic was believed in ancient medicine and is still believed in some parts of the world to be a near-universal cure for minor illnesses. I resolved to have more garlic in my life and have since always had a bottle of garlic olive oil and a jar of garlic salt in the house. The former with salads, the latter livening up pasta or sprinkled on grilled broccoli (you must try it on grilled broccoli).

Debs and I, convinced of the depth of benefits contained in this unassuming accessory to the vegetable rack, spontaneously decided to have lunch there in the restaurant, ordering a garlic mezze and it was one of the most – and this actually is a compliment - interesting meals I have ever eaten. A large slate arrived loaded with ramekins containing hummus, garlic bread, battered prawns, halved pittas, salami slices, a giant baked bulb of elephant garlic the size of my fist, and it was all excellent, pulling off the neat trick of managing to be savoured whilst being gorged on at the same time.

Suddenly in love with the stuff, we proceeded to the gift shop and spent half our weekly food budget in there on treats for ourselves and gifts for friends and family – chutneys, mayonnaises, dressings, butters, exotic-looking bulbs, seeds, black garlic, and even garlic beer. I bought two of the beers – one for me, one for my dad, with whom I compete to give the most unusual bottle of beer as a birthday present. A couple of months after giving him the bottle, I received a text from informing me that the beer was without any doubt the most disgusting drink he'd ever tasted; he was on a sailing holiday and after taking one swig had offered the bottle to his friend to confirm its foulness. Having received that confirmation, he unhesitatingly emptied the bottle over the side and watched a fish bob to the surface, face up. I'm joking about the fish, of course, but without further ado I knocked the top off my bottle and can indeed attest that the stuff is not beer in any real sense, but rather the sort of prank beer that a joke shop might sell. The only way to describe the taste is to say that it is what you would experience if you drank beer, chewed a clove of garlic, then drank beer again. The two don't go – like cod and mushroom, vodka and margarine, spam and liquorice. After tipping the contents down the sink, I noticed something stuck in the bottom – a pink clove which had clearly lived there for the best part of a year. There was no secret recipe, no magical notes added to the brew, it was simply a clove of garlic stewing in the bottle. Putrid.

But don't let that put you off the place, I can't recommend the whole experience enough.

I still didn't see a red squirrel, though.

**

There are plenty of other titbits I could give you about the Isle of Wight – places that are much more interesting to visit than read about. There is Amazon World – a tropical glasshouse (which clearly used to be a large garden centre) containing animals far more interesting than I was expecting (crocodiles, penguins, monkeys to name but a few), Ventnor (the only town to suffer when the Isle of Wight achieves its cartographical destiny of symmetry) where Debs and I had a low-key but passionately insistent argument conducted with as much marital diplomacy as possible in a public place about whether to buy a heavy-looking windbreak made of wooden poles and deckchair material (we bought it, and at the time of writing five years later it has never left the garage where it was placed upon our return home) and a tiny restaurant called The Boathouse at Steephill Cove, which was no more than a beach hut with room for only eight diners. According to its menu, it sold prawns by the pint, which is how I think more food should be portioned out. I could murder a pint of chicken tikka masala right now. There was also time just before the ferry to visit the renowned red-squirrel hotspot, Borthwood Copse. Still no red squirrels.

But the day came to return to the mainland. My next trip overseas would not only be unplanned, but also as far removed from home as possible. If the Isle of Wight was my nearest overseas destination, then the next time I saw the sea, it would be in a coastal city as remote as the world could reasonably offer.

5. Seattle

"When it rains, we pour."

Local saying

"Good morning, ladies & gentlemen, this is your captain speaking from the flight deck. I'd like to welcome you aboard this Delta Airlines flight to Seattle. We have a flight time today of 9 hours and 55 minutes. Boarding is now complete and we're going to push back soon, then after take-off we'll be flying north, pretty much up the backbone of England until we reach Scotland, before heading north-west over Iceland and northern Canada to Seattle." Now, I've never understood why pilots plot these kinds of circuitous routes to America. Generations of air travellers know that if you want to get from London to America, you need to head west along the M4, cross the coast at Bristol, then go straight for 6 hours until you can see the Empire State building. Yet for some reason, the pilots always seem to fly due north from London and I'll never understand why.

Anyway, the captain finished his ditty and I relaxed back in my seat and gradually realised that this was my first long-haul flight since I was a child. I had spent much of my childhood on aeroplanes; my father worked at British Airways and one of the things about working at British Airways back then was that 1) everyone at parties always asked if you were a pilot and 2) in an attempt to compensate for the criminally uncompetitive pay and rations that kept prices low, employees were able to travel the world for free. However, this deal came with conditions that a) passengers on staff tickets were dressed smartly enough so as not to lower the tone of the cabin's aspirational upper-middle class atmosphere and b) there was an empty seat on the plane in the first place. And flights always being oversold meant that on a significant minority of occasions, we as a family would be at the airport all dressed up but with nowhere to go. So, as a family, we frequently entered a twilight status called Standby. Standby is fun, if you like a little jeopardy in your life, but my father was not one of those people. Risk averse to an admirable degree, he's driven by fearing the worst case scenario and organising himself so it can't happen; an attitude which I appreciate, but you don't want to be with him at an airport when you're in his party and you're all flying on his Standby status. We would leave the house approximately six hours before the flight was due, and present ourselves at check-in, my father in full suit and tie, my mother in an evening dress, my sister in the bridesmaid's dress she wore for her uncle's wedding and me dressed like a professional golfer, and request that we travel to Sydney, or whichever far off destination was rightly deemed worthy enough to be justified by the existence of free flights.

"Is the flight full?" my father demanded immediately of the impeccably presented BA check-in lady, who would spool up and down the green computer screen in front of her. "It's oversold" she'd reply (every time), sending my father into a fit of fear and panic as he pressed his forehead into the counter and mumbled something into the floor. "Oversold by fourteen, let's hope we get some no-shows," continued our clerk, as she strapped mango-coloured labels shouting the word "STANDBY" in bold black letters onto our luggage, and whizzed the cases down into the conveyor system, hopefully to be seen again in a foreign country later that day. But there were always no-shows and we always seemed to board ok (apart from that time when our plane home from New Zealand stopped to refuel in Singapore at midnight and after stretching our legs in the terminal for half an hour we were denied re-entry to the aircraft on account of the fact that some fare-paying passengers had turned up, but that's another story).

I digress! I was distracted from my daydream by the awakening seatback screen in front of me (a welcome addition to a long-haul flight in economy since my last time there) and I was immediately energised to see the airline (Delta) had decided to jazz up their in-flight safety video briefing. An actress dressed in Delta stewardess uniform asked us to watch carefully and there then followed a series of delicious, nourishing visual gags that would not have been out of place in the film "Airplane!". It was the best thing I'd seen on a tv screen in years.[20]

Now I must explain again that this trip wasn't one I had planned, life just decided to send me to a destination I had never previously considered. This one was under the premise of work – my new job required me to go there for a week. My employer had charitably suggested that with the time difference between London and America's west coast, all staff travel out on the Saturday 'to allow for time

---

[20] https://tinyurl.com/ydbwryqd

adjustment and sightseeing' on the Sunday. I was very much looking forward to this company-sponsored tourism, but I didn't know what to expect of Seattle and I wasn't sure how the 'minibreak with new colleagues' dynamic was going to work. My seat buddy for this flight was a colleague called Tom. Tom requested a glass of red wine at the post takeoff drinks service and I felt it churlish not to follow suit. He asked for another with the meal and ordered one for me too even though I had not requested it. I sensed that Tom was a bit more devil-may-care with alcohol than I was. Then after a trip to the galley to find something to wash down his sleeping pill, he returned with a glass of red in each hand. And when I say 'glass', I don't mean thin blue plastic tumbler you get at water coolers, but a capacious beaker that seemed to accommodate half a pint. It was my third. I did not want a pint and a half of red wine in one sitting (if I had been poured a pint of wine I would have baulked at it), but I was planning on having a nap soon, and clearly the wine (red, remember) could not be left standing on a traytable for that. So I risked it, frankly a little bit pleased deep down inside that I was on a transatlantic plane and being given as much free wine as I could stomach. But somewhere off the coast of Iceland, something started to go wrong. My stomach began sending concerning messages to my brain about my oesophagus. A lump formed in my epiglottis. The underside of my chin became tight. The aeroplane cabin started to spin and I realised that I'd Gone Too Far. I stole a glance at Tom who was by now fast asleep. I'm not proud of what happened next.

I scrunched the neck of the bag shut and wondered what to do with it. Tom was in deep sleep between me and the aisle on his left and I needed to get to a bin. One course of action would be to press the call button and pass the bag to a stewardess with an apologetic look, but my boss was seated behind me and would surely see. The other course of action was the only option.

I gripped the bag in my right hand and placed my left hand on the armrest. My stomach growled as I heaved myself up. I reached the bag across Tom to the farside armrest, placed my left foot upon my seat and I swung my groin over Tom's hip and assumed a 'point of no-return' body position. Fearing the worst, I held my breath and hoisted myself over Tom's droopy body, chin to chin, praying that no-one would come down the aisle and knock the bag out of my right hand. With all the skill of a heist thief dodging a laser beam, I vaulted over in one movement, landing in the aisle like a cat off a garden wall. I made for the washroom and disposed of the evidence in secret. I have never told Tom, nor indeed anyone about this. Until now.

**

I left the hotel the following morning jetlagged about six hours after waking up – secretly pleased that I'd spent the night sleepless in Seattle – to meet colleagues in the lobby to board a bus with SEATTLE written above its windscreen. For 20 minutes we chugged along the rain-soaked highways and byways before crossing Lake Washington on a floating bridge to enter downtown Seattle. And there in front of me was the vista of what could have passed for New York. A jungle of graphite skyscrapers, with the iconic Space Needle crowning the lot. What a day was ahead! We all pressed our noses to the glass to take in the skyline until the bus dived underground into a concrete tunnel, coming to a halt at what resembled a London Underground station whose roadway perplexingly doubled as a tramline. Dismounting, we climbed steps to burst up into the city from the underbelly, vitalised by the energy and comings and goings of the place. It didn't take long to get that Manhattan feel – advertising hoardings crowded us, pedestrians rushed hither and thither, traffic honked. We were somewhere in the world.

As a group, we'd decided to head for Pike Place Market, and I was particularly looking forward to seeing it for one specific reason. I'd spent the first three years of my career interviewing retail managers. One of the prewritten questions on my interview sheet was "How do you motivate your sales staff to give their best every day?" Suddenly – I think it was about 2003 or 2004 – absolutely every single retail manager started to give the same answer: "We do the fish thing."

The "Fish! Philosophy" to give it its proper name, was birthed in 1998 by a management consultant named John Christiansen and is marketed to this day as a 'technique to make individuals alert and active in the workplace' which basically means keep their brains switched on during menial jobs that have the power to make them die of boredom. Watching the fishmongers in Pike Place Market, Christiansen noticed that even though selling fish wasn't much fun – it was repetitive, cold, smelly and had long patches of inactivity, the fishmongers in Pike Place Market gave it their all and sold a lot of fish. Intrigued to see how, Christiansen videoed the men at work and made a film, wrote a book, printed t-shirts and doubtlessly engaged in many other moneymaking activities to spread the word. The Fish! Philosophy gives four central ideas which range from the laudable "Choosing One's Attitude" through the questionable "Playing at Work" the uplifting "Making

Someone's Day" to the impressively unspecific "Being Present". I gathered this was mainly to do with creating an element of theatre in Pike Place, which livened the market up a bit and drove footfall. So when fish were sold, bells would be enthusiastically dinged, stout fisherman would spontaneously burst into sea shanties, and – I guessed – when fish weren't being sold, countless volumes of salmon and cod and hopefully the odd bucket of shrimp or a gangly octopus would be hurled in every direction through the market hall, narrowly but deliberately registering a near-miss with the heads of overstimulated tourists. The idea appeared to be that a self-perpetuating cycle would be created where the fishmongers' theatrics would encourage the shoppers and the tourists to pass by and buy more fish, which would make more theatrics happen, and so on all the way to the bank. I couldn't wait to see it in real life.

Despite all my hopes for the place, the flurry of Pike Place's fish market consisted of two stalls, staffed by bearded men in gumboots and orange aprons. Tourists were understandably unwilling to buy raw fish on account of having no real use for it back at their hotel, and so a standoff ensued with tourists poised with cameraphones at the ready until a local turned up needing to buy some salmon. I waited about fifteen minutes until eventually an older lady in a red anorak shuffled up. Dollar bills were exchanged, small-talk was mumbled (during which I desperately hope the lady at some point exclaimed "what's that got to do with the price of fish?") and finally, we had a show. The lady was gestured to take a few steps back. The dead fish was passed backwards to the rear of the stall, as an American football might make its way to the quarterback. The fishermen lined up as though in a barbershop quartet. With a well-worn routine, they inhaled, then with a dramatic lean-back, burst into a loud "Heeeeeeeeeyyyyyy, hooooooooo!" The fish was launched from the back of the stall and caught at the front by an assistant who unfussily bagged it and passed it to the lady. She nodded her thanks and ambled off. The tourists had their photos on Facebook before the lady had the fish on the hob. It all seemed very underwhelming. Then nothing happened again for another ten minutes and I didn't know what to do next. Bored, I explored further stalls, hoping Pike Place Market wasn't exclusively dedicated to fish retail, and I can confirm that that was very definitely the case, because the next 30 stalls didn't have a fish in sight. The first stall I saw was displaying local fossils and sparkly stones that had fairly obviously been found on some local beach but prices started at $25. I passed on to the next stall. The man here had curled wire coat-hangers into the shape of various animals - beetles ($5), fish ($20), turtles ($25), geese ($45), but somehow the acquisition of a piece of clutter made out of rubbish that I couldn't transport home for the cost of three days of food didn't manage to ingratiate itself to me as an idea. A stall of "amusingly" worded t-shirts was next. A prominently displayed sign read "Please do not take photos of the t-shirts". I didn't, but did note down the quote that heads up this chapter. The stalls were seemingly endless, merchandising various low-cost knick-knacks for the tourist trade – little wooden pretzel bowls made from trees from one of Washington State's many forests, horrible orange and purple swirly tie-dye scarves worn by the sort of people you avoid at parties, a plethora of plaster-of-Paris Space Needles, coasters in the shape of Washington State and more tourist tat that I simply couldn't be bothered to reach into my wallet for.

I was beginning to give up on the place and head back to the downtown. Then I came to Gary Davis's stall.

I would quite happily sacrifice 99% of the world's tourist souvenir merchandise to mass market tat if the remaining 1% of it were of Gary Davis's ilk. In a world where assured mediocrity has become the norm, I yearn for Gary. Gary was a humble man, hunched beneath his cap on a cold January afternoon, surrounded by photographs of Seattle and local rural scenes. Photographs he had taken. Not because he thought a tourist might give him $50 for one, but because he needed to do his art and let it out for the world to see, money or no money; it was why he was alive. Of course, there were plenty of Space Needle photos to pay the rent, but there were also those sorts of images that the Pacific Northwest specialises in that made me stop and look a while: Sea ferries chugging in front of pine slopes with bleached-white clouds cradling the virgin sky. Pacific tugs heaving their load in the mist. A snowcapped Mount St Helens[21] perched benignly over logging fields. Gary and I chatted for a while, finding a mutual sanctuary of appreciative aestheticism amongst the more commercial agenda of our environs. I loved Gary for being here, doing his art, amongst the tie-dye scarves preying on the tourists hunting airborne fish, and he seemed to appreciate that I appreciated his endeavours too. I bought one of his prints, and if ever you come to my house you will see it hanging in my downstairs loo. But I didn't buy any fish.

**

After an hour, I had come to realise that the appeal of Pike Place Market was beginning to sag and so stepped off into

---

[21] Yes, that Mount St Helens, the one with the eruption you learnt about in school.

the hubbub of this New York of the west to see what I could see. I was faced with a café directly opposite Gary's stall – a pleasingly vintage emerald and cream shopfront with a large window either side of a wooden door. Just below the roofline, running the width of the shop were nine square panes of glass, each filled with a large, white capital letter. S – T – A – R – B – U – C – K - S. The queues were out the door. My brain reminded me that Starbucks started up in Seattle. This must have been the first ever one.

I remembered my first ever Starbucks. It was 2001 – just as the coffee shop chain boom was starting. Debs and I were out shopping, and after exhausting Leamington Spa of its retailing opportunities, we noticed one of these new Starbucks coffee shops that we'd heard mentioned, so in we went. There was a middle-aged man at the counter making quite a scene.

"I don't know, I just don't know! There's too much choice! I'm not doing this!!". He barged past us and out into the drizzle. We approached the counter with the undeserved burden of breaking the ice with the member of staff who had just been shouted at.

"What can I get you?"

A Starbucks virgin, indeed, a coffee-chain virgin, I replied with the only words hitherto available to me for exactly this situation: "I'd like a cup of coffee please."

Eyes were invisibly rolled at me in a well-worn way and eyebrows were visibly pointed towards the hoarding up behind her. "What kind of coffee would you like?"

I panicked, unaware that coffee could come in so many forms. I'd only heard of one.

"Cappuccino please."

"Tall or large?"

"Medium please." This answer received no comment. What was the difference between tall and large anyway?

"Skinny? Wings? Extra shot?"

"I'd just like a cappuccino in a mug please," I replied, slightly tired of this by now and suddenly realising what had been frustrating the middle-aged gentleman before me.

And so it continued. I finally formed a verbal contract with my server before it was Debs's turn to be interviewed on her preferences. Too scared to order anything else, she took a cappuccino too and we selected a couple of fingers of cake as well. I offered a £10 note and was given in return two mugs, two saucers of cake, and a £1 coin.

"Where's my change?"

"Two cappuccinos at £2.50, two slices of cake at £2, VAT is included. Enjoy your coffee and thanks for the profit!" Actually, I made that last bit up, but it was hard not to feel a sense of swindle about the whole affair. The coffees and cake were gone in twenty minutes and £9 was a lot of money for a pair of students to briefly sit down out of the rain. I've never been friends with the brand since.

Yet evidently my perspective on Starbucks is not shared, for the growth of the company is one of *the* great stories of corporate success. As dawn broke on January 1st, 1971, Starbucks didn't exist. Three college mates, led by a man named Jerry Baldwin, opened the first store in March of that year, agonising between shortlisted names of the geographically relevant 'Cargo House' and the instantly forgettable 'Pequod'. But Starbucks – named after the chef in Moby Dick – stuck, presumably because at nine letters it fitted nicely in the window panes above the door. And

Starbucks was one shop in Pike Place Market for much of the next 20 years, warming up fishmongers' fingers as they hopped from foot to foot inside their pens of crushed ice. Fifteen years later, Starbucks was still unknown outside downtown Seattle; coffee shops were not a 'thing' – coffee was an ancillary item on a menu in restaurants and cafés where the more serious, profitable and fundamental business of mealtimes was pursued. Sales of coffee were falling and in 1986, Baldwin had to buy out his bean supplier. Starbucks was operating a grand total of six shops at this point, all of them in Seattle. Baldwin decided to give up and sold the business to a rival coffee shop operator, Howard Schultz, who ran a competitor chain called Il Giornale but evidently thought that Starbucks was a more catchy name because he adopted the brand and gently expanded, opening the first foreign Starbucks before the year was out at the other end of the train line to nearby Vancouver. Suddenly, Starbucks was an international brand. Three years later, Starbucks had 46 shops across the Pacific Northwest and was getting through three tons of coffee beans a week. Coffee was beginning to trend, new stores were guaranteed profit and by the mid-1990s, there were 1,000 Starbucks and Schultz decided that if coffee worked in the USA there was no reason why it shouldn't work globally. 1996 saw Tokyo take the first Starbucks outside north America – I can't imagine how difficult it must have been to take a North American brand selling a South American crop with the cultural resonance of southern Europe to eastern Asia – but it must have worked because five years later the store count was at 5,000 and they even had one in Leamington Spa. As I write this in 2019 we're at something like 20,000 – more if you count the hutches in train stations and counters at petrol forecourts and in-office coffee points that Proudly Serve Starbucks Coffee. No one has counted, but I'll bet there are more Starbucks in the world now than churches, making it a religion of sorts – St. Arbuck presumably being its patron saint.

So that's the 'how'. Quite *why* Starbucks grew from a corner shop in one of the world's most remote cities to a global brand superpower is an interesting question. I don't have a degree in coffee, but I have a theory. In the early 1990s, Seattle wasn't the important city it is today. In the early 21st century, it became known as the corporate headquarters of some of the world's most significant internet businesses - Microsoft, Amazon, Expedia. Then when the internet went global in the early 2000s, Seattle could suddenly do business with the wider world much more easily than its remote geographical position had previously allowed and the city's businesspeople regularly needed to talk to Chicago, New York, London and beyond. But Seattle is in an inconvenient time zone for a large multinational to be headquartered. New York is three hours ahead and London, eight. And if you want to be speaking to someone in one of these cities, you'd better get up early in the morning. So you probably needed a few coffees to wake you up, and after six months you were addicted and begging Starbucks to open a branch near you.

But I have never warmed to Starbucks. I believe the sense of student injustice was something of a forerunner to my disquiet around the brand, but I think my main gripe about Starbucks is that what it offers me is somehow unexceptional. I don't know about you, but when I leave a Starbucks, I don't feel modestly uplifted somehow, in the way that I do when I leave a Costa Coffee or a Prêt A Manger. Somehow the coffee tastes as though it's a lower grade, because that's cheaper for Starbucks to buy and therefore more profitable, but the brand has enough fans already to not need to trade up to a more expensive bean. So there's that, and also the niggling sense that Starbucks's raison d'être is that the Starbucks in Rotterdam is meant to offer the same fare that I can expect in the Starbucks in Rotherham. So, standing in front of the *original* Starbucks somehow didn't seem to mean much to me – how could The Original Starbucks mean more to me that any of the other identical Starbucks in the world? If I was going to see the same Starbucks as I'd seen in Leamington Spa, I didn't want to go in. But if I was going to see some glorious blueprint of how a real Starbucks was meant to be, then I didn't want to see it either. Colleagues queued for a black Americano that they pretended was special, but was in fact identical to the one they have in the office at 11am on a Wednesday - but I walked by in the hope of seeing something new, some place I'd never seen before. I hope you expected nothing less from me; this book's not called The World Less Travelled for nothing.

**

I climbed the slope away from Pike Place Market and turned not left for the Space Needle, where every tourist goes, but right, for the Columbia Center. My hasty pre-departure read of Tripadvisor ranked ascending to its viewing platform as the number one thing to do in Seattle, ahead of going up the Space Needle. Apparently, it was taller and it gave a better view too. But I didn't want to rush, for meandering unhurriedly through the downtown of a new foreign city is one of life's great pleasures. Also, my winter coat had given up the ghost a few months previously and I had planned to take advantage of America's legendary bargain shopping.

So, I walked through the downtown, admiring shop windows and slowly but with great disappointment realising that Seattle had basically three types of shops:

1) Shops that are not for the likes of me and never will be. These shops have large windows displaying tiny, neatly displayed clothing and accessories on artful leading-edge mannequins that in some way represent the zeitgeist. There might be a male mannequin with a peaked houndstooth cap and a thin charcoal sweater and over the sweater, one of those thin patterned cotton scarves that it looks like a woman should be wearing. He has a bag slung diagonally across his chest, bladed pleats down the front of his trousers and shoes so pointed that you could use them to grout your tiles. Next to him on the floor is a model of a dog made of bubbles, and next to him is the woman whose hat brim dives down on the diagonal, parallel with the hem of her wool poncho, which draws the eye over her pencil skirt and down towards a pair of shiny wellington boots. She has a handbag that matches his and a cat under her arm that is made of roses. There are no price tags to be seen anywhere.

2) Shops that are not for the likes of me and I hope never will be. These shops have large windows that give a view into a grotty general merchandise store with a filthy floor and filthy customers. Aisles piled high with shiny brightly coloured plastic packaging, selling either something you were not considering buying, like oversized multipacks of sesame seed biscuits or a large object which before now, you had never considered acquiring, such as a fitness trampoline

(more fully and professionally assembled here than it would ever be once you got it home). Prices either aren't bothered with because it is obvious that this is a thrift store or are shouting "ONLY $10!" in giant red lettering at every turn. When you walk into the store your skin begins to crawl.

3) Shops that try to look like they're for the likes of me, but frankly aren't, no matter how hard they try. They have mannequins in sunglasses wearing big-ticket items such as a full set of hiking gear or a lounge suit, with a boast that they were for sale for just $600 but can now be obtained for just $450. There's normally a luggage set in the window too arranged in size order. No one has ever been drawn into spending their monthly disposable income on one object like this. Seattle's department stores excel in this regard.

But I was on the lookout for shop-type 4 – that sold *exactly* the thing I wanted at substantially less than I was hoping to pay. And my spidey senses started tingling and I stepped inside Old Navy. Past the endless jogging bottoms and messy t-shirts, it looked at me: a black quilted anorak in my size, dark enough to wear to the office, casual enough to wear around the kids with a detachable hood and a few trendy dangling cords and stoppers and I sensed this was to be my bargain. I was right. Was $50, now $15. I took it straight to the till before anyone had a chance to deprive me of it.

"Would you like an extra 33% off your purchase today sir?"

"An extra 33% off a $15 coat?"

"If you enter your email address into our database, we'll send you adverts from time to time, but you get 33% off today."

33% of $15 was $5. The coat would end up costing me £8. I gave a fake email address and a $10 dollar bill, slipped it onto my shoulders and marched out onto the street and towards the Columbia Center, striding with the confidence of a man who sensed that his day was on the turn. And now I was to do the best thing you can do in the city.

I passed Seattle Library - an exciting looking building that is all glass and full of jagged and diagonal edges so that it resembles an airline cargo container. I considered going in, but what would I find inside there but a library I could not use? I pressed on past anonymous grey office block after anonymous grey office block, each one giving off a little less of the New York buzz than the last. It was a good 20 minutes to reach the Colombia Center. The streets took on a more suburban, edge-of city feel. I started to see car maintenance workshops and dirty cafes. And now homeless people too. Suddenly, I felt acutely aware that this was their territory and that I was a rich tourist a long way from home. My pace quickened. I crossed a road behind a short-haired respectably dressed lady of about my age who I noticed was carrying a rolled-up sleeping mat. Curious, I looked ever so slightly more closely to notice worn hiking shoes, a big, dirty rucksack and a few more piercings than the average person I'd seen that day. I turned my head away so as not to be rude, but not before she had caught my eye and seen I was looking.

"Cheesedick! Hey, Cheesedick! What're you looking at Cheesedick?"

I had never prepared for how to respond to being addressed as "Cheesedick" and so, not knowing what to say, said nothing and carried on walking, looking dead ahead.

"Cheesedick! You want some of this? What's so funny Cheesedick?" She started bobbing and weaving her head around as though a boxer dodging punches.

I crossed the street. She was clearly bat-infested.

"Come back here Cheesedick! You want funny? I'll tell you funny. Cheesedick! Look at me Cheesedick! Look at me!!"

Soft drugs were legal in Washington State. And guns. This was America, where pedestrians are inexplicably legally entitled to walk down the street carrying a gun. I played out the worst case scenario in my mind and thought it credible that the last thirty seconds of a pedestrian's life before being shot might begin like this. I don't wish to reach for melodrama here, but I was pleased and proud to have never been shot and didn't want to lose my membership of that particular club today. I approached a ski equipment shop that looked out of both our price ranges, but crucially, in which her presence would be incongruous and mine, in my new coat, would not. I pushed the door open and stepped in. Because this was America, there was a greeter.

"Hello sir! What brought you in store today?"

I didn't want to say "I was scared I was about to be killed" even though it was the truth, because I'm British and didn't want to make a fuss. I have also never skied and didn't have any ski-related vocabulary in my lexicon. I noticed a pair of quilted trousers hanging from a rail.

"Jodhpurs. I'm looking for jodhpurs." What was I saying? I'd wanted to express that I was interested in buying a pair of trousers for skiing, jodhpurs were horse-riding, weren't they?

"OK, jodhpurs? I don't think we have any of those, I'm afraid. Where are you going skiing?"

I googled my memory for any American ski resort.

"Aspen." [22]

"OK, nice! Are you skiing, snowboarding, slalom, moguls?"

I really didn't have any options that weren't going to lead me even more out of my depth here than I already was. Yet at the same time, the skiing disciplines rattled off at me seemed to become progressively specialist as the sentence progressed. I had to go for one of the earlier options. And talk a bit more as well, be a bit disarming. We still hadn't established why I'd come into the shop.

"Just regular skiing. I'm not advanced level or anything, just thought that for, you know, when I fall, I'd need some salopettes." With relief, the word came to me.

"OK, well, we've got some Columbias just in – a new line, qualofil on the inside, taped seams to keep the meltwater out. How much were you thinking of spending?"

I wasn't thinking of spending anything, I simply didn't want to get killed. How much do salopettes cost, anyway?

"OK, let me get you a coffee – it's cold out there – and I'll introduce you to Avril who can take you through our range, OK?"

I spent the next twenty minutes with Avril, idly pinching fabrics, admiring IsoDry linings, and weighing up the benefits of Recco rescue reflectors. But Avril's patter gave

---

[22] From *Dumb and Dumber*.

me valuable thinking time. How was I going to get out of this situation? And was Cheesedick lady still out there, waiting for me with her weapon of choice? Or had she invited friends to meet me the moment I left the shop?

"OK, sorry to sound a sissy, but do you have anything in a mango yellow? When I started kayaking twenty years ago and bought my first watertight cagoule, I had to choose between turquoise and mango and bought mango because it was higher visibility in an emergency, so all my outdoor kit is mango now, it's kind of a superstition." This was a lie.

"Mango, we do not have. We have red, we have orange, but the salopettes tend to be grey / black because the top half is the bright colour."

This was my escape. I stuck my chin in my chest and proffered apologies about wasting Avril's time and asked for her business card so I could buy from her personally the next time I was buying snow gear in Seattle (which would be never).

I stepped back out onto the street, thinking I could throw the hot Americano dregs at my would-be assailant were she still hanging around. She was not.

**

Now, I've never been on the Seattle Tourist Board, but if I had a 76-storey, 295-metre skyscraper in my city with an observation deck at the top, and that 76-storey observation deck was judged by Tripadvisor to be the best thing to do in the whole city, then even if that skyscraper was owned by a private business, I'd be making movements to keep that observation deck open 365 days per year. I don't know if it was considered a tourist threat, the fact it was out of season, out of town, or that Seattle simply wasn't tourism-aware enough to care about these sorts of things, but when I reached the Colombia Center's visitor entrance I found the doors locked and a security guard waving me away from behind glass. I made the internationally recognised "oh, come on, I've travelled a long way for this" sign but turning my palms upwards and painting my face with an air of desperation, I was mirrored by the security guard adopting the same pose with an "I'm powerless to do anything" face. The walk here had been lovely, but clearly I wasn't going to go up the Columbia Center to the observation deck. I wasn't going to see the *Frasier* skyline. I wasn't going to look out over the Pacific Ocean or see snowcapped mountains on the horizon. Worse things have happened to me, but I wasn't happy.

I hopped from foot to foot, getting colder by the second as January's icy fingers reached through what I was becoming increasingly aware was a coat that had only cost me £8. Nearby, I noticed what I remembered from Tripadvisor to be the Smith Tower – an elegant 1920's skyscraper that made up in charm for what it lacked in height and, if my memory of Tripadvisor listings served me correctly, had a cocktail bar at the top too. Seattle's version of the Flatiron in New York, I figured. I tried the door. Not only was it locked, but the lights were off and the reception / security desk was unattended. I stood in the street and didn't quite know what to do next.

It was time to visit the Space Needle.

The Space Needle is without doubt one of the most recognisable skyscrapers in the world. Growing up in the

1980s I was in awe of these large buildings. There were only five tall buildings in the world worth knowing about (Eiffel Tower, Chrysler Building, Empire State, World Trade Centre, the Sears Tower in Chicago and maybe the CN Tower in Toronto if you were a real connoisseur of the genre.) Because there were only five, they were like a family: The Empire State was the husband and the Chrysler the wife with the World Trade grandparents just down the road. Empire State had a brother in Chicago and Chrysler's sister had moved to Paris after divorcing that CN guy from Canada. That was it, no other skyscrapers of any note existed. It was only when Frasier appeared on TV in the 1990s that the world was exposed to the Space Needle and we mentally added that to the family tree, as though the CN Tower had found a new partner. But in the mid-1990s, the eastern hemisphere discovered money and suddenly *they* were unstoppable in their skyscraper construction and we lost all idea of what the world's tallest buildings actually were. Looking at Wikipedia right now, the tallest buildings list is totally dominated by 21st century creations. The list goes as far as the 126th tallest and of those 126, only 21 were built before the year 2000. All but 24 are in the Far East or the Middle East. New York's beautifully sleek Chrysler Building – 4th tallest when I was last paying attention back in the 1990s – is now 83rd tallest. How did this happen?

You see my point, of course. The height of the building is becoming irrelevant, a devalued currency. The tallest building in the world right now stands at 828 metres in Dubai (from which I am sure, the views of the surrounding flat desert are magnificent) and I have no doubt that plans are afoot to smash the 1km barrier somewhere. But when that happens, I won't care. And I won't care because the height of the building is important only to the owner's ego (and let's be honest, it probably is a he). Which would you rather gaze up at: The dainty point and intricate curly ironwork of the Eiffel Tower or the stark concrete phonebox of the unemotionally-named Goldin Finance 117 in Tianjin[23], China, at nearly twice the height? Exactly. So the Space Needle (at 184 metres, not even the tallest building in Seattle) is right up there on the list of loveable skyscrapers, for me. I think the light spaceship colour helps against a frequently dark sky, and there's something about its proportions, its high waist and actual alien spacecraft perched atop that gives it the necessary *je ne sais quoi*. Viewed at night, lit from below against a dark sky it actually looks like a spacecraft hovering below the black clouds with a powerful beam of light lasering directly upwards into the beyond. Suddenly, I was pleased the Colombia tower was closed and the Space Needle was my date for the night. But first I had to get there, and here I was, standing at the other end of the downtown, carrying shopping, weary, cold and unable to see my destination through the cereal boxes of the city centre.

The Space Needle is not in the middle of Seattle, and for good reason; it was built to host the 1962 World's Fair – an exposition devoted to enthusiastically demonstrating that the USA wasn't in fact all that far behind the USSR in the space race that it had just lost. But World Fairs need more space than city centres can afford, so for this reason a site was selected about a mile away from the downtown and the grounds of the fair were divided into various different 'worlds' just like Disneyland – with a World of Science, World of Art, World of Tomorrow etc, and to say it was a success was an understatement; two million people

---

[23] https://tinyurl.com/y7lfo8k8

travelled to one of the world's most inaccessible cities, which then had a population of less than a tenth of that figure (goodness knows where everyone slept). The whole show made a profit, which was a pretty rare thing back then, and the Space Needle was the star of the show, literally towering over the whole spectacle; it had 20,000 people riding the elevators to its observation deck every day. It was one of the most extraordinary buildings in the world – tallest in the country west of the Mississippi and a hitherto unseen style, conceptualised as a compromise between two rival architects' visions of a tethered balloon and a flying saucer. The Space Needle was built to withstand wind speeds of 200 miles per hour (double the requirements in the building code of the time) and earthquakes of up to 9 on the Richter Scale. A monorail was even constructed to shuttle visitors to and from the downtown. But that was all a very long time ago. Now, the structure stands on the edge of a quiet park where the city centre meets the suburbs and it looks a little forlorn there, out in the cold. The monorail still runs, but I didn't see anyone riding it.

The sun was setting – sadly not in any sort of magical-orange-and-pink-sky way, but more in a daylight-giving-up-on-a-bleak-January-day way and I was keen to get to the top to take in both the day view and the night view. I presented myself to the visitors' desk and enquired how I got to the top and was presented with an intriguing option. If I committed to spending $35 in the revolving restaurant at the top, the ticket up was free. Because I was in Seattle on business, I was allowed up to $40 to spend on an evening meal. I asked to see a menu and, apart from noticing that they'd missed a trick in not, in the city of *Frasier*, offering tossed salads and scrambled eggs, to my predictable horror

I saw that a full meal was anything from $75 to $150. I agonised as the sun continued to set, then hit upon the capital idea of washing down a tapas of starters with a glass of wine. This was America, I reasoned, and the portions would be big. I was right. There was a complimentary breadbasket too, which was repurposed as a side for a bowl of clam chowder before a main course of mussels and chips, after which I was full. I raised a glass of prosecco and drank to beating the system. The view was a perfect cityscape of skyscrapers by night, but there was a sense of lack as I took in the view. When I got home, I suddenly realised - with a jolt as I was dropping off to sleep one night – what that sense of lack was. I went to my bookshelf and found the paragraph I was looking for that puts it perfectly:

"Seattle is an insistently modern city with glass skyscrapers lining up along the bay. But something was missing. I couldn't work out what it was, but somehow the experience felt incomplete. It came to me later when I was back at the hotel [...]. The problem was that while it had been an impressive view, it hadn't been very identifiable; it hadn't felt uniquely Seattle, which is what the tourist in me really wanted. There was only one building that screamed Seattle and that was the Space Needle itself. By standing on top of it, I had automatically removed from view the one part of Seattle I really wanted to look at."

Dave Gorman's Googlewhack! Adventure, Ebury, 2004

If you like, I can write about the following five days, but I'm not sure you want to read about jetlag and business meetings, so I'll spare you that. But I will explain that after five days in Seattle, I did rather develop the feeling that there wasn't much else to see, and what there was wasn't particularly new. I'd climbed into an aeroplane in London one rainy afternoon, having just ordered a hamburger, chips and a beer in the airport in English for about £15. Getting off the plane ten hours later, the first thing I did was order hamburger, chips and a beer in English in a modern airport-like restaurant for about $15 and eat it staring at the rain. Don't get me wrong, being on the Pacific rim is nice and I'm very grateful to have unexpectedly had the chance to go to Seattle, but in terms of new experiences, I found Seattle a little lacking – the culture, the vegetation, the language, the climate, and the weights and measures were all the same as in London. The city boomed in the late 20th century with the growth of big businesses and many of the buildings looked like a large, modern and clean hotel built in 1998. Everywhere we went was perfectly nice, but had a certain 'sameness' quality to it. Many parts of Seattle that I saw were like a food restaurant in a shopping centre, a bar in an airport, or that perfectly manufactured town in *The Truman Show*. With hindsight, I should have been as excited to travel there from London as a New Yorker should have been to spend the week in Leeds or Bristol. Seattle seemed to have reached its peak in the year 2000 and then wondered what to do with itself in the great change of the 21st century, much like America.

**

Eventually, I was sitting in Seattle airport's departure lounge with a beer brewed from Alaskan meltwater, listening to piped muzak and mulling over the fact I was about to voluntarily seal myself inside a metal tube and spend my next day being blasted across the entire American continent and the Atlantic Ocean. I've never been a nervous flyer, but as I've become an adult, I've realised that aeroplanes are built, maintained and operated by people just like me, who make mistakes and have bad days at the office occasionally. Statistically, flying is so safe that aviation experts are getting bored of coming up with new ways of describing just how safe: You're much more likely to die of a shark attack, or a lightning strike, or a car crash, or the flu, than because of a problem during a flight on a reputable airline. But if you're on that one plane out of one million that goes down, and are that one person out of 11 million passengers that dies, then that's enough, isn't it? If you're scared of flying, skip to the next chapter, because a few years ago, flicking channels late one night, I stumbled across one of those Air Crash Investigation documentaries and sat helplessly gripped while a narrator recounted the tale of a time a Captain lost control of his plane and the whole thing was faithfully reconstructed in ghoulish detail. Two incidents in particular have played on my mind every time I've had to fly:

The first concerned a British Airways flight from Birmingham to Malaga in 1990. During the uneventful climb after takeoff, one of the cockpit windows was suddenly sucked out of the plane and twirled uselessly onto the countryside below. The Captain, Tim Lancaster, had removed his seatbelt and so found his top half following the window pane out through the frame and into oblivion. Lancaster's bottom half refused to follow because his toes caught the handles on his control column and pushed it forward, sending the plane into a steep nosedive. His upper body was pinned to the outside of the roof of the cockpit by the onrushing air. His arms flailed helplessly as he stared backwards into the vortex of one of the screaming engines next to the plane's tailfin. A steward charged the cockpit and pulled on Lancaster's belt buckle with enough force to stop his toes from engaging with the stick while First Office

Alastair Aitchison – new on the job that morning – somehow pulled the plane out of the dive in a fog-filled cockpit and calmly landed everyone at Southampton airport twenty minutes later. Lancaster somehow survived, the passengers were told it was Malaga and everyone got off happy and enjoyed their holiday.

But if that was the best-case scenario, then the second, Air France Flight 447 was surely the worst. Seriously, if you ignored my warning and have got the heebegeebies from that last paragraph, then now's the time to skip on a few pages and I'll see you shortly.

AF447 took off from Rio de Janiero for Paris in June 2009. It disappeared.

Shortly after take-off, the captain, Marc Dubois, delegated the landing to one of his co-pilots, David Robert, and so gave the third - and most inexperienced - member of his crew, Cedric Bonin, the task of flying the plane across the open ocean in the dead of night. That sounds ominous now, but by 'flying the plane' I mean 'sitting and looking at the dashboard having typed "Paris CDG" into the autopilot a while before'. There wasn't much to do. Monitoring his instruments, Bonin saw that the speedometer was telling him that the plane was travelling at precisely 0 miles per hour. This was patently untrue, and the aeroplane's computer decided that it couldn't autopilot on bad data, so it switched the autopilot off and asked Bonin to earn his pay packet and fly the plane instead. We know now that the pitot tube – the pipe that sticks out from underneath the cockpit, points forwards, and by measuring the force of the air coming into it determines the aircraft's speed, had iced over and therefore was failing to give a valid speed reading.

But we will never know why Bonin did what he did next.

Flight records show that Bonin unaccountably and wordlessly pulled back on his control stick, sending the plane into a steep climb. His co-pilot, David Robert, was blissfully unaware of this, for this was not a Boeing plane, where the control columns rise up out of the floor like a moose's antlers and are mechanically connected so if one pilot yanks to the left, the other pilot's control column moves in tandem, but an Airbus, where the control column is a chunky joystick, much like the ones found in computer games arcades at the turn of the millennium. The left-hand pilot had his joystick by his left hand, and the right-hand pilot had his joystick by his right hand. Line of sight from one seat to the opposite joystick was not obstructed, but with joystick movements discreet and not replicated on the opposite joystick, it wasn't necessarily obvious to one pilot what the other was doing. Also, it was dark, so there was no visible horizon for the pilots to orientate themselves by. Within a couple of minutes, the plane had climbed higher than it was designed to fly and the air was too thin to support its weight. "STALL! STALL! STALL!" blurted the cockpit alarm, and the plane, wingtips level but nose above tail, began to arc downwards, like a stone that has just been thrown. Co-pilot Robert looked up in consternation when an unlikely thing happened. The pitot tube that had frozen up, thawed. The aeroplane's computer systems were reassured that the aeroplane was now in fact moving forwards again, so the stall alarm stopped. But the plane had stalled and, deprived of all thrust and dangerously nose-up, was now totally under the influence of gravity. Bonin carried on sitting there, projecting relief that he'd managed to silence the alarm, perhaps not wishing to disclose the potentially fatal cockup he knew he'd just made. Captain Dubois, wondering supine from his rest quarters why his bed was no longer level, entered the cockpit, at which point Bonin broke his silence and admitted he'd "totally lost control of the plane". Dubois immediately pointed the nose down again to get some airspeed back, but it was too late, for at this point they were 1,000 feet from sea level, considerably less than the 35,000 feet they should have been. "Oh putain, on va s'écraser! CE N'EST PAS POSSIBLE!" were the last reported words from the cockpit. The aeroplane had been above the middle of the Atlantic in a dark spot between Brazilian and Senegalese radar. Dakar's air traffic control didn't raise the alarm until a couple of hours later when the plane didn't turn up on its screen. A few hours after that, the poor relatives waiting at Paris Charles de Gaulle airport simply read the word "RETARDÉ" on the information screens for hours on end while news reports filtered through on the 24 hour news screens in the terminal as Air France's Chief Executive declared a catastrophe. It took 3 days to find any wreckage.

It probably wasn't the best thought to dwell on before boarding. I gave my head a little shake and snapped back into the room. Suddenly I was uncannily aware of the airport's poor choice of background music: Tom Petty, singing: "And I'm FREEEEEEEE! FREEFALLING!"

6. Denmark

"Denmark is like a secret little place with its own special language."

Helena Christensen

Picture the scene. You are at your departure gate in Heathrow's Terminal 5, satisfied with your morning after a modest lie in and a taxi ride on leather seats, followed by a leisurely airport brunch of smashed avocados and poached egg on rye. You have now secured the nearest seat to the gate, facing the runway where every sixty seconds or so you are able to witness the miracle of 300 tonnes of complicated metal powering itself into the air at speeds man has dreamt of since the dawn of humankind while sipping a cappuccino as a large flatscreen TV tells you everything that's going on in the world. Perfect? Pretty much. This was me on 24th March 2015 as I whiled away the last ten minutes before my flight to Copenhagen boarded. There wasn't scope for much to happen that could prick my bubble of contentment, but the TV whooshed up a bold headline along the bottom of the screen.

"AEROPLANE CRASH IN FRANCE – ALL PASSENGERS DEAD"

I cannot bear to think about the sights and sounds inside that plane and will forever be relieved that of all the planes in Europe that day, mine wasn't the one that went down, but I couldn't help but feel that this was not exactly the best news for the airport's management to be broadcasting to passengers waiting to climb aboard at the gate. The news was all-consuming and yet too close to my departure to endanger my trip. Should I fly? I could stay at home with the perfectly legitimate excuse that I didn't quite fancy flying that day and no-one would fail to understand.

But life wasn't that simple; it never is. I was going to Denmark not for fun but because I had some people to meet about some business and failing to travel wasn't really an option. The tannoy bing-bonged, the less attentive passengers rushed towards the gate, oblivious of the news and it was time to decide: to fly or not to fly? As accidentally mentioned in the previous chapter (critics, I assure you, I didn't mean to end one chapter writing about plane crashes and then begin the next one in the same vein, that's just how it happened), I reasoned that one aeroplane crashing was unlikely – the statistics are something like one death on an aeroplane per 11 million passengers globally, so stepping onto the aeroplane in front of me was the safe option compared to climbing into an underslept taxi driver's car to shoot home along a motorway crowded with foreigners in hire-cars who had never before driven on the left. So I stood up and joined the queue, fixing my eyes on the screen for as long as possible for a potentially life-saving piece of information. What caused the crash? What kind of aeroplane was it? The only new piece of information offered was that the plane was an Airbus A320.

"Good morning ladies and gentlemen, welcome aboard this Airbus A320 British Airways flight to Copenhagen..." came the usually reassuring voice from the flight deck. I listened intently, waiting for the Captain – who had surely been made aware of the news – to either order us off the plane in line with regulations or make reference to the news but tell us not to worry. Sensibly, he did neither and gave us the standard patter of cruising altitudes and destination weather reports in his rich and fruity voice before signing off and suggesting we pay attention to the flight attendants' safety demonstration. I watched it this time.

I had brought with me Bill Bryson's *Neither Here Nor There* with the intention of reading the chapter on Copenhagen to see if there were any passages that might alert me to something worth doing in the city. I was flying with two colleagues, Stanley and Rick. In the absence of any meaningful conversation with Stanley, I'd mentioned to Rick that it looked like our plane was going to have to taxi from the west of the airport all the way to the east where the queue for the runway was, then take off to the west before turning round and going back east over the North Sea – which disappointed me as it meant that we'd miss out on a good 40 minutes wandering the streets of Copenhagen before heading on to the evening's hotel ahead of a big day at work tomorrow. Rick immediately and correctly noted me down as a nerd and remarked that he hoped the chat would improve in the limited time we had for strolling round Denmark's capital. This appeared to signal the end of the conversation, so I buried my head in Bill Bryson's Copenhagen chapter and started to read. Then it began.

"So, are you travelling for business?" enquired an American accent in my right ear. I looked up. He was in a suit, but seemed too young to be travelling in a suit on business. Probably about 20. On his suit was a name badge.

"Yes, a gentle day today but then working tomorrow. You?"

"I'm on a mission."

I drew the information together. He was 20, he was wearing a suit with a name badge, he was American, he was on a mission. It came to me like a solution to a crossword clue: Mormon. I gave a little inward sigh; I was on a plane and had the seat next to the Mormon and the Mormon was engaging me in a conversation about Mormonism. Bill Bryson's take on Copenhagen was looking like it wasn't going to get read before I reached the city. Why does time get eaten up like this?

My dim awareness of Mormonism was that it was thought to be a pretty dodgy religion, broadly connected to mainstream Christianity but I wasn't sure how, or why it was dodgy. We did a little chatting in which I learnt his name was Zac, and before long I found myself saying the six words you are on no account ever meant to say to your Mormon neighbour on an aeroplane:

"So, tell me more about Mormonism."

Well, the next few minutes of my life was as educational as it was hilarious. Zac gave me a basic rundown and I can honestly say I have never heard a greater amount of such clearly obvious nonsense be taken as true by so many people. Mormonism in a nutshell is the belief that in the early 1800s a teenager named Joseph Smith claimed to have been visited by an angel named Moroni who informed him that, buried in the ground near where Smith was right now, was a story about an Israelite population that moved to the Americas and there witnessed the second coming of Christ in AD 400. One of these Israelites was called Mormon and in a language called 'reformed Egyptian', Mormon had engraved this story into a set of golden plates and buried it. Smith dug it up, along with some Rosetta-like stones which happened to be buried right next to the plates and helped him translate the messages on them into Smith's very dialect. A dozen people signed a statement saying they'd seen the plates which is the thread Mormonism hangs from nowadays because when asked to produce these gold plates, Smith was unable to, stating that Moroni had now taken the plates back up to heaven and so regrettably this was not going to be possible.

The translation of these plates became The Book of Mormon[24] and the Mormon church was formed in 1830, believing that Joseph Smith was an infallible prophet. So the whole of Mormonism is built on the word of Joseph Smith, and if you had any doubts at all about any one of the elements of Smith's story – that there was an Israelite population in America in AD 400, that Joseph Smith really was visited by an angel called Moroni that no-one else saw, that these priceless gold plates actually were the medium used to record the goings-on of the day in the Dark Ages and were then buried underground in a secret location in rural upstate New York, that Moroni did reappear to take them away before they were able to be generally shown around, that they were written in a language hitherto and ever since unheard of – then the whole of Mormonism comes tumbling down like a house of cards. I don't mean this as a diatribe against all religion; Christianity is a record of the acts and words of Jesus Christ in public, recalled and retold by

---

[24] Many hundreds of pages long, remember. I'm amazed to think how many gold plates must have been not only buried but also dug out by Smith to capture all the original text.

people who were actually there watching him, listening to his words and later written down as history which still tallies with secular accounts of the day and contemporary archaeological evidence of the places mentioned in the Gospels. But Mormonism in its entirety goes back to Joseph Smith 200 years ago and his private and supernatural revelations of what was alleged to have happened 1,400 years before.

I asked Zac how he could believe that Mormonism was true enough to get on a plane to Denmark for and evangelise in Danish to Danish strangers when the whole thing sounded pretty ropey to the objective ear at the outset to even the most desperate believer. Zac answered that the very first words of the Book of Mormon were that when reading the Book of Mormon the reader should pray about whether what he was reading was true or not and if after prayer the reader felt it was true, then it was true and he could believe it. That's why Zac believed the Book of Mormon. That's why Mormons believe the Book of Mormon. I asked Zac how a statement of fact could be true for one person but not true for another – especially in the context of a monotheistic religion that believes in absolute Truths and Rights and Wrongs, but Zac didn't seem to have any answer beyond this other than the fact that because it was true to him, that was the important thing. I eased off a little in my argument, beginning to feel just a little sorry for Zac. Here he was, months out of his teenage years, being sent away from his hometown of Salt Lake City where everyone's a Mormon and unbecoming a Mormon is only for the brave, on a mission to a small country on the other side of the world, and his most attentive listener was the guy on the plane who was slashing his faith apart before the wheels had even left the tarmac. The conversation ended cordially, I flashed my Bryson, Zac pulled out a copy of 'The Dummies Guide To Proselytizing Your Oversized Mid-Western Sect to Vikings In Their Native Tongue' and we read in silence until, thankfully, we landed safely.

**

I fairly sprinted off the plane in that zesty walk everyone does when competing to be towards the front of the Passport Control queue. The formalities completed, I set about aiming to make my way to the heart of the capital. It wasn't that easy.

One of the annoyances of travel, particularly at airports, is how hostile the simplest tasks can be for the traveller to accomplish when immediately immersed in a foreign culture. I have had several memorable occasions such as this. In 2008, wishing to convey myself, my wife, our two month old baby, three suitcases, three hand-baggage bags and a collapsible pram from the baggage reclaim area of Nice airport to the hire car desk, I discovered that Nice's luggage trolleys were chained to each other and releasing one required a €1 coin. Fresh off the plane from London, I didn't have a €1 coin on me, so dragged everything to a shop where I bought a chocolate bar with the €5 note I *did* have on me (because bureaux de change never give you coins), and made change. The trolley was loaded and pushed about 100 metres where we learned that the hire car was parked on the other side of the airport and it was necessary to take a shuttle bus there, on which trolleys could not, of course, be accommodated. So we transferred the contents of the trolley onto the rapidly-filling bus while its engine growled portentously and I was tasked to return the trolley to inside the terminal building and retrieve our €1. Unable to return through security to the baggage carousel where I had obtained the trolley, I had to find somewhere else to chain the trolley up. The walk was further than I wanted, bearing in mind my wife was on the bus with a baby and seven bags but I found a trolley sticking out through a hole in a wall and as I approached the back of it from the side, a little man in a short sleeved-shirt pushing a train of 50 trolleys started barking at me to get out of the way so he could dock his load. He did so, pushing all the trolleys through the hole in the wall and into another dimension while I stood there open-mouthed, and now suddenly deprived of anywhere to chain my trolley to.

Shortly after this, I had a similar experience at New York's spacious JFK airport, trying to find any seats at all near the check-in desks where the three of us could sit and give our baby his bottle, but there were none in the landside part of the terminal, we were required to go airside – despite the fact that our baby would really rather not have to wait the twenty extra minutes to queue for security - where all the shops and restaurants and cafés and seats were. On the way in to JFK from London, we again discovered the hard way that we were required to possess a specific type of American coinage to acquire a luggage trolley, and if we didn't have it (and we didn't) then that was that. I wrote and complained the day after I got home and received a reply six months later bleating something about FAA regulations and it all being like this with my safety and comfort of paramount importance.

Denmark's experience was a little different. Stanley, Rick and I needed to get to the city and all the signs were directing us to a train service that promised to convey us there quickly and at a reasonable price. We walked up to a ticket machine and I inserted the American Express card my company had provided me with to accrue all my travelling expenses – as I understood it, no other form of purchase and therefore reimbursement would be allowed. You've guessed the punchline: this machine didn't seem to have been introduced to the fact that American Express cards were widely used by travellers on international business and Stanley, Rick and I were therefore marooned at the airport with essentially no way to get to Copenhagen itself. None of us really fancied the walk, particularly Stanley who was a little flat-footed. I stress-tested the machine's casing with my forehead, Rick had an idea about a way he could pay for two tickets with a different card to keep the accountants happy and we boarded the train to Copenhagen. The journey from airport to city centre and all the newness it so quickly brings is my favourite part of international travel. I took my seat on the train and pressed my nose to the window, anxious to take in as much of Denmark as possible.

Sadly, the train route is not only the most boring view possible, there isn't actually a view at all. I don't mean that what you see is uninspiring, like when you ride the Eurostar from London to Paris and come up at Calais to be suddenly shown the most featureless hour of countryside it is possible to see from a train window, I mean that the constructors of the airport rail link in Copenhagen had felt it worthwhile to manufacture a large embankment on either side of the tracks to obscure the travellers' views of the country they had just come to see. We pulled into Copenhagen's central station with me not exactly feeling welcome to Denmark at this point, and the feeling did not improve over the next half-hour or so.

I'd consulted a map of Copenhagen before the trip (serendipitously, my local charity shop had thought to display a Copenhagen pocket guidebook in its window a week before I was due to travel) and had been able to form a rough plan for the afternoon. Right outside the station was Tivoli Gardens, which sounded like an immaculately presented city park, but was in actual fact something much better: a fully-functioning theme park, right in the centre of the capital city. I don't know why this idea hasn't caught on more, globally. Trafalgar Square is a well-proportioned space and it's pleasing to have an airy block of emptiness in the exact centre of a bustling megacity, but if, occasionally, something like a roller coaster were installed there, wouldn't we all appreciate the space a little bit more? It would certainly give us something to do on our lunchbreaks and it's not like there's less passing trade than in a countryside park off an A road, where roller coasters usually live. Wouldn't the Eiffel Tower be improved if we had the option of descending it by climbing into a seat and pulling a bar over our shoulders to freefall the 100 or so feet from the first floor to the ground, with only a whoosh of pneumatic brakes at the last second? We have giant Ferris wheels in the centre of most cities, so why not? Denmark had got it right in this regard, and I emerged from the station under a sky the same colour as the pavement, immediately walked up to Tivoli's entrance ready to pay whatever they asked for the privilege of looping the loop. "A sign on the gate said it wouldn't be open for a couple of weeks", reads page 133 of Bill Bryson's *Neither Here Nor There* (Black Swan, 2008) on his visit to Copenhagen. I wondered whether I was looking at the same sign, which said "PÅ GENSYN 1. APRIL". I didn't speak any Danish but I felt a sudden affinity with Bryson. April Fool.

Denmark isn't as far north as you might think. It's Scandinavia, of course, a word which makes us think of icy fjords, Lapland and the Northern Lights, but in terms of latitude, Copenhagen is no further north than Edinburgh. It is perhaps this more favourable climate that has made Copenhagen so amenable to the bicycle. The oil crisis of the 1970s prompted the city to introduce no-car Sundays as a way of in effect rationing petrol use and many residents quickly thought it the best day of the week. Cycling grew in popularity and studies were commissioned to realise the costs and benefits of cycling. The benefits can hardly be overstated: Every kilometre cycled brought a net gain for society of 1.22DKK (about 12 pence), compared to a net loss of 0.69 DKK in a car. Healthwise, it was found in a study of 20,000 cyclists aged 20 to 100[25] that cycling at a high or average speed increases life expectancy by between 3 and 5 years compared to 2 to 4 years cycling at low speed.

50% of all commutes within Copenhagen are done by bike. Copenhagen has 220 miles of segregated cycle tracks and 14 miles of on-street bicycle lanes – which is the right way round, if you ask me. 1.2 million kilometres are cycled in Copenhagen every year, double the distance covered by underground train journeys. 63% of all members of the Danish parliament cycle there. Copenhagen's main cycling route has 36,000 bicycles per day passing along it. A proper authentic cycling culture has emerged in Copenhagen and as more people cycle, more services are laid on for cyclists – 'cargo bikes' abound – pimped tricycles selling fresh coffee, sandwiches, ice creams, fruit and veg. If you're really lucky, you might spot Copenhagen's most famous commercial bicycle – the Sperm Bullitt. Denmark leads the world in this

[25] I hope I can still cycle at 100.

particular market as Denmark's liberal view of family values translates into national legislation that sperm donors aren't required to be traceable. In a *Daily Telegraph* article I have just read, 'John' – who without irony likened the process to giving blood - is paid £30 a pop as a patient to propel his popularly potent potion possessing the appropriate properties for procreating people at a place called Nordic Cryobank on the edge of Copenhagen's city centre, with seemingly no concern for the fact that he is becoming a father to many sons and daughters, none of whom will ever know him. For £30. But I guess everyone has their price. This enforced privacy has made Denmark something of a Mecca for foreign women wanting to conceive in a way nature did not intend for them. For these women, shopping for a father is not unlike shopping online, for they are able to view donors' photos, download an audio interview with them and see a photo of them as a baby before making their choice. "A lot of our clients typically want their donor to be at least 180cm [5ft 11in] tall and have blue eyes," explains Peter Bower, director of Nordic Cryobank, just a touch unnervingly. Danish clinics provide insemination services at a fraction of the price of the UK, and single women is Bower's fastest-growing market; a citybreak in Copenhagen wrapped around the appointment is the best option in many ways for a number of the 15-20 women per day who make use of the humorously named Stork Klinik. But it wouldn't do for mothers and fathers to meet each other as part of this process, so the sperm donated in one part of the city has to make its short journey across town to fulfil its destiny, and as Peter Bower wondered how this could be done with a low carbon footprint (seemingly oblivious to the huge carbon footprint caused by the creation of a human being where there would not otherwise have been one), the bicycle was the obvious solution. The sperm bike was born, as it were – a custom-modified bicycle with cooling container accommodated between the pedals and front wheel in housing shaped to very accurately resemble the head of a sperm cell, with the whipping tail flowing backwards over the rear wheel, seemingly driving the whole vehicle forwards. It's as eye-catching a sight as can be seen on any city street and it's good publicity for Nordic Cryobank too. I just wouldn't want it to crash into me.

All this cycling is perhaps why Copenhagen has what was upon its opening, the world's longest pedestrianised street – Strøget, at 1km long, linking Tivoli to Nyhavn, that short street filled with a canal and flanked by many-coloured timbered buildings that you have in your mind's eye when you picture Copenhagen. This was the route Stanley, Rick and I were walking now. Starting outside the grand and intimidating Københavns Rådhus (City Hall) with its clock turret, gold trim and intricate crenellations, we made it about 100 metres down the street before Rick announced that he wished to dive into a bar and drink a Carlsberg or two and possibly a little lunch as well. Now, after the delay at Heathrow, the forced conversation with the Mormon on the plane, the faff getting into town from the airport and the disappointment of Tivoli being closed, I admit that stopping and going indoors for an hour after sixty seconds of walking wasn't exactly what I wanted to do with my unexpected half day in a European capital city. Also, I hated Carlsberg so much that I once had to throw a crate of it away, so much did I not want to drink it, but Rick literally carried Stanley through the door before I could begin to articulate any disagreement.

Happily, this bar had three things going for it: 1) A quirky, atmospheric interior that I placed in a venn diagram between Tudor England and Lederhosen Bavaria; 2) It served Tuborg, a beer I hadn't heard of but was the biggest selling Danish beer in Denmark (and no visit to a foreign city is complete without a big glass of the local); and 3) It had an empty table at the window with a view of the street. Stanley slid onto the seat with his back to the window and Rick and I nuzzled the foam on our lagers and people-watched. We couldn't take our eyes off what we saw, as uncomfortable as it made us. Directly across the street was a tiny shoe shop, no bigger than my lounge, with shoes and boots displayed on little shelves from wall to ceiling and an island unit in the middle. It was a cold weekday in March and trade wasn't exactly brisk, so the shop was staffed by just one person who had absolutely no work to do and just spent her time standing there, quite literally looking pretty – we weren't especially looking at her, but it was hard not to notice. From time to time she'd flick dust off a slingback or lap the shop like a bear in a cage, but other than that she was just there, quite literally minding her own business, totally unaware that two men in the bar across the street had a direct view in. Rick and I agreed that we were both deeply uncomfortable in our own skin about this. I couldn't take any more, so I swapped seats with Stanley to face the interior and to congratulate myself on my self-discipline ordered another Tuborg, which I downgraded to a Carlsberg, I was feeling so ashamed of myself. The taste hadn't improved and I forced myself to drink it up by way of penance. That didn't make me feel any better so I ordered a Tuborg to take the taste away. Well, honestly. I paid in cash, and in my change received several coins which had the unique feature of a small hole bored through the centre. I'd never seen this before and whilst it seemed a little bit odd, I was glad it was there and that the Danes were thinking differently to the rest of the world.

I should note that for the record I ate a delicious and typically Danish open herring and bacon sandwich on Rugbrød – that dark sour rye bread that is so synonymous with healthy living and probably explained the slim build of everyone on Strøget, down which Rick and I continued our stroll, feeling like a couple of blimps. Neither of us had kept track of how much Stanley had drunk, but we had to physically carry him along the street.

I need to come clean with you about something, dear reader. Stanley isn't who you think he is. At the end of the next paragraph, read back over my mentions of Stanley and you can see that the clues were there all along.

The week before leaving, my friend Alan asked if I could do him a favour. His sister-in-law had a relative who lived in the United States, but more pertinently was ten years old. At school one day, he had been introduced to a fictional friend in a book by an author called Jeff Brown. Stanley Lambchop, to give him his full name, was fixing a notice board over his bed one evening, but during the night, the board fell down, flattening Stanley in his sleep. Stanley survived, and, making the best of a bad situation, used his new form to benefit from all sorts of new adventures: sliding under locked doors, employing himself as a kite, and visiting friends via envelope. And it was the visiting of friends that gave rise to the Flat Stanley Project in 1995, where a primary school teacher named Dale Hubert tasked his class to send Flat Stanley to a penfriend in another country and encourage Stanley to 'write back' with accompanying photos of his adventures. So, my friend Alan's relative had sent his Flat Stanley over to England where Alan and his wife had great fun taking photos of Stanley riding a big red bus, in a phonebox, sitting down to a plate of roast beef – that sort of thing. Then when Alan heard I was going to Copenhagen, Alan ran Stanley through the photocopier and asked if I might take Stanley on tour. I was only too happy to oblige, and Rick and I continued down Strøget, looking for somewhere that would scream "Denmark" to a ten year old in America where we could photograph Stanley. We came to Copenhagen's design district, for Denmark is known within design circles for taking the matter pretty seriously. I began to see brands I recognised and were dimly aware that they were Danish – Skagen watches, Georg Jensen silverware, Pandora jewellery, all of which suggested I become a customer, but cutting such a dash uses up a lot of cash and I didn't want to fritter it all. I was tiring a little of looking at shop windows. Then, waiting to cross a road, I noticed a brick tower sticking up above the skyline in the middle-distance, iron railings around the top and a handful of people milling about up there. I alerted Rick and suggested that we climb the tower, see Copenhagen, and get our bearings before we lost our marbles. I also wanted to get a photo of Stanley, I admit. Rick had his mind on another Carlsberg but I offered to pay his admission fee and this seemed to persuade him.

I had discovered the Rundetårn, the oldest functioning observatory in Europe, built in 1642 and pleasingly rated by TripAdvisor, I was to learn in the queue as I consulted my phone, as the 10th best thing out of 383 to do in Copenhagen. Astronomy became an increasingly important science in the 17th century as commercial shipping became more and more lucrative and Copenhagen became an important port, strategically situated between the Baltic and North Seas. Scandinavia, wanting to get ahead of the game and map the skies for the benefit of its ships, built the Rundetårn for precisely this purpose – above the roofline so as to benefit from the lack of light pollution. But the rise of the electric light and the increasing unwieldiness of modern telescopes spelled the demise of the Rundetårn as an observatory. Speaking personally, I was happy it now operated as a tourist attraction. Looking at it from a few blocks away, there was something unusual about the Rundetårn's appearance – its windows, which climbed the full height of the tower, weren't quite level with each other.

I bought two tickets for myself, Rick and Stanley and was immediately faced with a curious sight which explained why the windows were wonky. The path to the top of the tower wasn't a staircase, it was a ramp. A ramp. In a tower built in 1642. Why? Well, the internet tells me now that it was so a horse and cart could be driven up the tower, pulling carts of books for the library in the hall of one of the rooms in the main building, on which the Rundetarn had been stuck to the end. The ramp completes 7.5 turns and is 85.5m long at its centre, but of course 257.5m long along the outer wall. It was novel to be pacing up a spiralling indoor slope and to share the moment I looked over towards Rick, who, as not the most athletic of people, and had taken to tacking, much as a yacht does into the wind. His face had gone all red and shiny. "Carlsberg!" was all he could pant. Rick excused himself and entered the toilet located in a side room for what I suspect was as much rest as relief. I passed the time by googling the Rundetårn and discovered that the very toilet Rick was in was installed for use by the researchers and astronomers working on the observation deck and consisted of nothing more than a seat and a pan at the top and a shaft dropping some 30 metres down to the bottom floor then leading into the hollow core at the centre of the spiral. This shaft cannot be emptied nor does it have any ventilation to the outside, making it a curious piece of architecture on which Rick was clearly going to leave his mark.

I also discovered that not everyone walks up the slope of the Rundetårn. In 1888, a bicycle race to the top was organised and in 1902, a Beaufort car made it up the ramp in what sounds suspiciously like a publicity stunt, becoming the first motorized vehicle to spiral its way to the top, inspiring multi-story car park architects for much of the next century. Cycle races continue intermittently and have now broadened to include a clearly genial fancy-dress unicycle race, the most recent of which I could find evidence for having been in 2011; but I doubt the managers of the Rundetårn permit such an excellent publicity stunt to only take place twice a decade.

Rick and I finally reached the top and it was well worth the climb. Is there any better activity in a foreign city than going to the top of a tall building in the middle of the city and looking out? The Eiffel Tower was initially derided by Parisians but is now embraced. The Millennium Dome was the main event in London in the year 2000 with the Millennium Wheel / London Eye something of a secondary effort. But which draws the crowds now? Anyway, it wasn't ideal weather for observation deck viewing – it wasn't ideal for anything outdoors actually – but Rick and I hung around up there for a quarter of an hour or so, slowly moving clockwise around the railings, trying to identify what we could and taking in the city's oxblood brickwork and roof tiles, ruminating on how pleasant it was to look out across the rooftops, rather than down on them. We took a photo of Stanley.

Then, back down we went and ploughed on to Kongens Nytorv which my guidebook told me was the most pleasant of city squares and, being at the head of Nyhavn, was effectively the jewel in Copenhagen's centrepiece. But today, it was a building site, surrounded by green corrugated fences which inadequately masked piles of muddy rubble. Unsatisfying, but at least it ended our walk as disappointingly as Tivoli had started it. Rick and I stood in the street and considered our options; we'd reached our destination and now faced what was frankly a bit of a trudge back up the street that we'd just walked down to retrieve our suitcases from the luggage lockers at the station. Then I saw a baker's window full of little pastries and coffees being passed over the counter inside and I knew I couldn't leave the country without having sat down and had a Danish Danish.

**

Rick and I decided not to retrace our steps back up Strøget – after all, what we're interested in here is The World *Less* Travelled – and tossing our holey coin we chose to turn right up a sidestreet and found ourselves in the hipster district. We knew it was the hipster district because skinny little men with beards bigger than their shorts were riding scooters into basement cafés.

Now I'm no authority on fashion whatsoever, but I simply can't believe that the rules on what constitutes a normal and appropriate state of dress had changed so quickly in such little time as from 2012 to 2015. When I was a teenager in the 1990s, no more and no less had been expected of me than a pair of jeans and a t-shirt. Not an awful lot had changed in my twenties – it briefly became unsurprising to have a number on the back of your t-shirt like a footballer but that was about as directive as male fashion got. Then, in about 2012, someone seemed to flick a switch and it became immediately required of most men to be wearing drainpipe red trousers and a slim-fit shirt buttoned all the way up to the neck, which had to be obscured with a bushy beard. Superfluous waistcoats and bow-ties were encouraged, and geek glasses were expected, irrespective of what your optician said. I simply couldn't work out how this all happened in less time than it took to grow a bushy beard and I suspect that in 30 years' time we'll look back in horror at today's photos in the way that we do now at the 1970s when all the men were in tartan flares and had jaw-length hair and mutton-chops.

I don't wish to put down the hipster culture, though. New ideas, new ways of doing things and the disruption of complacent cultures are the heartbeat of hipsterism. With the technological advances of the 2000s, the ability to create and broadcast art in the widest sense of the word had become democratised. Why sell your financial future to a record company who will then tell you what sort of songs fit the market segment they have carved out for you for the next 18 months before consigning you to the scrapheap to make way for the Next Big Thing when you can instead upload your music directly to a global market forever and keep all the royalties if the public thinks your music is as good as you think it is? Why build a hotel and run it at 60% occupancy when you can charge a trivial fee for anyone with a spare room to let it out to tourists at a fraction of the cost? Why drive around for hours in your taxi hoping to pick up a fare when you can commission drivers to rent out their spare seats for everyone's benefit? Why post your manuscript to 30 publishers and collect 30 rejection letters when you can write a book you want to write on your unexpected travels to some of the world's smaller and more offbeat destinations, certain that it's going to get self-published at some point? No, I wouldn't jettison the hipster mentality from the world for any price, it's far too important a culture for the future of how the world is organised to be suppressed. It's just the uniform individuality of everyone's on-trend appearance that gnaws at me, and the fact that they always look like they're wearing the outfit for a bet.

Rick and I continued along Copenhagen's snaking, slightly claustrophobic streets in the fading light with the distinct sense that our sightseeing was over for the day and that this walk was more about the journey than the destination. We crossed the road, and at the other side were greeted by a policeman holding a machine gun. Neither Rick nor I knew how to interpret this; Scandinavia isn't renowned for its armed police. What was one doing on a public thoroughfare, and armed with a machine gun, at that? We pressed on, glancing around for danger. I noticed a Star of David engraved into an exterior wall and then it clicked. Days before, Copenhagen had made international headlines right where I was standing.

In September 2005, Danish newspaper Jyllands-Posten took a deep breath and, under the banner of contributing to the debate about criticism of Islam, published 12 cartoons depicting the prophet Muhammad, in the full knowledge that this was considered hideously blasphemous in most Islamic traditions and that western Christian / eastern Muslim tensions were still very much there. To say it was a form of terrorist-baiting that showed dangerously poor decision-making is very much a subjective point of view, but the Danish Prime Minister at the time declared the whole thing to be Denmark's worst international relations incident since the country was captured by Hitler, and he was right in this respect. Upon viewing the images, Danish Imams toured the Middle East to whip up hate, and without any hint of hypocrisy in any way, prepared and presented a dossier of the 12 cartoons to anyone who would let themselves look, resulting in prominent media attention across the Muslim world. Danish Muslims petitioned their government to take action and filed a judicial complaint against Jyllands-Posten, which was dismissed by the courts, on the grounds that Jyllands-Posten wasn't breaking any Danish laws. Diplomats from Muslim countries requested to meet Denmark's Foreign Ministers but had their requests refused. There were protests across the world for the first two months of 2006, escalating to violence with 200 reported deaths, attacks on Danish and other European diplomats, and attacks on Christians. The issue polarised western-Muslim relations and came to symbolise relations between Islamic communities and the rest of society. Some non-Muslims responded to the protests by endorsing Denmark, launching "Buy Danish" campaigns and holding Carlsberg and bacon parties in what was either a generous show of self-sacrificial bridge-building to the Danes or an incendiary act of gloating. The cartoons were reprinted in newspapers around the world in a sense of journalistic solidarity.

The tensions have never fully subsided, but the Krudttønden Cultural Centre decided to mark Valentine's Day 2015 with an exhibition lovingly entitled "Art, Blasphemy and Freedom of Expression", in the immediate aftermath of the *Charlie Hebdo* attacks in which 12 journalists were predictably and fatally targeted after many years of poking sacred radical Islamic cows. French Ambassador to Denmark, François Zimeray was in attendance, and notorious Swedish Artist Lars Viks, who bravely/foolishly decided to allow three of his drawings of the prophet Muhammad be published by a local newspaper in 2007 (and has subsequently been forced to live under police protection following death threats and a memorable offer from the al-Qaeda affiliated Islamic State of Iraq of $150,000 for his murder), was a guest speaker. I think I have telegraphed the climax of the story for you if you didn't already know it. Omar El-Hussain was a 22 year-old, born in Denmark to Jordan-Palestinian parents and known to Danish 'intelligence' services, having been sentenced twice for violence and possession of an illegal weapon, before he was sentenced to two years for an indiscriminate knife attack on a man riding a train in Copenhagen in 2013. In September 2014, prison officers reported concerns about El-Hussain's bizarre and fanatical behaviour in jail, finding that he had become "extremely religious".   But he was released weeks later, just before this Valentine's Day exhibition, having only served half his sentence. El-Hussain attempted to enter the exhibition through a back door, but was stopped by film director Finn Nørgaard, whom El-Hussain shot dead before unleashing 200 further shots through the window of the centre. Zimeray believed all present would die, just as in the editorial meeting at Charlie Hébdo four weeks previously. But the five police officers present returned fire and El-Hussain fled.

Shortly after midnight, El-Hussain appeared drunk as he clutched his gun in front of the Great Synagogue where I was now standing. He fired nine rounds of bullets into the building, hitting the head of Dan Uzan, the Jewish community member on security duty and two police officers. Uzan died. El-Hussein ran away again, four hours later appearing outside an apartment building that the police had under surveillance, El-Hussain having visited it between the shootings. The police called out to El-Hussein, who replied with gunshots. The police reciprocated. El-Hussein was killed and flowers were placed in the street by well-wishers, which no-one knew how to react to.

Well, if you'd told me the day after the Charlie Hébdo attack in January 2015 that within two months there would be a related killing and that I would be a passer-by at the spot where the attack would take place and that I would on that day fly on an Airbus 320 which was also a day where an A320 would crash killing all aboard, I can assure you I would have taken out a pretty large insurance policy and mended some broken friendships before leaving the house. Isn't life fragile?

**

The hotel booked for that night had caused great excitement and mirth as it had emerged that some Tripadvisor reviews for this hotel mentioned the fact that on top of the mini bar in the reviewer's room was a shallow dish displaying a small selection of sex toys for the occupant to avail themselves of if they so, er, desired. Rick and I (not to mention Stanley) were infused with a conflicted sense of foreboding and also eagerness to see if the hotel was continuing to dare to offer this service. We hopped into a taxi, paid the exorbitant fare, checked in, ran upstairs to our rooms and discovered with a touch of dismay as we dumped our bags that the tradition had been discontinued, or that we'd just got unlucky. We will never know. The rooms were just totally vanilla, normal hotel rooms, nothing amiss.

Back downstairs, a rendez-vous with colleagues from all parts of Europe was in full swing. We were about fifteen in total but we all conversed in the international language of alcohol while we waited for the promised buffet to appear. I was having an excellent time, and as conversation turned to what Danish cuisine could possibly feature in any buffet, I suddenly remembered my colleague Laura who wasn't able to arrive until late in the evening and had asked me to ensure there was a plate of food in her room on arrival. I made my excuses and wandered back towards reception, where a scene was clearly in progress.

"I cannot believe it!" erupted a short, angry German man at the presentable blonde face who I will call Tania behind the reception desk. "Are you seriously telling me that I travel 1000 miles on a day where all the flights are cancelled, where I miss my daughter's birthday, and this is where you give me to rest my head for the night?" Tania cut him off too soon, "I'm sorry, sir, we have a big group staying tonight and all the rooms are fully booked, so…"

"So you're telling me I have to sleep *there*? In that room? Do you know what I'm going to do tomorrow? I'm going to see the *board.* I'm going to go into the boardroom of [some company I'd never heard of] and present to the CEO and his counterparts, and you think *this* room is the place where I should prepare for that? It's like a children's room! I'm not sleeping in it! You have to do something and you have to do something pretty fast lady, because you have one seriously pissed off customer here!" I stood there awkwardly with my room key in my hand. All I wanted to do was ask for a plate of food to be in Laura's room when she arrived. Why do the shortest queries always get stuck behind the longest transactions? If Tania's colleagues could hear what was going on, they were not coming to her rescue. Tania's eyes bored into the computer screen as she jabbed her buttons, unsuccessfully instructing the room booking system to make something happen. Tania didn't deserve to suffer like this. "Excuse me?" I ventured, trying to sound less like the awkward Brit that I was and more like an English knight in shining armour "But I couldn't help overhearing your conversation. I checked in twenty minutes ago. My suitcase is on the floor of a perfectly fine room upstairs and I'm happy to sleep anywhere. Do you want to swap?"

I'm not sure what reaction I was expecting. Maybe for Tania's face to light up before regathering her businesslike composure and for the German man to launch into a preamble of "No, I couldn't possibly..." before, amidst a sea of obliging noises, it was agreed that I was without doubt the best person in the hotel and subsequently offered drinks on the house all evening by way of thanks. What actually happened was Tania answered "Yes, thank you, you can go and get your bag now and bring it down," and the German man continued to bitch and grumble that it had come to this. That was it, and I silently climbed the stairs, almost with a sense of reproach. German man seemed to be easily irritated. I knew that, of the two of us, I would sleep better that night.

**

The following day contained the work that had made the trip necessary in the first place and about which you have no desire to read, but it had been agreed that after business there would be a boat ride around Copenhagen before food and drink and further drink could disintegrate into bedtime. I can recommend the boat ride immensely, though will counsel that sundown in March is not the best weather for a cruise on the Baltic Sea. The boat was one of these wide barges with blue plastic seating covered by a curved transparent roof and a small section of open deck at the stern. It was here that several colleagues and I stood in the wind for several minutes with blue lips and dancing hair, taking in the sight of Copenhagen's slate-grey water until it simply became too cold to continue and a featureless, open expanse of sea lay between us and any sights.

But when the sights came, they were worth seeing. On a map, Copenhagen is not dissimilar to Venice or Amsterdam, with a main waterway submerging the central passageway of the city and radial canals running off it to make picturesque streets for the tourists. No boat tour of Copenhagen would be complete without a view of the city's famous mermaid statue, but my, what a trudge it is to get there; I was pleased I hadn't walked to it the day before because it was about a mile the wrong side of Nyhavn on the edge of a little park on the way to nowhere in particular. It took about ten minutes for the boat to chug through the damp wintry air to the pile of boulders on which she sat, facing away from us, with her tail obscured from us by her plinth, rendering her an insufficient sight for a photo with Stanley. I have no idea how she had become so famous. It was another ten minutes back again to our starting point when the tour *really* began: landmark waterfront building rapidly followed landmark waterfront building and we were treated to Copenhagen's remarkable ancient and modern architecture at a pace I could barely keep up with. So please excuse me if you are a Dane and recognise any of the following as being in the wrong order:

Copenhagen Opera House came first (I think). It's a modern, boxy, glass building; a cuboid flat-pack box with an overhanging, near-horizontal roof that looks like the builders had the plans turned at 90 degrees when they built it. A tinted glass façade gave onto the canal, allowing us on the water to see the calm snugness of the main bar area. It is about as pleasant a large modern building as you can hope to find; wrapped in expensive-looking wooden planks of varying lengths and shiny glass. Even so, I was astonished to discover later that construction cost an eye-popping $500 million. Let me give that number some context. Wembley Stadium in London, built at the same time, cost approximately double that (let's say exactly double) and seats 90,000. This means that (with dollars converted to pounds) each Wembley seat needs to attract £11,111 in revenue during the course of its life to pay for itself, and at a ticket price of, say, £60, Wembley will have raised the cash it cost to build it after 185 sell-out events. At one event per month, that's 15 years – a fairly reasonable timescale once you consider the operating costs which will chip away at the profit and the 77 year lifespan of the former Wembley Stadium. Now that you know these numbers, do you have a ball-park figure for the approximate number of seats in Copenhagen's Opera House? Remember, it cost half what Wembley Stadium cost to build and Wembley seats 90,000. You were wrong – Copenhagen Opera House accommodates just 1,492 people. That's a modest auditorium: 25ish seats across and 50ish seats deep (I have just checked on the website by pretending to book a ticket). By comparison, Aylesbury's Waterside Theatre (picking a small-town provincial theatre at random) seats 1,200. You know from school that 1,492 x £60 = £89,520 revenue per performance and that $500 million divided by $89,520 = 5,620 sell-out performances for the revenue to equal the construction costs. At one sell-out performance per week, that's going to be 108 insufferable years of Danish opera, played out in a modest city of one million people, capital of the 113th largest county by population, consisting largely of islands separated by a dark and icy sea. Does that sound like a viable economic investment to you? And that's before we get to the esoteric, highbrow nature of opera – an art form that will never pull in the masses and is clearly not cheap to produce. I hope the place breaks even though; it's a lovely building, best appreciated I think from the outside.

The sights continued – a quite magnificent dome resembling St Paul's Cathedral done in green which I'd've been able to tell you more about if I'd been able to hear the guide's crackly voice over the ear-whistling gust of wind sent at the precise moment she identified it to me. Then came The Black Diamond – a 21st Century glossy rhombus that was probably related to the Opera House in some way and looked like a swish headquarters for Scandinavia's largest audit firm or something, but I was edified to hear was Denmark's National Library, which is a great place to go if you have lots of free time, like reading and are fluent in Danish. It has an auditorium that seats 600 people, which must annoy the Opera House's financiers as the two undoubtedly compete for the same customers on some days.

Then came the Dome of Visions, which almost identical in size and shape to the The Dome from The Crystal Maze, yet standing there in the outdoors, on the Copenhagen Seafront. I only just repressed a strong urge to shout "START THE FANS, PLEASE!!" at the top of my voice into the inky sky. The Dome of Visions's website describes its purpose as "...about putting action into words and following through on new ideas in construction and urban thinking and planing [*sic*]" but was really a tropical garden inside a giant greenhouse, an environment I would gladly have swapped my night-air and metal floor combination for there and then.

Next up was one of the most horrible buildings I have ever had the misfortune to lay my eyes upon. After the intentional waterfront wonder of all the architecture I had just seen, I found myself suddenly staring at a pigeon-grey oblong tank – four times wider than it was high – with large square windows framed with concrete, evenly spaced so as to resemble a giants' mortuary. I couldn't get over how ugly it was and I found myself gesticulating wildly in disbelief that anyone could allow anything so foul to be constructed in the midst of buildings conceived and constructed with such care and attention. I practically gripped strangers by the elbow and pointed at it saying "Do you see this thing here? How, in a country that values high art enough to spend £100 per citizen on an Opera House, did they let this get built on the same seafront?" It had the beauty of those Hotel Formule 1s that you see off the ringroad of downbeat French cities that I hope you never to have to spend a night in (I have and it wasn't great – the duvet was sewn to the foot end of the bed). I literally couldn't believe it until, mercifully, it was pointed out to me that the Danes had not lost their mind nor the sense of taste for which they are rightly famous, for this was the head office of Maersk – the largest container ship operator in the world, which drew in some $50 billion in revenue in 2014, roughly the same as Disney. This building was not an architectural blight, it was a deliberate intent to reconstruct the design of a fully-loaded container ship at dock – Maersk's stock in trade. The world made sense again and the relief was tangible.

Then we passed Sluseholmen, which can only be described as an inner-city seawater lido – not a combination of words that encourages even the most visionary of leisure entrepreneurs to build it, but it was quite the tidiest thing I'd seen in a while. An area of harbour approximately the size of an Olympic swimming pool had been surrounded by decking, and a pleasing red and white striped lighthouse drew the eye to high diving facilities and shallow splashy children's pools. The whole thing looked like it had been made of Lego. It was clearly a marvellous facility, but I can't say how much you'd have to pay me to jump into an semi-industrial stretch of the Baltic Sea from a great height no matter what the air temperature. At the time of writing, the Slusehomen's Wikipedia page states that "...the harbour baths are a result of a consistent effort to improve the water quality in Copenhagen Harbour to an extent that allows for bathing to take place. [...] In the event of unusually strong rains, sewage may spill into the harbour and cause pollution with E. Coli bacteria, closing the harbour baths temporarily." But this didn't seem to have deterred a clutch of youths, taking it in turns to take the plunge (goaded on by slow hand-claps from the passengers of our passing boat that I encouraged), surely oblivious to the threat of hypothermia, bacterial infection and the fact that it was after dark in a month that had an 'r' in it.

But the takeaway views of the boat tour were the church spires peppering the city like, well, giant pepper mills, and best visible from the open water at the city's centre. Copenhagen perhaps does spires better than any other city I've seen; each was remarkable in its own right: There was the hollow, lumpy turret of Nikolaj Copenhagen Contemporary Art Center (formerly the Church of St. Nikolaj), the tight corkscrews of the Børs stock exchange (admiring the structure from the roofline up, you can see the spire is made up of four dragon tails twisting together), the diminishing fortification atop Rosenborg Castle, the opulent folly of Christiansborg Palace, but my personal favourite, the spire of the Church of Our Saviour – unique in that it accommodates a spiral staircase *on its outside*. You can climb it – a golden handrail the only thing separating you from an exciting but messy death. I decided this was the best church spire in the world. Uplit, the spires looked at their best and I feel fortunate to have been shown them after sundown.

Time was nearly up; we were ferried back to Nyhavn by way of a backwater so narrow the captain was forced to make a handbrake turn at one point and we all pressed our hands against the underside of a bridge to prevent a collision. Then we sprang off the boat, ready for dinner, during which I was reminded of Stanley.

Well, Stanley was the life and soul of the party that night, let me tell you. There is nothing like a common friend to bind together a group of strangers and Stanley, whilst quite literally lacking any depth of character, was that common friend. And so, at a suitably large table, Stanley provided the entertainment while we all killed time until the food arrived. Everybody wanted to have their photo taken with Stanley. The men tucked him into their shirt pocket and gurned a thumbs-up, the women gave him a cuddle and showed the camera their teeth before, as so often happens in this situation, one thing led to another and Stanley was being kissed on the lips and generally cherished by the ladies in the group who were now bonding with him as though he were the entertainment on a hen night. Stanley was inverted and inserted into wine glasses, had a steak knife drawn across his throat in a manner we all agree echoed the TV Series The Killing – and had bolognese rearranged into mock vomit as Stanley displayed the aftermath of all this hedonism.

But the restaurant was just the amuse-bouche to the evening. The panna cottas were consumed, the bill paid and half of us proceeded to exit to the street to get cold whilst waiting for half the remainder of the group to navigate unnecessary delays and accompany us to sample some of Denmark's nightlife.

I don't know what I was expecting from Denmark's nightlife – probably reserved, involving tall and narrow glasses of Carlsberg and revolving around the writings of Kierkegaard – but strolling up Nyhavn, we found ourselves judging establishment after establishment and ruminating upon whether this bar or that bar should provide the memorable backdrop to tonight's adventures. In *Neither Here Nor There*, Bryson described Nyhavn as "a street full of dive bars where you would expect to see Popeye and Bluto trading blows" but was being dragged forcibly upmarket by visionary restaurateurs. And now here I was many years later seeing that Bryson had called it right; many bars had sought to equip their pavement-spaces with not only patio-heaters but also complimentary blankets with which their mid-to-high income patrons could snuggle down and warm up with some of that fermented grape juice we all enjoy so much. In the event, for indiscriminate reasons, we settled upon a basement bar not much larger than a one-bedroom flat with walls panelled in wide vertical planks of pine and a sticky floor and a student air throughout. We ordered Tuborgs in plastic schooners and attempted small talk over the cacophony of a Europop / grunge mix that the DJ was selecting. All this time, Stanley poked out of my shirt pocket and his personality received a hearty second wind as we again revolved our conversation around him while trying to figure out something worthwhile to talk about, as is so often the way in noisy bars. Stanley was once more photographed in a variety of compromising positions, at one point ashamedly bowing his head over an ashtray crammed with cigarette butts when we suddenly realised something unusual: cigarettes.

Cigarettes have never been my thing – I think I can be one of about 1% of people in the developed world who can honestly claim never to have had a puff of anything at all – but they were unquestionably ubiquitous; smoking was frankly the norm in this bar. Smoking was legal in pubs in the UK until 2007 and I had now become resigned to the fact that smoking simply does not happen in pubs any more, anywhere in the world. But the liberal stripe in Denmark's national culture that thinks nothing of its low marriage rate or its men gifting their sperm for £30 as though a blood donation has it that small bar owners should not suffer bankruptcy as a result of the inevitable downturn in trade following the national decision to outlaw smoking in bars, so it came to pass that bars smaller than than $40m^2$ were not required to comply and it was a bar of this size that I obviously found myself in now, prompting synesthesia for my student days.

But these were not student days, any more - we in our group were all in our 30s now, had happy family lives, and were getting too old for this sort of thing. But for a couple of hours on that night, we all felt young again. Then Stanley disgraced himself, we called it a night and sought the *hygge* of our hotel.

**

The following day was full of yet more dreary business, but at the end of a day of PowerPoint and emails I piled into a taxi with colleagues and we sped to the airport where we spent an hour exchanging as many soon-to-be useless weird Danish coins for Tuborgs as possible before it was time to climb aboard the little piece of home that was a British Airways plane and nestle into my seat.

I exited out of a peaceful, nocturnal Heathrow into a dark and cold winter's night to find about fifty taxis all patiently lined up and waiting for passengers who were very plainly not there. I wondered how long the driver at the front of the rank had been waiting and how the driver joining the back of the queue must be feeling.

I wanted to go home to Reading – a long way in the wrong direction for any London taxi driver – which of them wanted to drive back from Reading at that time of night? I would surely be their last ride of the day. I approached the taxi at the front of the queue from behind with much less confidence than any customer willing to spend a significant pile of banknotes should. The sudden apparance of my face at the window clearly startled the driver. But I had a disarming gambit lined up: "Excuse me, can you take me to Reading? You do go south of the river at this time of night, don't you?" It had exactly the desired effect. The driver paused, mid-Mars bar, and smiled.

"Is Reading south of the river? Really? *South* of the river you say?"

"Yup, we're north of the Thames now. We'll cross it on the M4. I'll point it out to you if you like…"

"Jump in, you sound like a fun ride."

Well, I can report that the chat was great. My cabbie had a sharp mind, an open mindset and a pleasant demeanour – a Neanderthal opinionated cabbie he was not. I asked how long he'd been waiting at the rank (an hour), I asked where his home was, hoping he'd say Reading (it was east London). He told me that Heathrow was nearer London City Airport than Reading (a fact I checked before I went to bed that night and he was right). I asked how business was and the floodgates opened. Business was bad; it was almost impossible to make a living driving a taxi any more. He'd only been a taxi driver for the last five years; before that he'd run a company producing clothing for blue-collar workers, but since the admission of eastern European nations to the European Union in 2004 it had become cheaper for his customers to buy clothes manufactured there and import them en masse, tariff-free. He wound the company up and bought a taxi, impeccably timed to coincide with the game-changing and unforeseeable launch of Uber. I fancy modern life's disruption hasn't finished for him yet. I wondered whether with self-driving cars clearly the future and bicycles clearly the present if Copenhagen was anything to go by, the notion of driving yourself around in a petrol car would one day become as ancient an activity as donning a cloak and climbing into a carriage to tug at the reins of a horse.

I regretted not seeing any of Denmark outside Copenhagen – I wished I'd had the chance. Which of us can say that our capital sums our country up? There is plenty more to Denmark than I am letting on; I would have liked to explore Greenland or the Faroe Islands and probably would have done were I setting the agenda for this book, but these were never the options; I can only say it as I saw it, and I saw Demark as a country where city squares install rollercoasters, remote statues are erected to mermaids, church steeples have spiral staircases on the outside, coins have holes in them, and you can still smoke in little bars. As wonderfully peculiar s place as the world can offer, and so close to home.

7. The Vatican

"I love the language, that soft bastard Latin,
Which melts like kisses from a female mouth,
And sounds as if it should be writ on satin,
With syllables which breathe of the sweet South,
And gentle liquids gliding all so pat in,
That not a single accent seems uncouth,
Like our harsh northern whistling, grunting guttural,
Which we're obliged to hiss, and spit, and sputter all."

Lord Byron

A peculiar thing happens to you as a young adult that no-one tells you about as a child: Christmas changes. Christmas as a child is of course an intensely sparkling festival of chocolate and battery-powered toys and long may that tradition continue, but as you enter your twenties and acquire a job and from its salary enough possessions to attain a hygienic level of happiness, the concept of receiving gifts loses its value and the real joy of Christmas becomes not so much the gain of objects, but the gain of time. Time with the family and of course the knack of losing track of which day of the week it is from December 27 to 31. For me, the turning point was 2007 when I was approaching 30 and the idea was floated by my parents and my sister that since we were now all fully-qualified adults, there was a degree of madness to forking out hundreds of pounds every December on pasta makers and coffee pots for each other that weren't wanted and hadn't been asked for. So instead of giving each other superfluous atoms this Christmas, why didn't we instead sink the present budget into a week in Paris and just give each other a token present when we got there? We all agreed that this was an exceptional idea and so spent several glorious days strolling up the Champs Elysées, ascending the Eiffel Tower, dining on a pink steak and thin fries in a pavement conservatory restaurant, picking through the shops in the Marais district and generally treating ourselves to life-enriching experiences. It was a wonderful substitute for present-giving and I suggest you try it one year.

But the complication with it all was that Debs was carrying our first child and we knew that the fiscal stricture of life with small children would mean that there probably wasn't going to be a recurrence of this type of Christmas anytime soon. So subsequent Christmases then presented the problem of "What shall we do for presents if we're not going to buy each other pasta makers or go to Paris?" Every year, we have sought to give each other cost-neutral, high-value gifts and it's been a pleasing challenge to find something every year that adds value to a loved-one's life.

In the run up to Christmas 2014, Debs and I had an idea. With us now exiting the baby/toddler phase of life we requested of our parents a weekend of babysitting and a budget airline plane ticket each that would cost no more than something they might have bought us in Marks and Spencer. We asked that the destination would be dictated by the convenience of flight times and the affordability of the fare. We discovered on Christmas morning 2014 that we were going to Rome.

Five months later, we were at our gate at Gatwick, trying to make sense of the jumble of codes on our boarding passes – LGW, FCO, EZY5256, SB and so on. As we stood there (for there are never enough seats at departure gates), a fellow passenger spotted the 'SB' on my boarding pass and told us that this stood for 'Speedy Boarding' and that we were therefore entitled to board first, with the rich people. So we marched to the desk, and were waved through like VIPs to descend a ramp where we queued for a bus which after a short delay, we boarded. Then we sat there for a good ten minutes with our tall hand luggage between our feet, as another bus behind us filled up with the peasants who hadn't paid for Speedy Boarding. With no warning, the bus behind us suddenly pulled out and made for the plane, unloading its passengers onto the ramp and up the steps into their seats. I was glad we hadn't paid for the Speedy Boarding privilege.

But we had been gifted seats 1A and 1B and for this, we were grateful. It meant we had a front row view of the aeroplane door we'd just walked through being closed and locked by a 19 year old who I suspected hadn't always come top of her class in everything and I hoped she'd done it right; if she hadn't, I would clearly be the first to know. Once this was accomplished, I realised the downside of sitting in seat 1A – my legroom wasn't enhanced, as I thought it might be, it was reduced by the compartment at the bottom of the door containing the emergency chute. I had hoped to have a snooze on the flight, but this now being impossible, I reached for my guidebook and read up on God's own country[26] instead.

The Vatican possibly wins the award for the world's most quirky country; here are some facts about it to get you going:

The Vatican's national economy is unique in that it consists almost solely of funds raised by the sale of museum tickets, tourist souvenirs, postage stamps and various Catholic publications. All this totalled a tidy $450 million for 2008, the most recent year I could find figures for, which means that the Vatican could buy a pretty impressive football team, if it so desired.

It has a population of 842 (only 42 of whom are women) – about the same as an average secondary school. 74% of the country's citizens are employed as clergy.

The Vatican has its own international phone code. Rather sweetly, they've simply taken Italy's +39 and inserted the divine number in there, making it +379.

The Vatican's cash machines offer Latin as a language option.

18% of the Vatican's population are the Swiss Guard – a sort of ceremonial Renaissance-looking army in stripy navy and yellow uniforms and feathered hats with the nominal task of protecting the Pope. The Swiss Guard had their moment in the sun in 1981 when it was realised the hard way that they actually had a very real job to do and couldn't just stand there looking like toy soldiers all the time. As Pope John Paul II took a stroll amongst the crowds in the warm afternoon sunshine of St Peter's Square on 13 May, a man called Mehmet Ali Agca – whose life would be an excellent subject for a film – rose from writing his postcards, pulled a gun out of his pocket, and shot The Pope four times. Agca

---

[26] The Vatican, not Yorkshire, obviously.

threw his pistol away and prepared to run, but was grabbed by a nun (perhaps the most wonderful part of the story) and an adrenalin-fuelled circle of tourists. He was sentenced to life imprisonment. The Pope recovered and visited him in prison in the year 2000, where he promptly forgave him, and Agca was released and extradited to Turkey, where he was immediately imprisoned for the 1979 murder of a journalist and two bank raids before that. He was released on parole in 2006, but a Turkish court then announced that it had decided rather harshly – and a quarter of a century after the crime – that it didn't recognise time served in Italy, and so he would have to serve his Italian sentence again in Turkey from day 1. He was released in 2010 and is now at large in the world again and could pop up anywhere at any moment, as he did on 27 December 2014 when he publicly showed up at the Vatican, requesting to lay white roses on John Paul II's tomb and meet the new Pope, Francis. The request was denied, and the Swiss Guard now carry guns.

The Vatican also has its own radio station, which has an interesting story to tell in itself. It is broadcast by its own transmitters in Rome, one of which, the Santa Maria di Galeria transmitter (do you think Maria di Galeria *really* hoped that one day she would have a radio mast named after her?) emits electromagnetic signals that are far stronger than allowed by Italian law. In March 2001, local residents claimed that radiation from the transmitter had brought about increased rates of leukaemia and brought to general attention a study[27] from the Lazio regional Department of Epidemiology that claimed in a suspiciously contradictory way that whilst links between broadcast transmitters and leukaemia were generally accepted, and that "the risk of childhood leukemia was higher than

---

[27] http://tinyurl.com/yc3n85x8 if you want some further reading.

expected for the distance up to 6km from the radio station [...] and [that] there was a significant decline in risk with increasing distance both for male mortality and for childhood leukemia [...], no causal implication could be drawn." The residents' claims were not accepted by Vatican Radio, which in response quoted something called the 'Lateran Treaty' - agreements signed by the Italian President at the time which basically exempted the Vatican from any effects of Italian law. In a legal sense, Vatican Radio was putting its thumb to its nose and waggling its fingers at the leukaemia suffers living within the shadow of its transmitter that was churning out radiation significantly above reasonably acceptable health limits. The President who had signed the treaty was Mussolini. So that's nice.

Of course, the Vatican's most famous fact is that it is the world's smallest country – a walled enclave within Rome, very little more than a city square surrounded by architecturally impressive buildings, two-thirds of a mile long and half a mile wide. Some in the world are of the perspective that the Vatican doesn't count as a country because it's just one big church and it should have a separate government before it can be called a nation, but I have no truck with such antidisestablishmentarianism[28]. However, upon opening the inflight magazine, I read about a couple of places in the world that made me willing to call into question whether there were places in the world even smaller than the Vatican which could qualify as countries.

In 1967, an eccentric former army Major named Paddy Roy Bates decided to seize HM Fort Roughs, a disused anti-aircraft gun platform eight miles off the coast of Suffolk, from a group of pirate radio broadcasters; Bates had the

---

[28] I thank you.

intention of setting up his own station at the site. Bates was largely ignored in his quackish endeavour until 1975, when he noted that in 1967 an English court had ruled that Fort Roughs was in international waters, and so he took the unusual step of attempting to establish Sealand – as he called it – as a nation-state by writing a national constitution and designing a flag and coat of arms. No-one really takes it seriously as an official country, but it has its own coins and stamps, hosts a marathon (on a treadmill) and sells titles of Lord and Baron for anyone silly and willing enough to part with money for the honour. I'll just leave this here:

https://www.sealandgov.org.

But as bizarre a 'country' as Sealand is, it pales into insignificance beside a tract of land call Bir Tawil that borders Egypt and Sudan: Bir Tawil is the size of London, and Egypt and Sudan are practically at war about who *doesn't* own it. When the British arrived in Africa to draw up their conveniently right-angled boundaries across the ancient tribal lands, both Egyptian and Sudanese governments were understandably irked and in 1902 a new wiggly border was drawn going back and forth over the straight boundary, creating both Bir Tawil and an enormous, resource-rich expanse of land to the east called the Hala'Ib triangle which was significantly larger than Bir Tawil, inhabited, and had a coastline. Both Egypt and Sudan wanted it and so Egypt arrived at a point of believing the straight, east-west border to be legally binding, whilst Sudan preferred the wiggly border, meaning that both became insistent that they didn't own Bir Tawil. To this day, Bir Tawil is, despite being a totally empty stretch of desert, *Terra Nullius* – a Latin expression used in international law meaning "nobody's land". It's a non-country.

∗∗

Anyway, on to the Vatican! Before travelling, many people had advised Debs and I that if we wanted to properly 'do' Rome then we couldn't do better than buy a ticket for an open-topped bus tour. We thought this was an excellent idea and so on a warm Saturday morning in the late spring of 2015, presented ourselves at the bus stop next to Rome's central station, *Termini* (how refreshing it is to me, a Londoner, for the capital city to just have one big train station), ready for one of the ubiquitous buses to appear and whisk us away at the top of the front deck to drink in the sights of the world's most historically impressive city. Well, of course, nothing of the sort happened. Debs and I stood next to a kerbstone for the first 40 sightseeing minutes of the of the weekend while half of west Africa pleaded with us to buy selfie sticks, hats, bottled water and anything else they'd managed to lay their hands on. Every ten minutes an overloaded tour bus appeared and deadened its engine while the driver stepped out for a fag and a little lady in a light blue shirt and dark blue skirt held out her hands and pleaded with us in hot Italian not to attempt to board on account of trade union regulations concerning rest breaks or something. After a small eternity, another bus pulled up, from which enough people alighted to permit our access, but of course all the popular seats on the top deck were taken, meaning we had to settle for sharing a rear-facing seat at the back of the bottom deck with some teenage German tourists who had made the ill-advised decision at the start of the day to buy a cluster of marshmallows arranged into a posy resembling a wedding bouquet which admittedly looked pretty at 10am but clearly was destined to become landfill or a cause of diabetes before noon.

We were given complimentary headphones to plug into the armrest which we were told would provide a commentary. Between long sections of *The Godfather* score, a pleasantly disconnected tour-guide voice pointed out notable buildings that we could nearly see by swivelling our necks like owls and peering backwards through a window. For the next half-hour, the bus grinded in traffic along anonymous boulevards towards the Colosseum. The Colosseum is without any argument one of the most impressive structures in the world and we circled it, as through a giant traffic management system (which it effectively is) and resolved to come back the following day and step inside. Of more interest to us at that precise moment was that an endless stream of tourists was cascading down the steps from the top deck and out of the bus. Debs and I stood up, alerted by a sudden tug to our ears from the headphones, and jostled with our fellow tourists to be first up the steps. When we finally got there, our friend in the light blue shirt and dark blue skirt was in the process of fixing awnings in place over the seats to protect us from the sun. Complaints were registered in about seven different languages that protection from sunburn was all very well, but that buying tickets for an open-topped bus tour in a sunny city crammed full of world-famous sights and then discovering that the bus had an opaque ceiling wasn't quite what we had paid for. With a palms-up shrug, the awnings were put back in their places of rest and our frenemy disappeared down the stairwell, leaving behind an energising sense of international camaraderie as the tour got going.

The bus wove its way around Rome – the traffic was not nearly so terrifying as I had been led to believe – and I realised as the journey passed that much of Rome, indeed any city, has many more unknown streets and buildings than world-famous ones and it was these nowhere streets that the bus tour was showing us. I was able to follow the route with my finger on the map, such was the stop-start nature of large city traffic, and realised that whilst The Vatican was indeed on the other side of the city to where our hotel was located, the two points were only separated by two miles as the crow flies and could easily be walked in about half an hour. If there is one thing I can advise you about Rome it is this: you can walk it all. It is not like London, where if in Canary Wharf you asked a passer-by how to walk to Hyde Park you would be looked at like you were out of your mind – everything in Rome is available on foot, and with gorgeous sights along every street there is no reason to descend into a giant mechanised worm and burrow along underground, or pay a driver to seal you into a metal box where you can't hear or smell any of the sights. The Colosseum to the Vatican can be walked in 30 minutes. Why were we on this bus in the first place? We were to find out later.

**

After what felt like, and was, half a day shunting along Rome's clogged arteries, the approach to the Vatican was across the Ponte Vittorio Emanuele II, one of the more renowned bridges across one of the more disappointing capital city rivers, which opened out to Via della Conciliazione – a wide street that runs dead straight up to St Peter's Square and gives a classic view down the centre of the square to the Basilica behind it.

I admit, both Debs and I were disappointed not to be required to show our passports to get in (we'd brought them, of course), but we dismounted the bus and joined the scrum of pilgrims. The Via della Conciliazione offered us an impressive collection of tourist shops, and in search of miniature Vatican and Italy flags to add to the collection we wandered into one. But instead of finding flags, we were faced with walls of olive oil, wine, frilly packets of spaghetti, coffee table art books, imitation rosary beads, crucifixes and iconography until we saw the one thing that stopped us in our tracks: penis pasta.

Now, of all the countries from which souvenirs can be acquired, the Vatican is as rare as is available on account of its size. You can bring anything home that you'd bought in the Vatican and it will have value because it's one of the few things in your home, even in your town, that is *vaticana*. Of all the objects available for purchase in the world, penis pasta is about as rare as is readily available in any high street. Imagine if I set you loose for a day in Rio de Janiero or Tokyo or Paris and asked you to return by nightfall with a packet of penis pasta, my bet is that you'd struggle, but might manage with a lot of embarrassing gesticulation. But here the product was staring me in the face in the one square mile of the world where I would have thought that it was less likely to be available than anywhere else. It was very tempting to buy a packet just for the chutzpah of having done it but I then realised that I would neither be able to eat it nor give it away and I only had hand baggage for the flight home. But it reminded me that it was time for lunch.

Mediterranean city centres do lunch better than anywhere I've ever been. Wooden shutters are pushed open on stone buildings in ancient cobbled lanes, square tables are lined up a third of the way to the middle of the street and what was the pavement is filled with dining accessories that summon holiday memories just by looking at them – waxy red and white checked paper tablecloths the exact size and shape of the table, to which they are attached with specially-made clips, spring-loaded napkin dispensers, large square parasols promoting the region's beer in bright colours, sponsored ashtrays, a menu on an easel facing the street for passers-by, rectangular tubs of geraniums on the ground demarcating the edge of the restaurant, little saucers on each table containing five olives and two toothpicks, a wooden basket of warm, freshly-sliced bread, little foil pats of butter, a set of salt, pepper and a drizzling-bottle of olive oil containing a little woody bouquet inside, tall wine glasses, short wine glasses, water glasses, large rectangular placemats – all of which made for a very inviting scene as waiters rushed in and out. This was to be our only meal in the Vatican and it was Italian in all but name. I ordered a ham and artichoke pizza and a glass of Castello, savouring both for as long as possible because the perfection of the moment was worth extending. Holidaymakers and day-trippers were all around us, both at large and at leisure, dining modestly, basking in the sun and happy to be alive. Is this how all Romans lived, or were they just too busy to take the time for lunch like this?

It was after leaving the restaurant and approaching the Vatican museums that Debs and I realised why we'd paid for the bus tour: the bus ticket permitted us to jump the museum queue. If this was the eternal city, it was doubtless so named for the queues – they stretched halfway across the country, snaking round several street corners at the base of the ancient city walls. Debs and I pontificated[29] on how long they would have to queue for and whether any work of art was worth such a long queue to see with the naked eye.

I admit, my interest in classical art isn't great, but the Vatican museums do contain the Sistine Chapel and in anyone's book the ceiling of the Sistine Chapel is worth seeing. It took four years to paint, apparently, but that's nothing because my lounge ceiling has had a brown watermark on it for eight years and I'm still in the process of painting it (the process, of course, beginning with the realisation that it's a job that needs doing). But of course, it wasn't possible to just pop our head into the Sistine Chapel and have a quick peek, first there were several tonnes of statues to slalom around and thousands of portraits of ancient people sitting in front of a dark greeny/brown background to "admire" first. I apologise if marble statues and oily canvases are your thing and you've bought this book hoping for an honest critique of the Vatican Museum's contents; I am going to fall short in this respect. But what the museum lacked in any sort of qualitative sense to my untrained eyes at least, it made up for in quantity. There were more works of art than I have ever seen in one day before, with what was surely a large percentage of the world's marble statues. Some of the statues were people standing up, some had body parts missing, one was standing naked with a sword in one hand and a severed head in the other, most were just a head on a plinth, like The Head in *Art Attack*[30]. I took one photo of a shelfful of 12 of

---

[29] Pun fully intended.

these marble heads, and 10 of them were recognised by Facebook's algorithms as being faces requiring tagging, so that means that the art was clearly of a very high quality.

The afternoon passed. Debs and I feigned interest in each of the 137,000 rooms we were forced to pass through to get to the Sistine Chapel as hundreds of strangers swirled around us – it was worse than Ikea. Some of the rooms had their ceilings painted – one was a large domed affair with a sort of 'angels in the sky with gold trim' look to it which I craned my neck up at for a good couple of minutes and was impressed enough with to wonder why the Sistine Chapel was world-famous and this ceiling wasn't. The next room's ceiling was bare plaster decorated by a couple of cracks, which made me feel lots better about the plight of my lounge. We passed windows which gave views over Rome so magnificent that every tourist bar none stopped and admired as though it were the greatest painting in the place – which in fact it may have been.

At a point where we'd almost given up hope and run out of water, it was time for the Sistine Chapel.

The first thing that struck me about the Sistine Chapel ceiling was the amount of detail. The ceiling is 130 feet long and 40 feet wide and every bit of it is coated by an intricate Biblical scene. The ceiling was split into 33 separate panels (11 x 3) which I suspect was by no co-incidence the age of Christ at crucifixion. Each of these panels depicted an entire Biblical scene, so gazing up at the ceiling was like playing a giant game of *Guess Who?* There was Jonah, having his thigh gnawed by a fish oddly smaller than he was, round the corner was, we were told, Daniel (though the absence of a lion in that tableau made me have my doubts) and in

---

[30] https://tinyurl.com/y93vmk93

between them was Moses holding aloft a snake. Also up there was David slaying Goliath, but virtually every other scene was of a Biblical character so obscure that it was unreasonable to have a guess at who was depicted. I snuck a look at the guidebook and was surprised to find that there were characters called Zerubbabel, Abiud and Eliakim up there. If ever you're watching Pointless and the subject in question is Sistine Chapel Figures then there are three answers right there.

We stood in the chapel for about twenty minutes, realising as we craned our necks upwards to drink it all in that a sort of crowd convection current was at work: as time passed, benches at the sides of the chapel were vacated by tourists who had had their fill and their places taken by the standing tourists from the middle, many of whom massaged their necks as they sat down. I took my seat and much more comfortably raised my eyes to gaze at the flesh tones above but was increasingly noticing the attendants every few minutes loudly ordering silence and no taking of photos or videos. But their edicts were in vain as crowd churn rendered their instructions irrelevant almost as soon as the words were out. For what reason would you, upon having being given the responsibility of curating one of the greatest paintings in the world, create a rule so fatuous as to ban the crowds – who you have charged an admission fee to observe the painting with their own eyes – from taking any image (even when no flash was used) of the painting to take home? I can only think official souvenir sales were in mind, which gave me the idea of acting all Christlike, turning over gift-shop tables and proclaiming something about dens of thieves, but I didn't want to have it on my record that I'd been thrown out of a country, even if the country was only the Vatican.

**

Now, it was an interesting time to be visiting the Vatican, because the place was quite literally an unholy mess. You'll remember that in February 2013 Pope Benedict XVI shocked the world by becoming the first Pope in 600 years to resign. His official resignation statement explained that his waning physical and mental powers were the reason, but it's widely held that there was more to it than that. In January 2012, Italian television aired a programme throwing light on the internal workings of Vatican politics with the not-entirely affirming title *Gli Intoccabili* (The Untouchables). Benedict's butler, Paolo Gabriele, had leaked many confidential documents alleging corruption, abuse of power and a lack of financial transparency at the Vatican, exposing the highly politically-charged atmosphere around Benedict. In March 2012, Pope Benedict appointed a commission of cardinals to investigate the leaks, but the leaks were so numerous that a journalist named Gianluigi Nuzzi was able to publish a book in May 2012 entitled *His Holiness: The Secret Papers of Benedict XVI*. The 'Vatileaks' (as they are known) alleged financial corruption, power struggles inside the Church over attempts to comply with international money-laundering regulations, the blackmailing of homosexual clergy by individuals outside the Church, and bribes made to secure an audience with the Pope. Paolo Gabriele was arrested upon the publication of the book and put on trial for aggravated theft in October 2012. Gabriele claimed to have stolen the documents to fight "evil and corruption" and put the Vatican "back on track". This sounds laudably honest, but it wasn't much of a legal defence, and Gabriele was swiftly found to be guilty, and sentenced to 18 months in jail, unusually in the Vatican itself, rather than the customary arrangement of an Italian prison, due to concerns that he might leak further secrets. Gabriele was personally visited and pardoned by Benedict XVI on 22 December 2012, which clearly put the matter to bed and ensured no further consequences. I'm joking, of course. Benedict – a bookish theologian by trade, was cast into a world of overseeing a highly politically-charged office and was in that respect out of his depth. He'd lost control of the governmental aspect of the Vatican and wasn't in a position to manage the unfolding crisis at the centre of which he undoubtedly was.

It is to the Vatican's credit that it was able to elect and appoint a new leader within one month of Benedict's resignation (something the United States could take note of as they conduct their two-year long soap opera to vet all candidates before appointing the least suitable rich man in the country). And the new leader Pope Francis was the tonic that the Church and indeed the world needed from its Christian leaders; he was starkly different from all Popes in living memory. Setting out to create a "Church for the Poor", he shunned the Popemobile and limousines used to ferry Pontiffs around, preferring a 20-year-old Renault 4 with 200,000 miles on the clock that he drove himself. Then he replaced his outrageously extravagant gold throne with a simple white chair, got rid of the red carpet trimmed in gold on which it sat, threw out his red velvet and gold-embroidered cape in favour of just the plain white robes meant to be worn underneath it, traded in the famous hand-crafted red loafers for his everyday black lace-ups, and had his solid gold Papal ring melted and replaced with a silver-plated one.

A Washington Post poll in December 2013 showed Francis to have a near-impossible 92% approval rating from American Catholics, with 95% of all Catholics thinking the Church was moving in the right direction, up from 26% ten years previously. All of which backs up my father's theory about why only good or nasty people seem to be appointed to positions of such high authority: "It's basic physics, son; there are two things rise to the top – cream and scum."

We emerged from the Sistine Chapel into St Peter's Square where many thousands of foldable chairs were being set up for the following day's ceremony at which, we later discovered, two nineteenth-century nuns, Marie Alphonsine Ghattas and Mariam Barawdy, would be canonised. This was much less arcane than it sounded; it was a politically significant event. These two women were to become the first Palestinian saints in modern times, and therefore Palestinian President Mahmoud Abbas and 2,000 pilgrims had travelled to the Vatican specifically to attend the ceremony, which meant we were lucky to get a hotel room that weekend.

But we were unaware of that as we did what every tourist does and entered St Peter's Cathedral, which is as massive and ornate as you'd expect it to be, with Renaissance paintings covering every vertical surface. Standing at the entrance to the Cathedral I took the obligatory photo of the inside and noticed through the viewfinder that three blades of celestial light shone down through windows in the great dome behind the altar. Surely the Father, Son and Holy Spirit don't lay that on for all the tourists? The altar itself is a four-poster affair, covered by a sort of bronze gazebo which looked like it could be employed as an extractor fan should the altar ever be used for barbecuing, which I doubted it ever would be, but I would be sure to attend if it happened.

Then, stepping outside again, Debs and I wondered what to do next, as frankly we had to all intents and purposes exhausted the Vatican of its diversions and so resolved to spend the next 24 hours wandering the streets of Rome – a pastime so enjoyable that it would be remiss of me not to give you a flavour of the experience now.

**

Ancient history doesn't warm my blood, but I will say this, if you travel to Rome, a ticket to enter the Colosseum and adjacent Roman Forum is worth the effort of the visit alone. Imagine an immaculate city park with all the features you'd usually expect – rose beds, fountains centred in circular pools, rectangular lawns giving onto fine clifftop views of the city and so on, but now drop into this park crumbling away amongst the arid pines ancient Roman ruins, as though a stone-age spaceship had broken apart in the atmosphere and its debris had all fallen here. There were 1,400 years of temples and monuments there, as well as the majestic pile of columns and arches that made up the original Caesar's Palace[31], a jutting column of which I'm pleased to say I identified as a much-photographed monument without any knowledge of what I was looking at. I'm not sure I've spent a finer hour in a park anywhere in the world and I insist you go there if you visit Rome.

The Colosseum inexplicably wasn't something Debs or I had been that bothered about going inside until we discovered

---

[31] The real one, not the casino in Las Vegas.

we'd accidentally bought a ticket for the Roman Forum *and* Colosseum without meaning to and found ourselves queueing up at the gate. The building is so – to employ an overused adjective – iconic that it is easy to forget gazing upon the arcaded light and shadow that the whole thing is one giant execution chamber, dedicated to some of the most gruesome, painful and humiliating deaths the world has ever seen. Countless people were thrown to their end here for choosing to adhere to a peaceful, loving and forgiving way of life that was a threat to the brutal dictatorship of the time.

We exited the Roman Forum at the rear, far away from the Colosseum, climbing a set of steps that looked comfortably within our physical appetite but proved not to be so at about halfway up, twisting around to our right once we'd left and found ourselves in a narrow backstreet to make a pass to the right around Piazza Venezia, at one end of which was a wedding-cake of a building in brilliant white that brought to mind a Roman Empire equivalent of the White House in Washington DC except that this one had Italian flags out front, winged horses on the top and a glorious blue-sky backdrop. It is called the *Altare della Patria* and it looked pretty impressive to me, though it is widely hated by Italians for being monumentally ugly. Referred to by locals as "the Giant Typewriter" or, I am pleased to have discovered since writing the above lines, "the Wedding Cake", it's a monument in honour of Victor Emmanuel - the first king of a unified Italy – and contains Italy's Tomb of the Unknown Soldier and eternal flame. Much of Rome's historic medieval quarter was bulldozed to make way for it in 1885, hugely controversially at the time if only because all that gorgeous brown/gold stone abutting the Roman Forum was turned to powder and replaced with glaringly white imported marble. Critic Peter Davey, writing in the *Architectural Review* in 1996 described how the building was "chopped with terrible brutality into the immensely complicated fabric of the [Capitoline] hill". The thing is unarguably boxy, sticks out like a naked Milkybar on a plate of spaghetti and doesn't even have a dome or a tower to grace its flat roof. I daresay if I were a resident of the Capitoline Hill in the 1880s I'd've objected to it, but as a tourist, I wasn't disappointed that it was there. It was certainly as memorable a sight as any other building in Rome.

Now, you'll have noticed that I have a little history of bad luck when it comes to tourist attractions in foreign cities. Earlier in the book you'll recall I had a sauna to remember in Helsinki, but the back story to it is that on two previous visits to Helsinki, I tried to have a sauna but was thwarted – the first time by my hotel receptionist telling me that using the sauna would cost an unimaginable sum of cash for a half-hour session, the second time – a different hotel – I was told that the sauna was being renovated and as such was out of order. Shortly after that in Seattle, you'll remember that both the Columbia Centre and Smith Tower were closed when I tried to climb them, then in Copenhagen the Tivoli amusement park had chains on its gates and the Kongens Nytorv – apparently an exceptionally pretty city square – was shrouded in builders' hoardings, out of tourist view.

So I have found out the hard way that that boarding an aeroplane and fizzing through the sky in a rocket-powered jetcraft to view tourist attractions in a foreign city is not the same thing as those tourist attractions actually being open and accessible once you get there. And now I was able to add the Trevi fountain to my list of disappointments. It had been drained for maintenance, which is perfectly allowable, though less forgivable when I found out upon posting a photo on Facebook that a friend had visited Rome the previous year and found it in exactly the same state, with remarkably little progress from that state in evidence now. The builders had considerately laid a metal gangplank across the basin across which we were welcome to clomp in order to gain a better view of the scaffolding obstructing the elegant stone façade but there didn't seem much point. So I didn't throw a coin in, which I think means I am now not allowed to return to Rome.

We wandered the short distance through cobbled lanes – much of central Rome is cobbled lanes – to the Pantheon. You may have expected better from a travel writer, but I'll admit I was mildly startled to find the Pantheon in Rome at all, because in my head at least, the Pantheon was a famous set of ancient crumbling columns in Athens. Then another part of my head alerted me to the fact that that's the Parthenon and I wasn't such a fool to have confused the two, especially since we all know that all of humanity's eyes glaze over in any pub quiz when the question begins "Which Roman/Greek god…" (Apollo's usually a good guess). You can tell it's very ancient just walking up to it. The stone is darker than its surrounding buildings, seemingly dirtier, more worn – and with good reason because the building dates from about 25 BC which must make it one of not very many BC buildings still standing in the world. We approached from the rear of the building, and so could easily see the famous dome – the world's largest circular dome for 2,000 years, until surpassed in 1881 by, of all things, the University of Derby[32]. Large chunks of the soffit had tumbled away over the years, making the dart

---

[32]   https://tinyurl.com/y7fmumwy

underneath it unnecessarily exciting. We walked into the square in front and after absorbing the architecture for a few minutes decided the best thing we could do was sit down and drink something cold and bubbly like the locals were doing. When in Rome…

The Pantheon is right to be thought of as a Greek building: the name comes from two Greek words: "pan" (everything) and "theon" (divine). Originally constructed as a temple dedicated to all Roman gods, it was commissioned by a Roman statesman and architect called Marcus Agrippa who must have been a heck of a motivator, because the façade's granite columns (each weighing 60 tons and 12 metres high) were quarried in Egypt, dragged 60 miles throughout winter against the clock to the Nile where they were loaded onto some very hefty barges just in time for spring floods to recede and tug the precious cargo down to the delta where they were somehow transferred onto seafaring vessels to traverse 1,000 miles of open sea to the Tiber estuary, where they were loaded onto more boats on which colossal energy was employed to make everything go upstream for 20 miles to Rome, at which point the stones were still half a mile away from the building site. This was all a Stonehenge-like act of worship to gods who, at the time, didn't have any theological argument in favour of their existence other than a hunch that there must be something out there.

I know all this because the above was printed on the back of the café's menu and I took a photo of it, even though I didn't know I'd be writing this book one day as I did so.

One final tip on Rome before I go. If you venture at any point onto Rome's Metro (a colossal undertaking in that pretty much every metre of it rumbles close to some ancient buried artefact too precious to be destroyed) then there is one station at which you would be well advised to alight: *Spagna*. Spagna has two exits, one at the Spanish Steps (about which too much has been written for me to need to record anything here) and Villa Borghese. Villa Borghese is Rome's principal urban park and is marked in the guidebooks as the one to visit. Usually parks are many acres of flat lawns, carved up by asphalt footpaths that lead nowhere in particular until you find yourself at the other side of the park and needing to walk back again but this time with depleted energy. I find parks in a sense to have a sort of 'nowhere' quality. Don't get me wrong, I wouldn't want to turn them over to developers to build apartment blocks, it's just that I don't quite see what parks are for. Well, flat, empty parks, at least.

But it was in Villa Borghese that I realised how my problem with parks could be remedied. I'd simply got the pace wrong. There was a hut and shelter in the centre of Villa Borghese that housed bikes for hire and Debs and I took a couple and set off to see the place. This was much better than walking; for walking in a park is something of a trudge; the landscape barely changing minute to minute and the whole thing taking too long to see. But two hours of bike hire proved to be ample to take us to see the well-spaced attractions within it - the Zoo (we stared at the terrapins in the pool by the entrance – why do you only ever see terrapins at the entrance to zoos?), the boating lake, the Galleria Nazionale d'Arte Moderna, the monument to Ahmed Shawqui (an Arabic poet, but I didn't know it), the Galleria Borghese, the Villa Medici, a terrace with a heart-stopping view across Rome, a water-powered clock given the luxurious name of hydrochronometer (useful for Scrabble). There was also an exact replica of Shakespeare's Globe Theatre which was surely too big to miss but we did indeed contrive to miss it. Such is life. I hope that if you go to Rome, you manage to find it.

So the Vatican was complete. It is absurd to call it a country; it is smaller than your nearest ASDA car park, but it is without debate a country and whilst not trying to visit the world's smaller destinations but realising I was doing so, I was glad it had ventured onto my path. But if you are thinking of heading there, take the weekend for it at least; memories of Rome aren't built in a day.

8. Monaco

"Behind every great fortune lies a great crime."

Honoré de Balzac

I spent my 21st birthday in Monte Carlo.

A year living next to a steel factory on the France/Luxembourg border was about as much as I could take, so Debs announced that as a form of therapy, her plans to visit an old schoolfriend in Nice where she'd grown up would include me. As soon as it was mentioned that the third day of our visit would be a special occasion, it was immediately decided that we would all go to Monte Carlo. Once there, we stood in front of the casino for a handful of minutes, then got a bit bored and took a decision to take a bus up the hill to Monaco's clifftop exotic gardens in which we strolled around for a bit, had a bite to eat and then returned to France. On paper, it sounds a lovely day, but I remember riding the train home and feeling that I hadn't really seen Monte Carlo. I had some unfinished business.

16 years later, in possession of a pair of wedding rings and pair of children, Debs and I decided to visit Nice again. We couldn't think of a better reason other than that it would be

guaranteed to be hot and that a city by the sea would be bound to have lots of things to entertain the little smashers with. In the hills above Cannes (glitzily-named Super-Cannes), we'd also been told that a church was hosting a well-reviewed art display telling the story of the spread of Christianity (we went – I'd like to say how good it was, but sadly the Super-Cannes evangelistic expo was atrocious[33]). But I was determined to return to Monaco and see it properly. Also, I admit, the flights were cheap. I shan't trouble you with all the numbers here, but having the previous year spent £X on a family Easyjet flight to Malaga from Gatwick, the British Airways website informed us that flying to Nice from Heathrow on their airline would be a third of X. This seemed suspiciously low, so we booked it immediately.

I think we can agree that air travel has now been fully democratised. The May 27, 1955 issue of *Collier's* magazine that I am looking at now advertises a plane ticket from New York to London at $290 – or $2,450 in today's money. Assuming the return trip cost roughly the same amount and there were a few add-ons, then I think we can safely say that the full price was over $5,000, or over $10,000 if there were two of you.

Right now, the New York to London price I have just had quoted on the internet is £208 – a 92% price reduction. And the journey is now six hours, a 50% saving on the 13 hours in took for propellers to grind through the sky in 1955. Nowadays, I can choose, if I wish, to spend a £50 note on some new denim, or a day in Nimes. I can fly from London to Manchester to watch Manchester United play for less than the cost of the match ticket. You take my point –

---

[33] It's rare you get the opportunity to pun on Supercalifragilisticexpealidocious.

flying, perhaps the closest thing to a miracle that man has ever achieved, has become remarkably normal.

Yet no-one seems to have told this to the operators of today's airports. Still, to my great disdain, whilst the tickets are so cheap, airport shops still labour under the misapprehension of flying as a luxurious lifestyle that only the very richest can afford. With an hour to kill at Terminal 5, I was open to the idea of treating myself to a little something for my holiday – a thin polo shirt perhaps, or a brown leather wristband. But I was confronted instead by a long line of high-end white box shops retailing perfume that was manufactured for a penny and sold for £100, shoes for women with more credit cards than feet, jewellery that cost more than I earned in a month, innumerable handbags (targeted, remember, at passers-by who were already laden down with bags as it was) – and that was just the shops for the women. The only shops targeted at men sold high-end suits or electrical gadgets. It seemed that every shop was trying to market itself to this imagined traveller of 1955 – every product had the whiff of one of those overused retailing adjectives 'luxury' or 'deluxe'. One bookshop even had a section entitled 'Luxury Books'. I fail to understand how printed information can in any way be luxurious.

You can't fly to Monaco, you have to fly to Nice, and I'm pleased to report that it's only a 90 minute hop. But in reality it is a world away. Pilots fight to fly the route to Nice for the simple reason that the approach to Nice Airport is officially the most scenic airport in Europe to land at, and with good reason. Nice Airport is built on a headland at the end of the city's famous seafront, the Promenade des Anglais. The runways are parallel to the beach and according to wind direction, the ire of local residents or whatever it is they use to decide which way planes proceed along a runway, the fact is that you either approach Nice Airport with Monaco and Nice on your right or with Cannes and St Tropez on your left. Either way, you also have the mountains of the lower Alps on one side and a perfect sea on the other – it really couldn't be prettier, and you're close to it all too – just before you touch down, you can see people sunbathing on the beach you will be lying on in a few minutes. It looks like a little piece of Malibu with its tended verges and pineapple-like palm trees busting up from the ground.

But it was raining in Nice when I arrived. I genuinely hadn't expected this – over the years, I've spent a cumulative month of my life in Nice and had never seen a drop, yet here I was in July at the start of my summer holiday sitting on the tarmac and watching raindrops race each other down the window pane. I sensed it was 'dry rain', as my late grandmother so memorably used to describe it, and a scan of the vegetation confirmed everything was as water-starved as I had hoped. Maybe, as we used to say as children, it was God crying; Nice had been the scene of a terrorist attack just two weeks previously where a coward with an aversion to people smiling hired a lorry and drove through a seafront crowd as they watched fireworks pop over the bay to celebrate the values of liberty, equality and fraternity. 85 people were killed; many, families with children.

This was in the back of my mind throughout the week I was there. The following day, I was reading on the balcony in the late morning and, looking over the top of my book to drink in the view across the port and seafront, I suddenly saw a ball of smoke about the size of a car rise from the city centre. Then I heard a boom. Birds flapped into the air.

"Dad, was that a bomb?" enquired my eight year old son from the next room, jolted into consciousness from the television. I didn't quite know what to say, so I made speaking shapes with my mouth until some words came out.

"I don't know." It was the best I could do. "I'll check on the internet. Probably not…" I hoped he would believe me.

For much of the next hour, I raked Google, Bing, Yahoo and just about every other internet search facility I could summon but found no mention of a bomb going off in Nice. Which was unnerving because I had plainly just seen a bomb go off in Nice, two weeks after a terrorist attack. Why else would there be a boom and a large, rising ball of smoke in the heart of the city mid-morning on a weekday? I never found out the answer. Whatever it was, it clearly wasn't newsworthy and I may just be the first person to write about it now.[34]

To get from Nice to Monaco, you have four options:

1) Car. This is absolutely not an option. For hiring a car and driving it through a French city and onto a winding Mediterranean coast road with children in the back is literally the single most stressful thing it is possible to do. France is legendary for its drivers' casual attitude to road safety. Debs and I have first-hand experience of this, as passengers in a car being thrown over blind brows and comfortably over the speed limit by a French friend until, as he was admiring a house on a bend in the road, he drifted across the centre line to where a small Citroen was in

---

[34] It's now two years later, I'm editing the book just before publication and have just found out it wasn't a bomb. They do this every day, apparently: https://tinyurl.com/y9tysqvv

a filter lane was waiting to turn across oncoming traffic, and we were very much the oncoming traffic. "*Attention!*" I shouted, in French, as the Citroen rapidly filled the windscreen, but it was too late – the driver and I headbutted our airbags, our wives in the back headbutted the front seats, both cars were written off, and we still have flashbacks about it even now when we fall asleep, nearly a decade later.

Later in the holiday, we did indeed hire a car for a few days and I was reminded again why hiring a car in France is a Bad Thing. In a gloomy concrete shed behind a rental office, I edged a ton of unfamiliar metal out onto the street, indicated to turn right (promptly activating the windscreen wipers as I did so) and before having reached the end of the road was forced into several emergency stops, firstly by a swirling cliché of Japanese tourists, then a shoal of Segway riders, then by an old lady walking her poodle down the middle of the street, and finally a beachbound family stepping into the road with fully inflated lilos held at head height, rendering my approach invisible to them. Driving in France is no fun.

2) Helicopter. I'd been tipped off that if ever I was travelling to Monaco for business (ha!) then it was actually cheaper to take a helicopter than a taxi. I can see a certain panache in touching down on a helipad in Monte Carlo, but somehow it just wasn't our style and unlike a taxi, you pay for the seat, not the vehicle, and there were four of us.

3) Train. I'd been advised that trains from Nice were everything you want about travel: Fast, cheap,

reliable, comfortable and a pleasing sense of exoticism too. Subsequent journeys through Nice station have revealed this to be true. But weighing against the train journey was the immutable fact that the train ride from Nice to Monaco was largely through tunnels and we wanted the view from the coast road. And so we decided on option 4.

4) Bus. This was the way to travel. Cheap as chips, sea views, and someone else doing the driving. What was not to like? It was the only logical choice.

I can report that climbing aboard the 100 bus from Nice's port, you begin without doubt the most glorious bus route the world has to offer. If ever you do this journey, sit on the right of the bus and take your camera. We crept out of the old town and around Nice's handsome port and a premium restaurant called Le Plongeoir that had its tables laid out on a high diving board platform that sits on top of the cliff-face (apparently the food goes down very well). After that we climbed the corniche to labour up Mount Boron in the way that a roller coaster climbs its first lift-hill, and rounded the headland to summon the most incredible view that it was possible to see through a bus window. We were no longer progressing along suburban roads at street level, but hanging high on a shelf halfway up a mountain with spangles jumping around on a hazy blue sea a thousand feet below. The sea was dotted with boats whose pristine whiteness improved the scene even further. Half a mile across the bay was St-Jean-Cap-Ferrat, rising from the water much like Uluru from its desert. The bus window framed the scene as though a priceless painting. The boats became even more impressive the nearer to Monaco we came. At one point, they became ships, big enough to land a helicopter on – and every single one had a wooden deck at the stern just above the waterline, for those that wanted to dive headfirst into a deep sea containing octopi, swordfish, squid and all sorts of other unpleasant menu items that you don't get in your local municipal pool. There was a full-sized cruise ship anchored a safe distance out and a millionaire's yacht that had a waterslide built into its port side. It was hard not to be impressed.

**

I wasn't sure when we entered Monaco. I don't know what I was expecting by way of a border; somehow a full pat-down with sniffer dogs was beyond what my mind's eye had played out for me, but perhaps I was looking for a structure much like a motorway toll booth, with police officers in sky blue short sleeves, circular caps and little white gloves, who would flag the bus down and inspect the driver's papers before waving us through, generating a frisson of excitement amongst the attentive tourists. At the very least I expected a street-sign saying simply MONACO on it, but there wasn't even that. I'm still not sure of the point where I entered Monaco, but I saw a raised red and white striped barrier at about the right point in the journey, so maybe that was it?

The first moment I knew for sure I was in Monaco was when I saw the football stadium. There really isn't that much to write about an empty stadium, but it is home to the Monaco football team, who once made for an interesting quirk in sporting law. For this is not a national football team but a club side, AS Monaco, who play in the French league, much as Cardiff City do/did in the Premier League in England. Everyone unthinkingly accepted it as fact that AS Monaco is a French football club apart from one man, a Scot named Fergus McCann.

McCann owned 51% of Glasgow's Celtic football club and in 1996 he sold one of his players, John Collins, to *Les Monégasques*. Collins was an exceptionally talented footballer – he was Celtic's first one million pound player when they bought him and would go on to score against Brazil at the World Cup a couple of years later (and not a lot of footballers can say they've done that). But his transfer to AS Monaco came twelve months after the most disruptive incident in commercial football history.

Collins was out of contract with Celtic and under the European Union's famous 'Bosman' ruling which ordained that when a footballer's contract with their employer ended, they were, like every other worker on the planet, a free agent who the releasing football club couldn't charge a fee for if another club wanted to buy him. So Monaco wouldn't have to pay Celtic a penny. But McCann argued that Monaco was a country that wasn't *in* the European Union and thus AS Monaco was out of its jurisdiction. "Monaco is a rightly proud country that has exercised its right not to be part of the EU, hence the laws of the EU do not apply," thundered McCann to Scottish newspaper *The Herald*. "We were admitted to the French league in 1926 and we regard ourselves as French," replied AS Monaco's president Jean-Louis Combora as he lit another Gauloise and reclined to absorb the view over the Mediterranean from his Director's box. Celtic lost the ruling and Monaco got richer by successfully exploiting a loophole, not for the first time.

**

I alighted the bus in Monte Carlo and led the family to the casino to see if I could take in more Monte Carlo than I did on my 21st birthday. The gardens in front of the Casino de Monte Carlo were as perfect as could be hoped – lush, tropical even, yet still respectful of their Mediterranean location. I'm told that towards the end of the twentieth century, speakers were hidden in the leafy canopy, playing birdsong on a loop. I looked but couldn't see any evidence and was just beginning to appreciate the neatly manicured nature when a large white golf-ball-like building started to loom in front of me. I was interested at first – it resembled several of these linked geodesic roofs like you see on the Eden Project in Cornwall or the Epcot Centre in Florida. Intrigued, I wandered closer – the buildings were a stylish work of art in their immaculate garden settings. It was at this point that Little Miss Procter, who hadn't long detached herself from her 'I am 4' badge, decided that she needed a wee.

If there is a more inconvenient place for a pre-schooler to start urgently hopping around cross-legged than the approach to the Casino de Monte Carlo, then I can't think of it. We made for the geodesic buildings to discover they were labelled 'Les Pavillions de Monte Carlo'. I had in mind a semi-public space with tourist information, perhaps a water fountain or a Starbucks, and surely the necessary facilities for a comfort break. I couldn't have been more wrong. There was an outdoor walkway between buildings which contained, predictably, shops. Not just shops, of course, but pointless shops that don't serve any real purpose other than to give mega-rich people somewhere to convert some of their grubby money into less liquid assets. I saw brands I'd heard of – Alexander McQueen, Yves Saint Laurent, Chanel – but mainly brands I didn't know existed, let alone were the pinnacle of their respective product categories – Chopard, Stardust, Lanvin. None of them looked as if they wanted to risk letting a waist-high child enter and urinate on their floor. I could understand this, but it didn't help our predicament. We rushed past more anonymous brands – Czarina, Balenciaga, Zendrini, towards the casino.

I don't know what it was that made me think the casino would be likely to let a 4 year old in, but I figured they'd be more accommodating than a small shop which sold only high-heeled velvet boots. I didn't have the guts to stride up the steps and explain our predicament to the uniformed doorman, but happily saw a man in a red polo shirt with 'Can I help you?' written on it. He tried to offer me a map, but I cut him off with a brisk "Monsieur, savez-vous où ma petite fille peut faire pipi?" He gestured towards a rectangular hole in the ground in front of the casino that contained the highest point of an escalator and we plunged into the coolness of what must surely be the most expensively-appointed multi-storey car park ever built. This was Monaco, not France, of course, but some of the French traditions lived on, the most notable one at this point being that there was a sign on a locked door declaring the toilets closed. A cleaning cart was in the doorway, but the cleaner had evidently disappeared for a cigarette break. The situation was getting very urgent and we resurfaced, asking again the Can I Help You Man what we could do now. He informed us there was a McDonald's not two minutes away down the hill through a park in the general direction of the sea. And so through the park we jogged, trying as much as possible to travel in a straight line irrespective of the neat and wandering paths to minimise journey time. I spotted an eighteen-inch gap between a railing and a wall and we went for it, emerging onto a busy road that needed to be crossed. Then I suddenly realised where I was. This was the famous Grand Hotel Hairpin – the 180 degree bend of the Monaco Grand Prix known the world over. I paused to look and was amused to see that the bend of this famous Formula 1 turn had a bus stop on it. We were quickly reminded of my parental duties again and continued down the hill under an almond-coloured underpass that also rang bells from the Grand Prix to a great white ship-like building at the entrance to the Grand Prix track's famous tunnel that contained the necessary relief.

Job done, we retraced our steps back to the casino to take it in. It is a magnificent building, without a doubt. An intricate façade with an ornate pair of turrets and nine windows across, framed perfectly by a perfectly turfed and fountained roundabout whose centrepiece was a convex mirror that allowed plebs like me to look out from the casino's doors and see the casino in my view, an idea I appreciate very much. Then there were the cars. Parked all around were innumerable cars of the sort that would get Jeremy Clarkson torturing metaphors in his pieces to camera. I'd like to identify each of these cars to you now, but nature made me a man more interested in the vehicle's destination than the vehicle itself and so I will simply report that there were many cars, all of which were significantly less tall than I was and came in multiple bright colours.

There isn't much to do in Monte Carlo if gambling or shopping with rich people isn't your thing and so we stood on the clifftop behind the casino for a minute and surveyed the port.

Monaco's port was not much different from Nice's port – a similar size, a similar collection of floating baubles. I don't profess to understand why it is vehicles of all things that rich people feel the need to possess to convey their immense wealth, but looking out over the gently rocking masts and bobbing hulls, I was reminded of how this wealth is so often created.

On the plane from Heathrow, the front page news story of the day was about a Monaco resident: Philip Green, in charge of British high-street bastion British Home Stores, which had just collapsed, making some 11,000 people jobless. Sir Philip, having made a success of an agglomeration of high street fashion bands – Topshop, Dorothy Perkins, Burton - bought BHS for £200 million in the year 2000, but sold it just fifteen years later for the arrestingly modest price of £1. Not only that, but he sold the pension schemes of these 11,000 people – and a further 9,000 pensioners - to a faceless business venture called Retail Acquisitions Limited, really just an assembled cluster of lawyers and accountants who hoped to attract further investment while keeping the lights on in the company's 160 stores, just 77 of which were able to pay the rent. Retail Acquisitions Limited failed to do this, and that was pretty much that, with the pension deficit standing at a cool £571 million, or £28,550 per employee if you paid enough attention in maths lessons as a child. The British government were open with their fury. Frank Field MP, Chair of the Work and Pensions Select Committee, called for the Serious Fraud Office to investigate after a parliamentary report accused Sir Philip of plundering the business.

Well, Sir Philip's £100 million, two-week old, 90-metre superyacht *Lionheart* was moored a couple of hundred metres under our noses in Monaco's harbour, significant sums of money having been spent tweaking the fixtures and fittings throughout its 12 reception rooms, beauty salon, gym and bar. A gold statue of Buddha had been handmade in Jaipur and flown in, a helicopter landing-pad was added, as were armchairs at £16,000 each that were decorated with cushions at £3,000 a throw. Ahead of its inhabitation, a staff of 40 were conveyed to the yacht in a fleet of silver Mercedes. The ceilings are panelled in (I wish this was fiction) mink. And once fitted out, there are of course guests to entertain: for his fiftieth birthday, Sir Philip flew 200 guests to Cyprus for a three-day party that included hiring Michael Aspel to deliver a live on-board This Is Your Life. His 60th was an even bigger affair: you're getting the picture by now, but the headlines are that it was in Mexico and Stevie Wonder and Rihanna were there to sing to him in person. Leonardo di Caprio was also present (which was a bit risky considering his character's fate in *Titanic*). His riches were as conspicuous as the CLOSING DOWN SALE signs filling BHS's windows up and down the land. And all this obscene wealth was created for him by shopfloor workers – struggling parents, students and people too old to be working spending long hours on low wages standing on aching feet in evenings and at weekends ringing tills which were never taking quite enough money under Sir Philip's stewardship to keep the company afloat, but were systemically siphoning money into Sir Philip's pocket before their pension scheme was a concern for him. MPs found that Sir Philip and his wife Tina extracted 'incredible wealth' from BHS, at least £300 million, much of it held in Lady Green's name. In 2015, she earned £8.5 million purely from interest on a £200 million loan she made to help purchase BHS which will run until 2019 – by which time the cumulative interest will pay for two more Lionhearts. At the time of writing, it was suggested that Sir Philip contribute significantly to the £571 million hole in BHS's employees' pensions. Whilst Sir Philip failed to respond with any convincing reply, the stunt comedian, Simon Brodkin – known for showering FIFA President Sepp Blatter with dollar bills – moored a motorboat alongside Lionheart from which he erected a banner over the ship's name, rechristening it the 'BHS Destroyer'. Apt.

**

Anyway, where were we? I think I was helping a child urinate in Monte Carlo, that's right. Such is life in the company of small children that having returned from McDonald's it was now approaching lunchtime and it was time to think about where to go for that. It had been noticed that McDonald's were offering toys from a popular film that had just invaded the minds of the world's young children and in the powerfully insistent way that little girls decide what they want to do next, we descended the Grand Hotel Hairpin again to find ourselves back in McDonald's for the second time that day. McDonald's was its usual long queue for identikit foodstuffs, though I should note that this McDonald's had a glorious sea view through rounded porthole like windows and with the food came a little scratchcard game that I think McDonald's's[35] head office must have decided would be good for their Monte Carlo restaurant.

There were three scratch panels and I was invited to firstly rub panel 1. I did so and was informed that I had won a free

---

[35] If you know for certain how to correctly apostrophise that, please write to me: @MrProcter

soft drink. I was pleased with this and as I weighed up the benefits of sugar water I didn't need against the time and effort of having to queue for it, I read that I was could now either stick at the prize indicated in panel 1, or twist and scratch panel 2 for what would either be a better prize or an announcement that I had gone bust. It was hardly Monte Carlo, but at the same time it couldn't have been more Monte Carlo. I risked my cola and scratched again. I was now told that I had won some music. This seemed like a curiously intangible prize, but, thinking that music was better for me than cola, I thought I'd go for it, until I read the small print, that is. To get the music I had to download an app, then once I'd got the app I had to create a login and password that was linked to my email account, then once I'd done that, I'd have access to one track by a band I hadn't heard of. This prize had now assumed the shape of something I was willing to gamble away, so I scratched panel 3. I had got lucky, I hadn't gone bust, but was now the proud owner of a portion of French Fries (or Monegasque Fries, as they would surely be called here). I'd just finished my current portion and another load was about as appealing as a second pint of Coke, and the queue at the till had got longer. Satisfied with my victory, I declared myself out and stared out across the sea thinking "I gambled and won in Monte Carlo."

What better thing is there to do after lunch than go for a stroll along the waterfront? Monaco's was particularly alluring as the view inland from the water's edge was more interesting than most places I've been. Monaco's jumble of cream-coloured tower-blocks rising up the mountainside to an impossibly close peak. It can be adequately recreated in your own home by covering your staircase with cereal boxes. I made blinkers with my hands to frame a seemingly vertical wall of these buildings, cramped next to each other, jostling for position. What are the millionaires doing in there? They can't all be channel surfing with cups of tea and wiping worktops when they've got their boat moored up at the bottom of the hill, so they must be empty much of the time. It must be a perplexing country to run when most of your residents don't live there.

I enquired at a booth selling souvenir knick-knacks if they had any Monaco flags to add to my collection and was told that they did but that they were ambitiously priced at €5 each. These flags, let me tell you, were the size of a postcard, and contained only two colours, I couldn't bear to be fleeced so badly. I considered offering a card worth a free portion of McDonald's fries but in the end I just sulked away, bitching bitterly to myself about the whole exploitative culture of super-wealth creation. I needed calming down, and as if by design, Princess Grace Kelly had envisioned a Japanese Garden on the plot of land across the road and twelve years after her death, her late husband, Prince Rainier, opened it in her honour and we strolled into it now, seeking some of the Zen-like calm it was alleged to offer. It was a perfect little spot, as Japanese-Garden-like as you can hope to find anywhere in the world. Tranquillity amongst the bustle, it was a grand stretch of countryside mapped out on a miniature scale – we felt like giants, picking our way between rocks and stepping over shrubs and bonsais. There was everything I hoped to see there – waterfalls, stepping stones, miniature beaches, lotus flowers, a little red wooden bridge underneath which koi carp glided, an unwalled oriental pavilion on stilts jutting out over the lake. I read some of the information boards and blurb on my smartphone about what I was seeing but couldn't help laughing at the absurdly far-fetched nature of the garden's symbolism: "Here, the Stone Fountain (Fusen-Ishi) symbolises a spring flowing towards the lake, ensuring long prosperity for the Principality of Monaco." The word 'ensuring' in that sentence seems to be overdelivering, doesn't it? Also, I didn't really follow how water running into a lake symbolised piles of banknotes, but millionaires with time on their hands and a creative streak have to design something, I guess. I walked as far as the eastern end of the garden (I wanted to experience the full oriental effect) where I entered the western world again in the form of an exposition hall and a large poster showing the way to somewhere named, somewhat paradoxically for a nation of 50,000 people per square mile, the Monte Carlo Country Club.

Inner peace restored, we headed inland, looking for something that might be identified as the centre. The casino and the port and the GP racetrack were all well and good, but I wanted a square with perhaps a fountain or a statue in the middle, or colonnade around the edge, perhaps a giant flag fluttering high at the top of a pole the height of a tall tree, but we couldn't seem to find anywhere like that. Monaco was just streets of grinding traffic and pharmacies and cushy, pointless embassies of distant countries and many hundreds of apartment blocks for rich people. At one point I saw a shop called "Fine Art Gallery of Russian Masters". A niche market, to be sure – but there were plenty of roubles in Monaco – I remember reading somewhere that the busiest flight route in the world, in terms of the number of aeroplanes making the trip in a measured period of time, was Moscow to Nice. But there was no landmark for the centre, nowhere where I could stand, knuckles on hips and say "*this* is Monaco." Not knowing quite what else to do, we headed back to the casino, thinking we'd head on to the port and beyond to The Rock – a high headland that looked like it would be worth a climb. Behind the casino were signs to some lifts whose shaft bored down into the rock behind the cliff-face and we thought it might be an idea to use it to get down to the port in case an out-of-the-way route made us experience something we wasn't expecting. It did.

The lift (which had a public toilet next to it, natch) descended, and when the lift doors opened, we found ourselves not stepping out into the sea breeze, but into a marble tunnel. Exquisite white marble too, with art deco doors at the end, all in all a very lavish subway – it certainly beat the damp concrete of England that I was used to. But then the curious thing: before the only exit to the outside there was a short flight of steps going down the last couple of metres. Now why would you install a lift in the cliff face that doesn't quite go all the way down to the bottom? More than that, I'm guessing the lift will be used by people who can't walk down a flight of stairs – people in wheelchairs, babies in prams, daleks. Hasn't the local authority noticed this? Surely they have the budget to sort it out. Perhaps they just don't care about people who need a little help in life. Anyway, we walked on down the hill to the port, where I noticed a sign on a jetty offering tourists like us the chance to pootle across the harbour in a little boat for a modest fee, thus being able to say they'd been on a boat in Monaco harbour. Of course, we arrived just in time to see the stern depositing a trail of bubbles leading away from the harbour-side, so instead we glumly plodded around the port instead along the backs of these land-loathing palaces, peering into each and every one, to see what we could see. It was generally cleaners rubbing and polishing surfaces but one boat in particular intrigued me.

I heard the sound of toddlers playing and immediately went into responsible-parent mode, fearing that there would be some terrifyingly low barrier or other nightmarish oversight that made a gruesome plop inevitable the moment a responsible adult's back was turned. I was relieved to see all exits were so responsibly barricaded that it was impossible for a child to get out, yet we pedestrians could still see in. If you have never experienced a two year-old's tantrum then you are missing out on one of life's most intense experiences; the problem with being two is that you are old enough to realise broadly what's going on around you, but still young enough not to understand it. So, while you have been watching your mummy put both her and your shoes on for the last two years, you suddenly work out that if your mummy is capable of doing it herself, then you must be too. So that becomes your mission, but as the task becomes more difficult you become more intense about your desire to complete it. Before long, you are discovering that pushing your heel into the back of the shoe is actually an impossible task because you don't yet know the trick of making a shoehorn with your finger. So you make growling noises until your mummy starts interfering with your project and trying to do it for you. It is only thirty seconds after you have lost your rag with this stupid shoe-pushing lark that you suddenly realise that you are wearing your other shoe that you haven't put on yet. So how did it get there? Mummy did it! How DARE SHE!!! You'd literally just told her that you didn't want her help with your shoe and now she has the audacity to go ahead and completely finish doing the other foot for you! Well, that really won't do at all. You bark at mummy as loudly as you can to GO AWAY and STOP IT because this foot is YOUR FOOT and it is YOUR JOB to shoe it. Mummy looks at her watch and patiently undoes your shoe for you and slides your heel out, which is frankly the final straw. You SCREAM at mummy with everything you've got and start stamping your foot hard to show your displeasure. Except your shoe's only half on and the stamp hurts the underside of your foot as the top of the heel digs in to your sole. You start crying and the cry turns into a wail as mummy moves nearer as if to try and help with that shoe again and That. Is. It. Steam shoots out of your ears and warm tears stream down your hot cheeks as you start jogging on the spot, roaring inarticulately. Lava would soar out of the top of your head if it could. Unable to jog on the spot whilst unbalanced, you fall over, catching the radiator valve with the side of your head on the way down. You scream so loudly that it hurts your ears and your mummy advances on you *again* even though you've made it perfectly clear that she is persona non grata right now. You see neighbours in the street looking in, concerned, and you are now beginning to feel the cold coming in through the front door so you roar at the discomfort. This carries on for an indeterminate length of time until you have no more heat left to give and you cool down and return to your normal self until the episode is repeated an hour later in a different set of circumstances.

Well, something approximating that was beginning to develop on the back of this multi-million-dollar yacht. I had never heard a toddler tantrum in French before, but I was now. Her words were as indecipherable as could be, but clearly something was grinding her gears and Monaco was going to know about it. I felt comforted, knowing that despite being in the very top echelon of the world's wealthiest people, you couldn't fully escape the slings and arrows of day-to-day life. So for the rest of the day, I started to list as many of the other of life's irksome frustrations from which cash cannot insulate you:

1) Power cuts.
2) The dawning realisation that you're standing in the slow queue in the supermarket.
3) Committing to press a part of an internet page on a touchscreen device at the very moment the page loads an advert into that space and you accidentally find yourself being linked through to the advert's website.
4) Trains whose advertised delay on the station's electric signs increases as you wait.
5) A shoelace snapping while you're walking in the street and having to drag a trailing leg half a mile to a place where you can buy a new shoelace while your foot flaps around in a loose-tongued brogue.
6) Rain in the destination where you'd planned to spend a sunny weekend.
7) When you only realise the remote control's out of reach once you're nicely squished into the sofa and a show featuring Piers Morgan starts.
8) Putting the kitchen bin out without having realised that you've dribbled a trail of bin juice over the hall carpet.
9) Your football team losing.
10)   Death.

Uplifted, we continued our stroll through the millionaires' playground and past the inviting open-air Piscine de Monaco (as it should be called, although it does in fact have the rather pointlessly aggrandised name of Stade Nautique Rainier III). We continued along the quay, strenuously resisting the temptation to run along whilst pretending to drive a Formula 1 car, complete with screaming engine noises and rapid gear changes, arriving at a life-size statue of a boxy 1950s F1 car with its driver standing next to it, helmet under one arm with the other extended, gripping the top of the steering wheel. A little sign informed us that this was Juan Manuel Fangio, who won the Monaco Grand Prix twice and that this spot was where the pit lane carved off from the main track. The seat in the car was empty and clearly intended for climbing into for a photo. Everyone in the family took the opportunity, and I'm sure you would have done if you had been there.

We were approaching the end of the afternoon and the sun was beginning to become mildly less hot. We were hoping to see the other part of Monaco that gets the headlines: Vieux-Monaco; the Old Town of narrow cobbled lanes and small pavement restaurants, of densely merchandised tourist shops where I hoped the fierce competition would bring down the price of my Monaco flag. Thoughtlessly, this tourist attraction had been placed upon a high rocky outcrop, meaning that to get there, we punters had to climb a path for ten minutes to elevate ourselves 100 metres or so in a hot climate. The path was bewilderingly separated into 10ft long sloping steps which eradicated all chance of a little white street train to take us up the hill – a service I was prepared to pay any price for – but after ten minutes of constant climb, we were at the top, in front of the Palace and looking back down and across the harbour and out again to sea, rotating my head thirty degrees inland to take in the forest of apartment blocks that are Monaco's signature. It was a perfect postcard of the country and we paused there for a lingering moment, sweat stinging our eyes and positively radiating body heat, to consider this the perfect place to drink the country in. This was the knuckles on hips moment we'd been looking for back on the other side of Monte Carlo.

Vieux-Monaco doesn't have the deafening bustle that defines other cobbly Mediterranean towns. We had the three central parallel narrow lanes pretty much to ourselves as we threaded our way between and past pavement restaurants and tourist shops. There really isn't that much to report from Vieux Monaco. Take a small British town, Newbury perhaps, or Otley or Tamworth and go there on a weekday mid-morning. Then walk down its main street and two other substreets running parallel and you get a similar idea of the sense of energy that I was receiving from the Vielle-Ville. There were things to do, for sure, a stately Museum of Oceanography with a dinky yellow submarine out front that the Beatles could have used as an onstage prop, a predictable Cathedral and the Prince's Palace, the official residence of the Prince of Monaco built in 1191 but appearing to have had as much cosmetic surgery since then as its country's residents. But none of the so-called tourist attractions really implored us to go in and risk being surprised by what lay inside. No knowing quite what to do with ourselves, we did what anyone in our situation would do: Sit down and have a drink. The cool beer hit the spot nicely enough, and noticing no further entertainment from the cathedral's edifice, I fell into the fruitless habit of so many of my generation: I idled into my smartphone, going down a wormhole of all things Monaco, seeing what this magic little box that contained all the world's information could tell me that I hadn't already discovered. A little switch flicked in the large part of my brain where totally useless information is stored and a remarkable fact was awakened. I jabbed the screen on my phone a few times and my memory was confirmed as correct: I had been watching the Four Man Bobsleigh during a Winter Olympics many years previously and was observing the usual central European teams go whizzing down the icy track with impressive speed and accuracy when it was announced that the next team to compete would be Monaco. And not only that, but that their sleigh was to be driven by (who else but) the Prince of Monaco, whose residence I was right now just around the corner from. I remember wondering firstly why Monaco even had a bobsleigh team (I suspect that male pride and the shape and size of the sleigh were something to do with it) and secondly where they trained (surely Switzerland for tax purposes). But there they were, standing next their maroon bullet on the start line, as ridiculous as a giant chorizo on a waterslide, preparing to push off. The camera zoomed in on the tightly-lycrad Prince Albert[36] as he snapped his visor shut and prepared to sprint. I remember fearing humiliation for the pompous Prince, and if I'm honest, a little bit of me was hoping for it too. Our Prince managed to run only about four steps before sheepishly climbing into the cockpit to drive, while the actual athletes behind him ran on for another twenty strides. I forget how long it took for the inevitable to occur and regrettably Youtube didn't have the footage, but the BBC website does record that the Prince did indeed crash the sleigh and his team slithered across the finish line with shoulders and helmets pressed to the ice, finishing in 28th place and a full ten seconds behind the inevitable winners, Germany.

I mused on the day as I drained my beer. There was lots to see in Monaco, but there was lots missing too. If Monaco really is the destination that everyone in the moneymaking world is striving to achieve, I wasn't altogether sure I wanted it. I had seen yachts that were verging on cruise ships, I had wandered amongst the finest cars ever made, I had seen actual people who at the moment I saw them had

---

[36] careful now

more money around their left wrist than I do in my life, but it all lacked a certain *je ne sais quoi*. It lacked soul. It lacked love. Where were all the things that make a community a community in this jumbled mass of tower blocks? Where were the newsagents, the charity shops, the playgrounds, the florists, the stand-up comedy venues, the municipal tennis courts? This place was a Principality, not a municipality. The country was a Private Beach multiplied by itself to the ultimate conclusion. I'd hoped to write more positive and colourful things about Monaco, but I'm sorry, I can't; there's not much there to write about: It's a dense forest of sunburnt phallic towers, populated by disaster capitalists propelled to their wealth by mistreatment of poor people, who never walk if they can drive and never drive if they can fly. If I had to choose between living here and living in an ordinary town in my home country, then give me Ipswich any day.

**

I'm sorry, I hadn't intended to be quite that negative about Monaco. It is in many ways a very fine place to live. It has an agreeable climate, it charges no income tax to its residents no matter whether they work as a barista or a barrister, it has Cannes to the west and San Remo to the east, mountains at its head and the sea at its feet. It has enough distractions to entertain the people who want to live there, it hosts a Formula 1 race on its streets, and you don't get that all in Ipswich. I'd hoped Monaco would be a place that was worth all the fuss, but it – quite literally – wasn't for me. We returned to France and, a few days later, visited somewhere similarly telling.

Marineland is a sort of Mediterranean SeaWorld and it is probably as close to SeaWorld as you can get without leaving Europe. I'm not particularly an animal lover (unless I'm eating one) so was pretty ambivalent about any zoo, aquatic or otherwise; we were doing it for the kids. So, we hobbled up to the penguins, glided through the shark tunnel, applauded the sea-lions, and generally did our best to appreciate every animal in the park. We took seats for the dolphin show and it was the best thing I've seen in a long time. I was expecting a dry explanation of dolphin's habitats and a well-worn preach on why conservation is so important, punctuated occasionally with a jump through a hoop or a series of squeaky clicks to a sleepy stadium, but Marineland had gone for the spectacular and boy did it nail it. I split my gaze equally between the wriggling cetaceans down below and the precious enchanted faces of my children as the animals danced upright on their tails, sprinted around the pool's perimeter, belly-flopped at the edge to drench the front row, flipped giant beachballs into row Z with their tails, nuzzled the arched feet of their trainers and speedboated them along before launching them many metres into the sky, and generally capered and cavorted around for a wildly entertaining half hour. It was the best thing I'd seen in a long time and despite the cliché, dolphins became the one animal I actually had feelings for. I liked it so much that I uploaded a five-second video of a series of splashing somersaults onto Facebook for my friends to see.

Then after lunch we proceeded to the giant killer-whale stadium – a seriously heavy-duty structure with a huge steel-reinforced glass tank in its pit and holding pens backstage where we glimpsed the occasional orca breaking the surface. Then the show began and it was similar to the dolphin show, except to say that orcas are much slower creatures and there was less agility on display as the beasts lumbered around performing a series of less impressive tricks – sticking their tongue out, fanning water over the edge of the glass with a flipper, nearly managing to execute a somersault but managing only to crash back into the water shoulder-first. The trainers didn't swim with the orcas and there was somehow less warmth in the occasion; it was all a bit less fun. The pool was the largest man-made body of water I'd ever seen – probably several times the size of an Olympic pool, but surely no container can be made large enough for an animal that's used to swimming 100 miles a day. I left the orca whale show feeling a touch downbeat and the children weren't that interested in the whales either.

Later that evening I checked Facebook and saw that my little dolphin video hadn't been blessed with any likes, but even worse than that, two friends – one of whom I knew to be an animal lover – both contributed a crying face emoticon. All my other friends had been too polite to remark anything. Clearly the corkscrewing dolphins that had been the highlight of my day were not only a more controversial feature of 21st century life than I'd imagined, but were regarded by some as a positively outrageous violation of animal rights, and I was guilty by association. I messaged both friends privately, apologising for upsetting them and asking them to open my eyes as to why dolphin shows were a bad thing. Both replies featured the same word: Blackfish. Bear with me while I explain, I'm going somewhere with this:

Blackfish is a 2013 documentary film about Seaworld-style marine parks and I urge you to watch the film and risk the enlightenment it brought me. The story begins in 1983, when American whale-hunters pulled in a two year-old who they named Tilikum and sold him to Sealand[37] in Victoria, Canada. Sealand wasn't the kind of marine park you have in your head when you picture SeaWorld or Marineland, it was little more than a netted cage suspended between two piers about the size of a couple of tennis courts. A ticket booth was erected by a jetty, and tourists would wander through and watch Tilikum and friends thrash about for half an hour, then the sun would set and Tilikum would be lured back to his pen that was about as large compared to him as your bathtub is compared to you and locked there for the next eighteen hours until it was time for the whole daily schedule to begin again.

One February day in 1991, Tilikum announced that he had had enough. In front of a paying crowd, 21 year old marine biology student, Keltie Byrne, working as a trainer, slipped and fell in. Tilikum and two friends dragged Byrne around the pool and tossed her from mouth to mouth, taking it in turns to pull her under then release her to surface and watch her make a beeline for the side. She made it there once, but, locking her arms straight as she rose from the sea, Tilikum grabbed her ankle and sadistically lowered her again for the game to continue. Horrified, visitors watched from the sides with hands over mouths, grimly realising that this was not part of the show. There was only ever going to be one outcome and the outsized Tilikum was identified by everyone present as the one who did the deed. Stories ran in the local press that Byrne had drowned in an accident after falling in. Tilikum was quietly sold to SeaWorld in Florida and Sealand closed down shortly afterwards.

---

[37] Not the small manmade country off the Suffolk coast.

In the summer of 1999, Tilikum's trainers entered the SeaWorld stadium to be greeted with the unusual sight of a chewed corpse lying on Tilikum's back as he basked in the morning sun. A visitor named Daniel Dukes had hidden overnight and fulfilled his now lifelong dream of swimming with Tilikum just like his trainers did in the shows. An autopsy found numerous wounds and abrasions covering his body but peculiarly concluded that Dukes's cause of death was hypothermia and drowning. No security camera footage was available for release. Animal rights campaigners suggested that penning these wild animals up in concrete baths probably wasn't helping their mental health and that maybe Tilikum wasn't entirely happy.

Seaworld continued with the shows. In early 2010, Seaworld's Senior Trainer, Dawn Brancheau was performing in the pool with Tilikum when he seized her arm and pulled it off, fractured her jawbone and ribs, crushed her cervical vertebra, tore her scalp from her head and severed her spinal cord. SeaWorld bleated in the ensuing PR war that Brancheau's fate was Brancheau's fault; she was wearing her hair in a grabbable ponytail, thus flouting regulations. Tilikum's mental state was in no way their responsibility.

The issue of keeping killer whales in captivity is a dark science; no-one can know for sure what is happening in the mind of an orca whale in captivity, but only interpret what they believe to be true and find evidence for that. We do know from brain scans that orcas are intelligent and complex creatures, and that showy, cramped living quarters where everything required for life is served up on a silver plate don't create the necessary conditions for happiness. Perhaps Monaco can learn something from that.

9. Wales

"There's no such thing as bad weather, only the wrong type of clothes."

Billy Connolly

Wales is my nearest country. By country, I mean 'has its own flag and football team', of course. It's a mere two hours from my front door, straight down the motorway; it could almost not be any easier to reach, and yet in something of an oversight, I had never been there. In fact, there had only been one occasion in my life where I'd had anything to do with Wales at all. Let me explain.

My phone rang one evening in late 2015 and when I picked up, my friend Andrew was there putting an interesting proposition to me. His brother-in-law David had applied for tickets to the following summer's European football championships and he'd got lucky, bagging four tickets for the quarter-final in which England were projected to be playing if they finished top of their qualifying group. However, he discovered shortly afterwards that his wife was pregnant and scheduled to give birth during the tournament. As such, he couldn't now commit to the trip he'd organised. Did I want to go in his place? The match would be taking place in Lille - just an hour away from Calais. I have made harder decisions.

Fast-forward six months and I was on tenterhooks in the week before the game and an emotional mess as, days after Britain shocked the world by voting to leave the European Union, England's football team exited Europe after melting against Iceland and as a consequence I now held a ticket not for England's quarter final, but for the rather less appealing fixture of Belgium v Wales. But I was financially and socially obliged to cross water for this game, and, in the hangover of the Brexit vote, resolved that if I were no longer to be permitted to identify as European at what was, quite frankly, a massive party in Europe for European citizens, then the only way I could think to square the circle was to go and be all-out Welsh. My circle of friends contained a music teacher from Aberfan called Paul, who agreed to lend me not only a Welsh football jersey, but a Welsh rugby top, a Wales scarf (which I agreed to wear anyway despite it being July) and a daffodil headdress (which sounded like an excellent accessory but turned out to be a joke). I accepted them all and promised some Calais alcohol by way of thanks. Thus, I came to be sitting in a car bedecked in Wales colours with an accountant, a vicar, and an IT manager for what was undoubtedly going to be a wild lads' weekend away, for I know nothing if not who the party animals are.

We crossed the channel, and late in the afternoon arrived at our modest hotel to drop our bags and were asked at reception if we cared to guarantee ourselves a breakfast the following morning for an absolutely unbelievably exorbitant charge of €14 each. This was clearly pushing the boundaries of how much a midmarket hotel could charge for breakfast and they clearly knew it, but what's a captive, hungry tourist meant to do? I explained this to my friends, who, none wanting to make an unpopular decision on the group's behalf, nominated me as the only French-speaker to conjure up an appropriate reply. Our unarticulated group-think was that in the light of Sterling's Brexit-caused crash which had cranked our price up even further, we didn't really want to pay £13.99 each for a hot breakfast in the height of summer, however if we declined the extortionate meal then it would clearly be poor form and force us to drive around looking for a patisserie on an empty stomach the morning after (we assumed) we had watched Wales lose - for Belgium were the highest ranked team in the competition and the match was being played about five miles from the Belgian border. Maybe the answer was in there somewhere. Without consultation, I explained to our host that the answer was fate: If Wales beat Belgium, we'd agree to be swindled for breakfast. If Belgium won, we'd drive off and buy pains aux chocolat for a reasonable price. We all agreed that this was the most diplomatic exit from the breakfast sting that could possibly have been achieved.

Now, I'm assuming you're 1) not a football fan and 2) tetchy that in this chapter about Wales we do not appear to have crossed the Severn Bridge yet, so I'll spare you a match report but suffice to say that one of the great British sporting moments of the decade took place that night. The winning goal (and goal of the tournament to boot) was scored in the goalmouth directly below and in front of us. Breakfast the following morning tasted fantastic.

**

One year later, the Procter family again faced its annual first-world agony regarding where to holiday. Much like the debate at the start of the Isle of Wight chapter, the context was right for a British break with as much sunshine as possible, but a week in Dorset / Devon / Cornwall somehow lacked the requisite 'foreign' quality that we wanted a holiday to have. Then the thought hit-us: Wales! It's not too far, it's foreign enough to make us feel abroad what with having its own language, and in southern Wales, we might just have a more favourable climate than in the north. It was decided. To distil many days of googling into six words, we found a cottage near Cardigan. Six weeks later, it was time to do something that had appealed to me since moving from west London to Berkshire: See what happened when we drove off the end of the M4.

Passing Bristol, large dot matrix signs rose either side of the carriageway explaining that one of the Severn[38] bridges was shut. No reason given, but it must have been pretty significant because it meant that two motorways' worth of cars were squeezed onto one bridge which meant the spectacular drive across the Severn estuary was instead a giant traffic jam. But the weight of traffic didn't collapse the bridge during the hour my family was on it, for which I will always be grateful. After the bridge came the long queue for the toll booths, during which I stopped to think about the sense of drudgery that must come across the people employed to sit in the little booths behind the barriers, take a succession of £10 notes, make change, then push a button to raise the barrier and keep that up for ten hours straight; it's work that must really take its toll[39]. They could do with Seattle's "Fish! Philosophy". Entering Wales cost me £6.70; it's the only country that I've visited that thought fit to

---

[38] A name that, phonetically, always encourages me to envisage a massive Communist waterway numbering system (River Six, River Seven, River Eight...)

[39] Hope you noticed that one.

charge its visitors an admission fee. But the entrance over the Severn Bridge was so spectacular, I was *almost* happy to pay it.

Over the next hour, the Welsh M4 gave me a breakneck tour of south Wales. Celtic Manor golf resort loomed on a bluff above the muddy estuary of the river Usk. The brink-of-closure and foul-smelling Tata steelworks belched their by-products into my car's air-conditioning system at Port Talbot. Road signs to places I'd heard referred to but never visited rose up along the hard shoulder: Llanelli, Llantrisant, Bridgend. I saw signs to Cardiff too, but sadly no panorama of its famous and initially controversial bay, about which I will now write because on the evening of my arrival in Cardigan I happened to read a newly-published article[40] about the regeneration of Cardiff's waterfront and found its content too interesting to omit in a chapter about Wales. So at the risk of being called a Severn bore...

Cardiff Bay was once the epicentre of Wales's booming export industry as locally mined coal was distributed to the world. But the fall in trade following World War Two coupled with the rise of long-haul cargo planes meant that much like Liverpool, Cardiff was facing the wrong way for sea trade with Europe and by the time of Thatcher's 1980s Britain, Cardiff Bay had become a giant expanse of ex-docks and mudflats.

The Cardiff Bay Development Corporation was set up in April 1987 to regenerate the 2,700 acre city centre, with the intangibly pithy aim of "putting Cardiff on the international map", and "establish the area as a recognised centre of excellence in urban regeneration" by which I think they meant "draw visits from other cities' urban planners to see

---

[40] http://tinyurl.com/y886nu4g

what we did and also attract sixth-form Geography field trips."

Key to the whole project was to build a barrage, necessary to trap water from the famously tidal Severn estuary, without which the bay would remain a muddy wasteland whenever it was anything less than close to high-tide, which was three quarters of the time. But the proposed barrage was not without controversy; everyone who was anything to do with Cardiff bandied about various words such as 'flood risk', '£220 million cost' and of course 'loss of wildlife habitat'.

After half a decade of political battling and a resignation threat from then-Welsh Secretary Nicholas Edwards, work on the barrage commenced in 1994 and was completed in 1999; it was one of the biggest engineering projects in Europe, creating a 200-hectare freshwater lake in the heart of the capital. Shops, restaurants and offices quickly followed, as did a rebuilt national stadium large enough to host the Rugby World Cup Final in the autumn of 1999 and six FA Cup finals from 2001 to 2006, both of which had a galvanising effect on investment in the city not dissimilar to an Olympic Games. Then the Wales Millennium Centre - an opera house and arts centre - followed in 2004 to make the rich people want to come, then in 2006 a new parliament building, a structure for which architects Lord Richard Rogers and his lesser-known partner Ivan Harbour[41] were briefed to create the most distinctive building in the country. The Senedd has won so many awards for architecture that you can see it now in your mind's eye, can't you?

---

[41] I swear that is his real name: https://en.wikipedia.org/wiki/Ivan_Harbour

So, the first decade of the 21st Century was quite a time to be alive in Cardiff. 16,000 new jobs and 5,000 new homes were created, 26 miles of road were upgraded; effectively a capital city's centre of gravity was moved, which is no mean feat in any country. The Welsh Secretary Nicholas Edwards (who you'll remember from the previous paragraph but was now inexplicably renamed Lord Crickhowell), talked the redevelopment up, telling the BBC that it had been "an immense success [...] we cannot contemplate Cardiff without the bay, it's the centre of the city, highly successful [...] and the barrage has protected Cardiff from flooding and tidal surges." Roger Thomas, who helped advise on the feasibility of the early redevelopment, was similarly gushing. "I hate to think what Cardiff would be like if it hadn't been done. During the next 20 years it [the bay] went through economic recessions but it has put Cardiff on the European and world map."

Not all agreed, though: Award-winning planning consultant Adrian Jones told the BBC that Cardiff's regeneration was a "dump plan" lacking in any "coherent urban structure of real streets or worthwhile public spaces", wasting money on vanity projects rather than providing much-needed public housing. "Public" being the key word there – despite the proliferation of posh waterfront flats built in the early years of the 21st century, they were mainly built by developers selling cramped flats on the private market for a fast buck, rather than actual comfortable homes with a bit of legroom, in which people might actually want to make their homes. Estate agent Mike Jones also told the same BBC journalist (to whom I owe a pint for this section) that he felt developers were overbuilding, with supply having outstripped demand for many years. The financial crash in the autumn of 2008 didn't help: "When the market was on a high in 2007/8 people were paying £250,000 for a 2-bed flat that 12 months later they were struggling to sell for £130,000. The bay has been spoilt to a great extent. I think it's such a pity they built so many flats." When an estate agent is complaining that he has too many properties to sell, something's gone wrong somewhere.

**

Anyway, an hour later, we dropped off the end of the M4 and as we experienced an hour of gloriously unfolding scenery in the drive from Camarthen to Cardigan, we started to get the feel of the country. The first thing to notice was that every road sign was bilingual. It's a curious thing, Welsh. Considering that Wales is one of only two countries to have a land border with the country that is unarguably the birthplace of the world's global language, Welsh is remarkably stubborn in the face of the globalisation of English. I saw the words ARAF – SLOW printed on bendy rural roads more times than I could count. Upon presenting myself at the reception desk at the cluster of holiday cottages that would be home for the week, I saw a No Smoking sign, translated into the unnecessarily verbose "Mae ysmygu yn y fangre hon yn erbyn y gyfraith". Ten words to say 'No Smoking'? And how could that sentence exist with so few vowels? Behind the No Smoking sign was the receptionist, who I was disappointed to note didn't speak to me in Welsh, didn't even speak English with a Welsh accent, which disappointed me greatly; I was firmly on the west coast of the country, impossible to be any further from England.

I've stayed in holiday cottages several times now and am starting to become experienced enough in the game to know the pitfalls. The thing about staying in cottages – unlike hotels – is that you never quite know what accoutrements will be provided for you. I neglected to mention in the Isle of Wight chapter that upon arrival at our home for a week, we not only flicked the kettle on after unpacking to discover that there was no milk, but no soap in the wash-hand basins either. This experience, and several similar over the years, has led me to consider all the 'maybes' that a rented cottage can provide. I'm sure you will agree that every one of these items could justifiably be provided or not provided in a rented cottage for a week's stay; consider the impact of living without any / some of the following for a couple of days:

Teabags
Decaffeinated teabags
Coffee (Instant? Ground? If ground, what kind of coffee-maker is it? Do we need to buy special pods?)
Washing-up-liquid, washing up brush / sponge? (I do hope it's a brush)
Kitchen roll
Loo roll (how much?)
Dishwasher tablets (what kind?)
Drinking glasses that are larger than a quarter of a pint
Washing powder
Fabric conditioner
Washing machine
Tumble dryer
Second pillow

I'm sure you can think of more.

Happily, all the necessities above had been laid on for us (even a complimentary bottle of wine!), and I can honestly say that the owners had thought of everything, because the building was equipped with metre-thick stone walls which we figured would prove handy in the event that Donald Trump succeeded with his wish of starting a nuclear war with North Korea that week, as it seemed at the time he was intent on.

We were shown to our cottage and unpacked as the preordained Tesco delivery driver arrived with the week's supplies, I noticed that our Tesco delivery lady was similarly RP as we made small talk and she answered our queries about what there was to do round here in the couple of hours before dinnertime. She told us to go to Mwnt.

Mwnt (silent w) is a beach, not a term of abuse, though to describe it as simply a beach here would be akin to saying Heathrow Airport is an airstrip. I could describe it as a secluded cove, hidden away at the end of a winding narrow lane, but none of that gives you the sense of scale in terms of what an enormous landscape feature is secreted between headlands on a remote section of coast. The sand was perhaps fifty metres wide and one hundred from front to back, but surrounding it on three sides was the most majestic sweep of steeply banked rock rising to such a height that death would most certainly ensue if you were to be foolish enough to topple off. It was the same size and shape as one end of Wembley Stadium. The steps down the cliff followed the course of a babbling cascade that at the base became a stream which swirled down the side of the beach. It was filled with children trying in vain to dam the thing up. The whole place was perfectly proportioned and decorated by crashing waves that crested at the ideal height for any of the dozen enthusiastic bodyboarders who were out there, ranging in age from about ten to an age and walk of life that can only be described as that of quite literally a silver surfer. Beyond the waves was the lively reflection of the sun on the sea, and beyond that, sunset. Dolphins are regular visitors here, the only place on the British mainland[42] that they frequent (I guess that being the intelligent yet illiterate creatures that they are, they decided they simply had to visit a country that they thought was called Whales). I am sure there are evenings where a pink sunset gives a rainbow under which the dolphins flip and dart, thereby creating something of a fantasy tableau. But more about dolphins in the dueness of course.

**

The first day of the holiday brought rain, which was only to be expected in Wales, but Debs and I had strategically accounted for this by planning a wet-weather trip to Dolaucothi Gold Mines, because a mine is nothing if not indoors. It transpired to be a perfect option for a rainy day, as we were able to spend two hours of it blanketed up inside the car sipping hot chocolate, dipping our fingers into bags of M&Ms and listening to the avuncular voice of Maurice Denham read The Magician's Nephew (the little-known but excellent prequel to The Lion, The Witch and the Wardrobe) whilst staring out of the window and being able to actually see Wales's guts. The first thing I noticed was that there were very few pubs. Not only that, but the villages we passed through – that would surely have supported one or two pubs back home in southern England - looked as though they'd never had a pub there at all. The average village contained a petrol station, a school, a strip of

[42] that isn't the north coast of Scotland.

grey houses, and that was it. I wasn't sure whether this absence of pubs was a good or a bad thing. On the minus side, it surely meant a reduced community spirit, fewer places to congregate; no public place free from rain. On the other hand, there was clearly less of a dangerously close relationship with alcohol (or less visibly so at any rate), and if society were to lose places for paunchy gammon-faced freemason golfers in polo-necks and Pringle sweaters to competitively compare resentment for their wives and children over £5 tankards of Taylor's Toebrew on a Wednesday night, then I'm not going to die in a ditch to preserve the pubs' right to exist.

The next thing I noticed was that everywhere was uphill. Every mile of the route in both directions seemed to contain a moment where it was necessary to yank the gearstick from 3rd back into 2nd and send the engine into overdrive so the car could scream up the sort of slope you wouldn't dare attempt on a bicycle. There never seemed to be a downhill section; it was like driving through an Escher drawing. It was also interesting to see that some of the little sat-nav cut-through roads advertised themselves at their entrance as having been paid for by the Welsh government, which I found disconcerting; why did the Welsh government feel the need to advertise the fact that they were building roads? Wasn't that the sort of thing a government was meant to do? The journey passed, remote wet hill after remote wet hill. I began to understand the meaning of C.S. Lewis's phrase 'always winter but never Christmas.'

Still, the rain decided to cease just in time for our planned picnic upon arrival (for there is nothing more dispiriting about holidaying in Britain than eating your picnic in your car) and the National Trust had helpfully laid out wooden benches for families to work through their sandwiches on.

Sat on, the benches had the feel of never being fully dry. The National Trust had converted this once working mine into a venue for a family day out which was a great deal more entertaining than the multiple and endless stately homes I was frogmarched around between the ages of six and 12 at a time when the National Trust hadn't fully grasped the notion of making their attractions appeal to children as well as adults, something I am glad that they have seen the light on this now.

After paying our entrance fee, we were ordered to exit the admissions building and upon entering a faithfully replicated miners' yard, locate the main central hut at which we would book our tour and then kill time until it was our turn. The yard had been dressed with various mining tools to entertain us: The sort of mining carts the Indiana Jones films had popularised, a scattering of outbuildings filled with various mining artefacts – detonators, rock crushers, a moveable girder overhead with a hook hanging down from a winch that the audio guide told me was called a travelling crane[43], and a classically imposing headframe with its giant wheels fifty feet up crowning the scene at the far end. In one of the outbuildings, gold-panning was encouraged, though in the drizzle it would better be described as grit-sifting. And there was a great deal of grit to sift through of all shapes and sizes; there must have been fifty grades of shale. After an hour or so of this diversion, we were given yellow mining helmets to don (which the children rightly believed gave us the appearance of oversized Minions) and it was time to descend.

Except we didn't descend. I'd rather hoped that access to the mines would be by some great elevator shaft, but the

---

[43] If only I'd known this back in that French classroom in chapter one, 17 years previously...

part of the mine we would visit was an open cast mine and to access it we had to counter-intuitively walk uphill and into what had the appearance of the mouth of a cave. Passing through perhaps fifty metres of rocky tunnel, we assembled in the gloom to be told the story of Edward Jones (Jones, what else?), a gold digger in the quite literal sense of the word, who'd prospected as far afield as South Africa but in 1888 ended up in central Wales on the back of a rumour that the Romans had mined for gold here and it was worth a shot.

Mining is dirty and dangerous work. Quite apart from the ever-present potential for catastrophe involved in spending your working day in underground tunnels that you are constructing with dynamite as you go, there is an absence of daylight for months on end to consider, the year-round cold climate, the constant damp air, and of course the plain fact that you will inhale a lot of dust and are therefore at a strong risk of contracting pneumonoultramicroscopicsilicovolcanoconiosis[44].

Mining for gold is one of the most labour-intensive activities it is possible to embark upon: Ten tonnes of rock have to be chiselled away from inherently collapsible underground tunnels to give one tonne of quartzite, which, when crushed, panned, melted, moulded and cooled, yields a square of gold the size of a ring. The enterprise was so unprofitable that the rarity of Welsh gold had to be somehow played upon to justify the high price. The marketing didn't work, and Jones gave up in 1894, leaving the site dormant until 1905 when the owners convinced a Cornish mining engineer named James Mitchell to have another go. Mitchell had experienced the South African gold rush first-hand and was

---

[44] Sorry, couldn't resist.

therefore thought to have something of a Midas touch (pun fully intended, thank you).

Mitchell's team hacked and blasted away at the rock for seven years until one fateful day when a boom of dynamite revealed an elaborate network of tunnels overhead. I'd like to have been a fly on the wall at that particular moment, because this was the fabled Roman mine which had, as was immediately apparent, been abandoned for the simple fact that their intensive mining activities meant that there was no gold left. Mitchell's ambitions had been quite literally undermined. He quit, and doubtless lost a fortune just as Jones had done a decade before.

We listened intently to our guide's lectures, learnt that the phrase "He can't hold a candle to him" had its origins in the mining industry: if miners thought the rock would have poor yield, they wouldn't pay a child to stand there gripping a candle all day. We all enjoyed simulating how dark it really was in the mine by all turning out our lights at the same time for theatrical effect (apart from one guy at the edge of the group who had failed to realise his light was still on and stood there, hands in pockets for a full half-minute, dimly wondering what was meant to be so amazing). We congregated in a drippy atrium known as 'the shower room' where we listened to a lecture that went on a little too long for our liking. Then we exited the mine via a steep rock staircase that needed all four limbs to climb, and out into the light where I realised the truth: This mine wasn't a happy place for tourists to have fun in, it was a monument to commercial failure. Jones and Mitchell collectively wasted efforts and lives in these tunnels all in the pursuit of gold. The place wasn't a hive of industry, it was a knackered old factory that had never produced anything but toil, bankruptcy, and death. I found myself wondering quite what all that risk and grind was for and didn't have a good answer.

It started to rain again. Debs and I took the family into the café where we attempted to lift our spirits via the medium of drinks of our choice and a plate of toasty-warm and buttered Welsh Cakes (which are delicious, you must try them). We drained a pot of tea, Master Procter finished a hot chocolate and Little Miss Procter had 1% of a strawberry milkshake that she had set her heart on the moment she saw it before changing her mind to request the chocolate version after one sip, of which she consumed 2%. I made idle chit-chat with the café staff who informed me that as a tourist attraction, the mines were only ever busy when it rained, to which I responded with an encouraging expression that it was lucky we were in a country where it rained so much. My enthusiasm wasn't shared.

**

Driving home, I gave in to a sudden urge to see Lampeter. I can't explain it. Well, I can of course, this sort of tangent is the very essence of this book. Some twenty years before, I'd been giving serious consideration to which university I would want to attend and with many factors to consider, declared that all universities were valid options at the outset until I'd deselected them for various reasons. Distance immediately put the kybosh on Scottish universities for me and as I worked through the remaining options (namely universities that had a winning combination of both a respectable academic reputation and low entrance-grade requirements), the University of Lampeter was in the top ten. It didn't make the final cut; I think when push came to shove the unknown-ness of the place put it in the relegation zone, but now here I was, proximate to Lampeter for surely the only time in my life, and I had to take the opportunity to see the place. Well, I have one word to describe Lampeter: Tiny. It is exactly one mile from end to end and its centrepiece is a mini-roundabout at a T-junction. The University is off the mini roundabout and was no larger than the average-sized secondary school I'd attended. A dozen (admittedly stony and historic) buildings populated a campus that really didn't suggest much of a student buzz. What young blade in their prime would choose to spend their formative years here? There seemed almost nothing to do when not studying, there was nothing nearby – the nearest town, Cardigan, (population 4,000) was one hour's drive to the west, and to the east, pretty much nothing all the way to Worcester. There wasn't even a train station. Who knew of a university town that doesn't have a train station? With relief, I declared Lampeter a near miss in my life and exited knowing I had seen about as much of it as I would have seen in three years there. I hold no grudge against the place, but I will never return.

**

Now, you'll recall from the last chapter that I'd got into hot water with animal-loving friends by visiting a Sea World-style waterpark and had subsequently become uneasy about observing sea mammals in captivity. It was now a year later, and time to right the wrong.

Apart from a couple of freak appearances in south west England, dolphins can only be seen in two places in the UK, northern Scotland and the very Cardigan Bay in which we were spending the week. Apparently, dolphins' whereabouts is primarily motivated by food availability, and Cardigan Bay obliges in this respect by not only reliably discharging a steady supply of salmon from the pollution-free river Teifi, but also welcoming the fish back later in their lifecycle, thus creating something of a dolphin buffet as the salmon go in and out. With no prior knowledge of the existence of dolphins when booking the cottage, Debs had heard on the grapevine that speedboats could be chartered to shuttle us punters at high speed to dolphin hotspots where we could Instagram them. When I phoned to book (a recorded voice informed me that my call would be recording for training porpoises), I was told of the catch: Because the dolphins are in the wild, they couldn't promise that, for what was a significant financial outlay for a one-hour excursion, the dolphins would show up. The Dolphin probability was 67% on a one-hour trip and, it was suggested with an unashamedly brazen commercial statement, that our odds would improve to 90% on one of their trips that cost 33% more. Or, put another way, that if we paid 33% more, our dolphin probability would increase by 23%. This was a fractional call, but we figured it a bad bet. After all, if a two-hour trip discovered dolphins 90% of the time, then that meant that there were always dolphins out there somewhere and surely since the statistics were initially put together, the tour operator's ability to spot the dolphins would have improved. We decided in the words of the song that as odds go, 2 out of 3 wasn't bad, and booked in for a one-hour ride.

The moment came to board in Cardigan's Gwbert ("Welcome to Gwbert, Cardigan's most unpronounceable locality this side of Mwnt" I decided the signs would read) where we met half a dozen strangers with whom we'd be riding and interviewed the departing passengers on the arriving boat as to whether they'd seen dolphins or not – convincing ourselves that a "yes" would mean that the dolphins had come out to play and a "no" would mean that statistically, it must now be our turn to see them. They gave us an answer we weren't expecting; they'd seen porpoises, but not dolphins. After a brief conference, we decided that we'd regard that outcome as a win; in the photos, they'd basically be the same thing.

As we boarded, we suddenly realised just how intense this boat trip was going to be. Our two guides, Chris and Tony, stepped ashore in matching red drysuits, wellies, and identical bushy beards that went many standard deviations beyond hipster in their length. I apologised for attempting to board without a beard and asked why such magnificent tufts were necessary. I was met with staring, glinty eyes that people who spend their days in nature specialise in. "You'll see."

We eased out of Cardigan Bay on what was a bright orange RIB with a sturdy steel stanchion above the stern and two enormous outboard engines below it. I could tell it was going to be fast, but I have never in my life felt more like Peter Stringfellow as we bounced across the open sea at a speed that would not disgrace a Porsche on a runway. I'm not easily given over to being emotionally altered by physical sensations but it was absolutely exhilarating and even Little Miss Procter, aged five, agreed it was the most fun thing she'd ever done. After ten minutes of wave-hopping, we were at Cardigan Island, which is a brown rock just off the coast with a turf cap, whose geology I'd be able to identify if I'd paid more attention to Mr King at Geography A-Level. Chris and Tony lazily lapped the island while they pointed out various kinds of seabirds, one of which was a nesting Fulmar, which, if you're a twitcher, is a sight that ranks up with albatross in rarity but unarguably looked almost exactly the same as a seagull. Perhaps it was. Really, we just wanted to see a dolphin. The throttle was engaged again for another ten minutes until, a good couple of miles out, the engine was cut and as we looked around, there they were: A pod of eight dolphins.

The dozen of us in the boat sat in sudden silence, consumed by our sense of sight. A dolphin arced out of the water, perhaps fifty yards to our right, and plunged nose first into the surf. No-one was reaching for their cameras yet, we all just wanted to see with our own eyes. Another flash of dorsal, then another as two broke the surface at the same time; a mother and her baby. You can look at cats on the internet from now until the end of time, but you haven't seen cute until you've seen a baby dolphin. They disappeared under their blanket of surf for perhaps a minute, which we all took as an opportunity to reach for our smartphones, after which the dolphins emerged again for photographs, albeit in a slightly different spot. We sat and watched for perhaps ten minutes. One popped up no more than five metres from the boat which drew gasps from everyone. Another pause. I turned behind me to speak to Chris/Tony's beard. "Do you ever get bored of seeing dolphins?" My captain looked back at me with those middle-distance eyes again. "Never. I've been doing this ten years, it's like the first time every day."

I didn't want the show to end. Then it struck me that the show wasn't going to end because it wasn't a show – this is where these dolphins lived, this is what they did with their days and they weren't going to go anywhere; these dolphins were natural and at home, not a circus display for profit like those I'd seen in France the year before. I was converted to the Blackfish way. With delight that it had happened and regret that it was now over both competing to be the dominant emotion, time ebbed away; the boat had to be turned around and we left the dolphins to carry on carrying on.

The boat was slowed again around Cardigan Island where we were told a seal could be seen. Chris / Tony gave a short lecture informing us that seals can hold their breath for up to fifteen minutes while they grub around on the ocean floor, but that being poor of sight, they could be attracted to the surface if we made enough noise and that Cardigan Bay's seals were particularly responsive to the music of Abba. And so, three families who had known each other for less than an hour and were quite literally all in the same boat spontaneously launched into "Anybody could be that guuuuuuuuy / night is young and the music's hiiiiiiiiigh..." climaxing in the awkwardly high-pitched and semi-screamed chorus[45] when surely Crazy, Kissed By a Rose, Killer, or anything else by Seal would surely have been more appropriate – particularly the opening lines of Crazy, with the Marineland dolphins in mind: "So you want to be free? / To live your life the way you want to be? Will you give if we cry? / Will we live or will we die?" But Abba worked a treat of course, our seal bobbed up for air and pivoted his head around like an owl as he trod water, looking slightly lost and alone, like an overgrown otter that had been washed out to sea. Didn't he know where his friends were? But it didn't matter, we'd seen a seal which was a welcome dessert to the main course of dolphin, as it were. Then our time was up and we headed back to shore. I rubbed my

---

[45] Incidentally, according to the QI Twitter feed, Dancing Queen is The Queen's favourite song. And shouldn't it be just?

beardless chin tenderly after the hour's assault of wind and spray; my skin stung and my eyes were watering. Never mind the dolphins and the seal, I was beginning to blubber.

**

A week in Wales is guaranteed to contain at least two rainy days and the following day was the second one. It forced us to rest, which can be a difficult thing to do on holiday with so much relaxation to get busy with. So we moped around the cottage in comfortable clothes while the little Procters discovered Challenge TV and reruns of Supermarket Sweep, Catchphrase, Gladiators, and of course, Family Fortunes. I idled into the lounge for half an episode to find Les Dennis resplendent in a beige suit, trousers pulled up to his diaphragm, asking the Perm family from Middlesbrough to name items a businessman might have in his briefcase. Ignoring the inherent sexism in the question, my mind went blank. I have only a laptop in mine; what were the tools of the trade for businesspeople in 1990? I didn't get any of the answers. Can you? Answers in the footnotes.[46]

In the afternoon, I got cabin fever and resolved to put the rain to good use and use the opportunity to get petrol, for there is never a good time to stop for petrol under normal circumstances. Debs wrote me a shopping list of items that appeared to have ideas above that of a petrol station – muffins, maple syrup, cashew nuts to name those I can remember. I filled up, then sought out a local paper to see if it contained any stories that I might appropriate as material to fill the following page with. As I queued to pay, I heard

---

[46] A calculator, documents, a phonecard, a pen, sandwiches. It was a different time.

the lady on the till in this rural petrol station at work; she was perhaps in her late twenties and was charm itself: warm, witty, kind-hearted, smiling with eyes that radiated warmth, and taking a genuine interest in her customers, making conversation with an interpersonal touch that was extraordinary; commenting on how her daughter loved that particular brand of biscuit that the customer was buying, asking the next customer if he perhaps had any silver coins he could pay with to provide change for subsequent customers, wishing everyone a good day and saying ta-ra as they turned to leave like they were old friends. My turn came, and my purchases were appraised, but I was so enjoying the customer service in contrast to the usual grump of the urban English petrol stations that I normally frequent that I was quite thrown by the whole interaction and kept making wrong-turnings in the conversation. It went something like this.

"Ooooh, Lime and Pepper crisps? I've not seen those before…"

"Yes [with doubt in my voice], it may be the last packet I ever buy."

"Mmmm, like those Pop Crisp things, the new ones."

"Oh, Pop Chips? They're delicious, aren't they? So moreish."

"Oooh no, I don't like them, I had to go and have a lie-down after eating my first ones."

"I know how you feel – I had to lie down and let the nausea pass after my first Pot Noodle."

"[Eyes brightening] Oh, I love a Pot Noodle. I've got a Pot Noodle tonight actually, going to have one with my jacket potato, I'm looking forward to that."

Now, I'm sure this lady had a perfectly fulfilled life with a comfortable sofa and a loving husband and the ability at weekends to pursue her love of windsurfing or whatever, but the apparent bleakness of her lifestyle revealed by that sentence was startling. Here she was with dazzling interpersonal skills that many large businesses would crave to employ, operating the till in a cottage-like petrol station on a low wage to feed her child, on a day that would build towards and climax in the consumption of a jacket potato with a Pot Noodle on the side. Surely she could 'do better' on the jobs market and afford a proper dinner, but where could she work round here to fund a lifestyle that would give her a reasonably nutritious and tasty evening meal? And how many other brainy, talented people drained out of the region to the bright lights of the cities because they didn't want this sort of life for their life? And why was the shop so ill-equipped with the modest things I was seeking to buy like a packet of ready-to eat croissants? I read the newspaper later (The Camarthen Journal, 16th August 2017) and started to find out.

On the front page, next to a giant photo of an otherwise unidentified man referred to as simply Nigel[47] urging that if readers "...live in Wales, they respect our way of life", was a sidebar promising delights on the inner pages, one of which was a story about a plan to build a Co-Op store in a residential area of Camarthen. Now, I know it's a journalist's job to whip up a bit of heat and controversy into an otherwise grey story, but this was ridiculous. The fact of

---
[47] Owens, celebrity rugby referee.

the matter was that the Co-Op supermarket group had lodged a planning application to build a store that would be open seven days a week and create 34 new jobs. Nothing in that previous sentence should really raise any local's hackles too much, but the article went on to explain that more than 700 people had signed a petition against the store on the grounds that, mainly, it may be popular and that people might come to the area to use it and so life would be a little less dull as a result. Please, people of Johnstown in Carmarthen, can you stop being so regressive and small-minded? If Co-Op had had a store there and were planning to close it, I'm pretty sure more than 700 of you would've signed a petition to try and save it, and you'd've been one of them, wouldn't you?

**

Now, I haven't written this chapter to be some sort of literary equivalent of a holiday slideshow and I hope you are entertained by the digressions and quirks of local life in all these slightly off-the-map places, but I am going to tell you now about a short trip to local beauty spot Cenarth Falls, because there happened the most peculiar conversation of the week and - please don't think I am reaching for melodrama here - of the year.

After switching on the Sat Nav in the rain several days before and finding that Dolaucothi Gold Mines was a full hour's drive away, imagine the sense of karmic rebalance I discovered upon finding that Cenarth Falls - another honeypot site on the holiday longlist – was a much more acceptable 14 minutes. With a couple of hours to kill on the last day of the holiday and having – and please don't think we as a family failed to enjoy ourselves in any way – exhausted the charms of the Cardigan Bay area, we bundled into the car for the short journey. Cenarth Falls isn't the tallest waterfall you will ever see, but I'm willing to bet that you probably see less than one waterfall per year and any opportunity to see a waterfall is a good one to take. Cenarth isn't a tall column, it's a sudden step down in the relatively broad river Teifi. As with all waterfalls, the noise is the most impressive part. Having stared at it long enough to justify the drive, we walked the riverside path upstream for perhaps ten minutes until we realised that there was no obvious spot to turn round, the scenery wasn't going to change a great deal, and there was an oncoming band of rain. So we returned to the car park next to which was a tea room where we decided to redistribute some of our supposed south east England economic heft.

The tea room wasn't the cutest I've ever sat in – the tables were tall Formica benches with the tabletops measuring about eighteen inches across, underneath which thick tubular steel legs descended vertically to the floor to which they were screwed. But the tea was hot, the Welsh Cakes arrived with butter melting into their centres, and the children couldn't finish their ice cream and so needed help doing so, which is what all parents secretly hope for when their children order a sweet treat. Then came a moment where one of the children knocked the bottom half of their hot chocolate over the table, whose modest size failed to contain the spillage much to the detriment of my beige shorts which were stained in the most unflattering place possible. The lady who ran the café was straight over with an armful of teatowels.

"Oh, don't you worry about that – is everyone ok? This sort of thing happens two or three times a week. They're children...I mean...this is what children do." Then she glanced down. "Those shorts are going to need washing tonight."

This broke the ice pleasantly and the conversation flowed from there on. Hankering after my student years where I canoed plenty of rural whitewater, I enquired whether kayakers ever shot the falls (they did), whether the rain which created the waterfall also reduced the café's footfall (yes, but without the rain there would be no waterfall but such is life), what else there was to do at Cenarth Falls other than look at the waterfall, walk past the waterfall and drink tea near the waterfall (not a lot). Conversation dried up. I filled the silence with the following:

"So, what's the hot topic in Wales at the moment?"

"Well, there's the Brexit of course – that was a good thing, we needed that." This was an opinion I hadn't expected to hear, or enter the conversation.

"Do you get a lot of immigrants round here?"

"No, not here; they don't go to places they can't pronounce[48]. The Pakistanis come in summer. The women don't speak. The man and the sons eat first, then the women when the men have finished, it's most peculiar."

I didn't quite know how to respond to that; I was torn between the twin ideals of firstly trying to be respectful of another country's culture and also speaking up for gender equality. Of more interest to me was the "we needed Brexit" viewpoint.

---

[48] A theory we can safely ridicule by asking non-Brits to pronounce the name of Britain's most multicultural town, Slough.

If I could literally open a can of worms right now, I would. I'm not going to go into the pros and cons of Brexit, largely because the whole debate about the European Union is nuanced and you're probably reading this long after Britain's exit from the European Union and you're in a much better position than I to judge whether it was the right thing to do or a stupid mistake. What I am going to comment on (here, but I didn't comment on in the coffee shop because I'm a chicken and I didn't want to have more hot chocolate thrown over my crotch) is the assertion that Wales needed Brexit.

From the year 2000 to 2016 – the figures for which I just happen to have at hand, Wales received just over £4 billion in European Union funding. Excuse me for ripping a hole in the narrative here, but exiting Swansea for the M4 a few days later I noticed an expensively complicated network of criss-crossing motorway junction flyovers that came with a large white sign declaring that they had been built with money from the EU. These signs are up all over Wales and doing a little research, I discovered that it is a matter of objective fact that Wales had financially benefited enormously from Britain's EU membership, being on the receiving end of a colossal number of funding programmes[49]:

Amongst other things, a centre for high-end research in Swansea University (£31.1 million), a Cardiff University Brain Research and Imaging Centre (£16.2 million) and countless others that are in a similar price bracket, a substantial proportion of which were in the education sector, because if there is one thing that can lift a region out of economic torpor then it is education. According to the Welsh Government itself (not the European Union), from 2007 to 2013 the European Union supported 229,110

---

[49] http://tinyurl.com/y7jw85cs

people to gain qualifications, helped 72,700 people into work and created 36,970 jobs and 11,925 enterprises. Then there are things like the Common Agricultural Policy, which provides around £200 million a year in single farm payments to more than 16,000 farms in Wales: That's £12,500 per farm, a significant amount of cash for any rural business. The European Union is Wales's largest export market.

A report published by Cardiff University's Wales Governance Centre[50] found that in 2014, Wales's contribution to the EU was £414m but it received £658m in funding – a tidy profit of £244 million, not bad for a population of three million. This investment is unarguably needed; West Wales and the Valleys (the funding region containing Cenarth Falls) is considered one of Europe's poorest regions, with GDP less than 75% of EU average. If there is one place in Britain that clearly benefitted from its place in the European Union then it is Wales, and if there is one part of Wales that benefitted most then it was here.

All this is pretty startling when you consider that Wales doesn't have the financial guts to stand as an independent nation in the way that Scotland nearly did – a stance reflected in a February 2017 poll that found Welsh independence was backed by just 6 per cent of its people. Support for a split has not hit 10 per cent in the last six years. At this point in time – spring 2019 – wanting to leave the European Union does seem like a mad position for Wales to hold.

**

---
[50] http://tinyurl.com/y9v4ujlt

There was one last place I wanted to see before it was time to leave the country: Oxwich Bay, 20 miles or so west of Swansea, which had been mentioned to me about a decade previously by a former colleague who had been there and described it as absolutely one of the top-tier beaches in the world, on a par with those in the Caribbean. So finely calibrated was the smoothness of the sand, the temperature of the air and clarity of the seawater, and the gentleness of the slope down to the water's edge, Oxwich Beach was practically perfect in every way, or so it looked on Google images. I had to go and have a look.

The drive there led us through a pretty village called Newcastle Emlyn which looked like a modest splat on the map but was in real life a charming, bustling village with a string of hanging-basket fronted white cottages on its bunting-bedecked high street provisioning a handsomely diverse range of colourful shops and facilities. Debs thought it probable that here she could avail herself of a coffee, so I parked up and managed tantrums in the back of the car while two cappuccinos were sought. During this wait, which seemed about twenty minutes longer than it probably was, I noticed that this busy high street had a Boots and a Co-Op, but there wasn't a single well-known coffee shop anywhere. No Starbucks, no Costa Coffee (the most ubiquitous shopfront in Britain), not a well-known coffeehouse façade in sight. And suddenly Wales made sense. This town had no chain stores because the people didn't want them, they were against the idea. The people of Newcastle Emlyn were against Costa Coffee. The people of Carmarthen were against a new Co-Op. The people of Cardiff were against investment in their rotting capital city.

The mindset of Wales was against, not for. Against England, against the European Union, against the wider world.

This was a place where ideas were opposed on the grounds that they polluted the very rich character and way of life that makes Wales what it is. Wales is a proud nation, but a small nation on the brink of poverty, with a gold mine that had run out of gold, an unprofitable steelworks under threat of closure, a pile of real estate in its capital city that was a bubble in mid-burst, but speak to any of your Welsh friends for ten minutes and their sense of national pride will bubble over. It certainly does when ten thousand of them are singing the national anthem in the quarter finals of the European football championships and you're in the crowd and have neglected to learn the words. Pride cannot be measured in money and paradise cannot be found in industrialised retail, but I suddenly realised that I hadn't seen a chain store in the full week I'd been in the country. I hadn't given a penny to some mega Luxembourg or Dublin headquartered institution whose aims were deliberately to overtake local cultures with their laminated shopfits and suck money out of communities and into offshore tax-dodging schemes. And I was grateful for that. Maybe I might have signed the petition against the Co-Op in Camarthen too.

To get to Oxwich, it was necessary to drive through the Gower peninsula, about whose scenery I had heard glowing reports, and we left the M4 hoping that the journey would for once be every bit as good as the destination. I wasn't disappointed; this part of Glamorgan was the first area of the United Kingdom to be designated an Area of Outstanding Natural Beauty and in the glorious sun of the last day of the summer holiday it was easy to see why; the composition of the countryside was heavenly. The soft hills were laid out like a crumpled duvet, the landscape peered downhill towards the sea and the vegetation suggested a touch of the tropics and plenty of sand in the soil. Everywhere I looked outside the car, I could see Gower's fine drives on the offside, cute cuts through outfields, smooth sweeps that befitted the elegance of one of England's greatest batsmen – I'm sorry, I appear to have drifted into describing the strokeplay of former England cricketer *David* Gower, so I shall return to the point, which is to say that whilst dreamily passing through this real-life landscape painting, I noticed something I'd never seen before: a road sign proclaiming a 25 mph speed limit. The sight of it immediately put me in a dismal frame of mind, because there's only one possible way that a 25 mph limit could have been arrived at – a meeting at the Speed Limit Awareness in Gower (SLAG) sub-committee where a thin-lipped woman in a trouser-suit said "thirty" and a fat man in a Homer Simpson tie said "twenty" and, neither budging, we were stuck with the mad compromise of having to drive at 25 mph. A camel is a horse designed by a committee.

I've always wondered whether speed enforcement is actually more concerned with making money than actually trying to reduce the number of people who have their lives seriously changed for the worse on the roads every year, and I strongly suspect it might be. I have three cases in point on this:

Firstly, if speed cameras are deliberately placed at accident black spots – as I would hope they are – then what would be the problem with displaying the speed limit on the back of the camera so we all slowed down? Surely by not doing this, they're issuing more speeding tickets?

Secondly, the twisty rural road from the holiday cottage I'd been staying in (Aberporth) to Mwnt beach, mentioned at the start of the chapter. The road was an absolute deathtrap – a winding single track road with hedgerows rising on either side to above car roof height. And yet, the speed limit for that road is 60, as designated by a 'National Speed Limit Applies' sign as the lane begins. If you told anyone you'd hit 59 on it earlier in the day they'd have looked at you like you were a psychopath intent on killing and shouldn't be allowed to drive. But you'd be perfectly within the law.

Thirdly, the one time I was sent on a speed awareness course, our host for the evening gave a brief introduction and then asked if there were any questions before he began. I put up my hand. "What happens to the £100 each of us has paid to be here?" The room was filled with the sound of people shifting in their seats uncomfortably. You see, when booking in for the course, I was given options of a morning, afternoon or evening session across a 4-day week at this venue, one of six available to me in the locality. Looking around the room, I counted 30 of us. 30 x £100 is of course £3,000, multiplied three times that day is £9,000, multiplied by four times that week is £36,000, multiplied by 52 weeks in a year is £1,872,000, multiplied by six venues is £11,232,000. And I wanted to know where that £11 million a year was going, considering the evidently minimal running costs. I was expecting an answer along the lines of road safety improvement programmes or general police coffers. The answer was neither:

"Your £100 sir, goes to AA Drivetech plc, who are the private company running this course."

"You mean a private company, with a CEO and shareholders and staff with company cars and annual bonuses and everything? My £100 has gone to them, and it's just £100 of the £1.9 million they're raking in this year just from this room, £30,000 of which you're being paid, the balance building a palace in the Cayman Islands? Presumably they had to bid for the contract to run this course and so have to catch a certain number of drivers to make a profit? Is that what's happening here?"

But I didn't say that because our host had the power of pass or fail over me and I didn't want to frighten the horses too much in that context, but you get my point.

Goodness, what an outburst! Anyway, we are now climbing out of the car at Oxwich Beach itself, where we discovered something that was going to have more of an impact on our enjoyment of this beach than any amount of sunshine possibly could and that didn't feature in any of the Google images we'd looked at before deciding to travel here: Wind.

You do not realise just how much of a downer the wind can put on your day until you are caught out in it. It was relentless; never changing speed or direction, it provided an onslaught that scuppered any thoughts of a sand-free sandwich, fruitful play with a beachball, the use of a lilo, or any of the usual seaside capers that we'd expected to be the memory of the day. Not only that, but the wind appeared to be blowing across a farmer's field that had just been spread with muck, so all in all, it wasn't everything we were hoping for as a family day out.

The beach itself was a gently sloping horseshoe between two headlands about a mile apart. It was about 200 metres from wave break point to the dunes at the back of the beach, where all the day-trippers had set up camp. The wind really was something else; it swept waves of sand at knee-height, sahara-like towards the water whither which Little Miss Procter and I trudged, where it completed the unusual trick of managing to send waves back out to sea before they could fold over and crash. The sea was shallow for quite a long way out – this was not a sea that could be swum in, just paddled in, ankle-deep for as long as was entertaining, which was not very long at all in the wind. We returned to join Debs and Master Procter who declared that they'd had enough of the beach and were ready to leave Oxwich and ready to leave Wales.

The lie of the land meant that rather than retrace our steps north to the M4, the quickest way home was to head east into Swansea and we were glad we did, for it gave us a chance to see Mumbles. The only thing I knew about Mumbles was that it was where Catherine Zeta-Jones was from, and the only thing I really knew about Catherine Zeta Jones is that she had humble beginnings but had managed to bag Michael Douglas as her career improved. This narrative was such a pleasing arc that I'd somehow got it into my head that Catherine Zeta-Jones was the same sort of person as the lady in the Cardigan petrol station who was so excited about her Pot Noodle dinner. As such, I'd come to visualise Mumbles, with its unappealing name, to be the sort of steeply-banked rows of terraced houses familiar to viewers of *Bread* or *Gavin and Stacey*. Well, it was about as far from that as it was possible to get – a sort of Welsh Malibu, where agreeably leafy boulevards and grand seafront houses gave way to the bustling strip along the seafront, behind which parks housed boating lakes featuring giant pedalo swans, crazy-golf and inflatable obstacle courses. The proportions and ambience of the place reminded me of the Promenade des Anglais along the front of Nice. I decided that I liked Swansea very much and that I could live there if required. It's just a shame that with the decision having been made to stop the European Union from funding Wales, Swansea, and indeed Wales, may never look this good again.

10. Basingstoke

"Away is good, but home is best."

Swedish proverb

Nick, what are you doing? It's the final chapter, you've taken me to the northern and southern edges of civilized Europe, you've shown me the Pacific and Atlantic Oceans, you've taken me far further than ever intended, which was nowhere. So why, of all places, does the book climax in Basingstoke? Basingstoke?

Well, this isn't, and never was, a book about destinations, it's about journeys.

The unstoppable march of globalisation somewhat reduced the wonder of travel to at times a grim certainty that you can always get an Egg McMuffin for breakfast while staring at Google images of your next destination, whichever city in the world you are in. Travel now doesn't mean what it did in the era when I went to Luxembourg, and whilst I've always tried to see the local colour in the places I've been – and hopefully point some of it out to you – I've become aware that the new experiences that travel always brings don't have to be sought out on the other side of the world.

You know by now that I didn't mean to write this book – the idea only occurred to me about three quarters of the way through my travels, and as I got deeper into the writing process, I became more perplexed about what to do for the last chapter. Which of the destinations should it be? Or should I abandon the 'accidental tourist' theme and get on a plane to San Marino / Andorra / Malta in order to write about another semi-obscure destination? Or should I just go for a walk in my hometown and write about what I saw while out and about? I had a gradual realisation over time that the answer was somewhere between the two – as it usually is. I would go not to my nearest town, but the next-nearest – one I'd never been to before - and write about that. My hypothesis was that I didn't need to change time zones to capture the spirit of travel. The joy of travel was probably there, on my global doorstep, waiting for me to discover it. So off I set, perhaps the first travel writer ever to make Basingstoke his destination.

It turns out I didn't have to go too far for my first adventure.

Because big trips need planning for, I wandered to my local supermarket one Saturday for snacks for the journey. It was after dropping a bag of wasabi peas and a couple of cans of ginger ale into the basket (the ideal travel snacks for a journey; you simply *can't* consume them quickly) that I turned and noticed some discount bins that contained a very hard-to-refuse bargain – many cans of proper foamy brown ale had been madly marked down to half their normal price, yet still had a good six months on their Best Before date. Before anyone else could get their hands in there, I picked up all 17 cans, took them to the till, and popped them into the carrier bags I'd brought with me. If I'd known I'd be buying 17 cans of beer that morning, I probably wouldn't have selected transparent carrier bags, but I figured I could get them home without anyone important noticing – maybe they'd be distracted by the large 3x3 bag of toilet roll I would be carrying instead.

As I approached my house, I noticed a middle-aged woman walking up my garden path towards my front door. She was just about to ring my doorbell when, suppressing my embarrassment at my cargo, I broke the ice and rather sheepishly said hello. I recognised her the moment she turned around: it was Theresa May. She was my local MP and, whatever else you may say about her, was doing the rounds of her local constituency, which is something I appreciated. But holding 17 cans of cut-price beer and a large pack of bog roll on a Saturday morning was not how I'd anticipated meeting a world leader. One of her colleagues standing three paces away from her scribbled something down in a notebook.

"Mr Procter?" enquired one of the most important people in the world, notably stealing a glance at my cargo. "Theresa May. I'm listening to my constituents and would like to hear about any issues you'd like to raise with me. Is there anything you'd like to ask or any matters you'd like to discuss?"

They say you get the measure of a man by how he reacts when taken by surprise.

You might think that someone who can write a book cannot be at a loss for words, but nothing prepares you for this sort of standoff. Many seconds into the long and deafening silence that followed the question, I mumbled some half-formed ideas about inequality and not fully able being to comprehend the ideology to which she'd subscribed that rich people should still be prioritised in their quest to accumulate even more needless wealth at a time when food banks were in use, and then reverted to a cliché and started moaning about the state of Britain's trains. The most powerful person in the land listened diligently to my answer, made notes as I spoke – pausing to wipe her nose with a disposable travel-tissue as she did so – and a few days later, to her credit, I received a signed letter on stiff cream paper responding to my points about inequality – mainly stating the measures already taken to reduce it by her government and, seemingly without irony, how the Conservative party were more interested in doing this than the Labour party. A similar 'we're making it better' formula followed about the trains.

Buying a train ticket in England is an unnecessarily difficult procedure; back in chapter 1 when I was a student living in France, every train station in the land had an identical touchscreen ticket machine positioned at its entrance, from which you could in half a dozen touches buy a ticket to travel from any station to any station for whichever day you wished to travel on. That was 20 years ago, but the idea still does not appear to have caught on in the UK. British ticket machines assume that the intent to travel more than 24 hours in advance cannot conceivably exist, and you are therefore restricted to buying a ticket for travel that day or the following day, but no further ahead under any circumstances. So, having previously found it impossible to acquire a ticket for travel to Basingstoke on the following Tuesday, I explained my frustration to my dear Debs, who, once I had calmed down, offered to buy my ticket on the Monday evening when she was passing through the station. Now, let me say that Debs is an intelligent woman. She received the highest grade possible in mathematics when taking her high school exams and then had the luxury of being able to abandon it as a subject and pursue modern languages at university, where she passed with flying colours and probably would have gone on to study an MA had I not distracted her. But even with all this intelligence, the machine still managed to trick her, and Mrs P bought a ticket for travel later that evening before realising the error of her ways and buying the right ticket. So on Tuesday morning I took all the tickets and receipts to the station and asked one of the members of staff to please refund the Monday ticket.

"I'm sorry, I can't."

I genuinely did not know what to say.

"You bought it from the machines. I can only refund tickets you bought from the ticket office."

"But…" I pleaded, sensing this conversation was going down a well-trodden path.

"If you buy a ticket from me, I can refund you. It you buy a ticket from the machine, you have to write to Head Office."

"But I don't want to write to Head Office. I want to talk to you now, because we're both here…" I flashed a winning smile and made my eye twinkle.

"Well, I can do it, but it'll have to be approved by Maidenhead, and it'll take up to 28 days."

This seemed a totally unhelpful way of processing quite a simple transaction and I was disappointed that the 'yes' in this sentence hadn't been unveiled in her first utterance to me. So I said:

"Thank you so much, that would be wonderful."

"Of course…" my ticket-lady continued, "…the responsibility is on you as the customer to buy the right ticket in the first place," thus introducing an element of doubt into the conversation that she had in her previous sentence eliminated. I pondered whether to take issue with her on this obviously hideous policy or keep quiet and hope the wind changed direction again.

"Fill this in."

A thin pad of A4 carbon paper was pushed under the glass to me and I was instructed to fill in every line and box of it. "ONLY THIS FORM CAN BE USED FOR ALL CUSTOMER REFUNDS WITH EFFECT FROM JANUARY 1ST 1996" proclaimed the bottom line of the form in capital letters. I stood there for ten seconds, wondering if the ticket-lady's good mood and burgeoning sense of initiative was going to extend to offering me a pen with which to fill the form in.

The silence was broken unexpectedly by a tannoy announcement in the middle distance: "PLATFORM 3 FOR THE 9.17 SERVICE TO READING." That was my train. Suddenly, I was on the clock.

"Can I have a pen please?" The lady, who I had decided looked like a Pauline, got up from her chair and wordlessly shuffled off into the back office while passengers on the platform got their belongings together and began to stand up and crane their necks down the track. I began to froth a little inside. Half an eternity later, Pauline came back. I wrote down my full address, every number that was embossed on my credit card and a full written apology justifying why I'd erroneously bought the wrong ticket and waited another half an eternity while Pauline fed all this information into a computer, using only her index finger to press one key at a time. After this, all tickets were threaded through a reader. Then Pauline stopped and did nothing while she stared at the machine. I saw my train arrive.

"Do you need anything more from me, or can I go and get my train?" I suggested as I began to calculate whether I had both the time and fitness level to run over the footbridge with two bags and a black Americano.

"Just wait."

My froth began to heat. The train stopped at the platform, Pauline oblivious to it.

"There you go, refund will be done in 28 days!" Pauline cheerfully concluded, genuinely thinking that this meant good customer service before adding "of course, one day the machines will take over, and my job won't be needed." This cheered me up for about half a second before I realised the grave truth in what she had said.

"Mine too," I replied, watching my train slide away.

**

But it wasn't the worst piece of customer service I'd receive that day. I had an errand to run in Reading first before I could take my train on to Basingstoke. Moving house a few years ago, Debs and I had bought a new sofa for the new lounge and a circular armchair that whirled around on its base, primarily for the children to play on. One fine day, the whirling had been a little too enthusiastic and the chair had clonked off its base. So I took the day's opportunity to pop into the shop where we'd bought it – let's call it Doncaster Furniture Store – where I was immediately attended to by a member of staff. Our exchange was thus:

"Hello, can I help you?"

"Hello, I bought a swivel chair from here a couple of years ago. It's broken. Can you help me get it fixed somehow?"

"OK sir, what you need to do is phone the store you bought it from and tell them the problem, and they'll arrange a repair for you."

"I bought it from this store."

"That's right sir, phone the store and someone will be able to help."

"But we're standing here right now. Can't you help? I mean, we're here, talking face to face, and I think we're getting on quite well."

"I can't help you sir, I'm Sales. You need to speak to Customer Service."

"Are the Customer Service people sitting in that frosted glass office over there, towards the back of the showroom but clearly visible inside?"

"Yes sir."

"As it's quite quiet right now, do you think you could go in there and speak to them?"

He paused. It was clearly The Right Thing To Do, but his training had not accounted for being confronted with such startling logic.

"Ok, but they'll probably say no, because they're not actually speaking to you."

"Shall I go in there myself?"

"I'm afraid customers aren't allowed in the office, sir."

"Do you see that this conversation isn't really helping the customer very much?"

"I'll go and speak to them, sir." He walked off.

"Do you need my name or address or something that identifies me?" He didn't appear to have considered that this information could in any way relevant to solving my problem.

"Actually yes, can I take your order number?"

"I bought it five years ago, I'm afraid I don't walk around with the knowledge of where the paperwork for my armchair purchase is in my head."

[Without a hint of empathy] "Can I take your name and address please?"

"Yes Nick, or Nicholas – spelt with an H – Procter – spelt 'e-r' at the end."

"OK, so P-r-o-c-t-o-r-e-r?"

This happens a lot. I give the salesman my address. Pause as he goes off to the office.

"I've spoken to them sir, they say they can't find you on the system."

"That's a shame, because I very definitely did buy it from here, and I'm pretty sure I can remember my home address, to where it was delivered."

"I'm sorry sir, I can't help you."

"Do you have a phone number you can ring that isn't the store, but a central customer service department or something?"

"I'll go and ask."

I took a seat.

"Sorry sir, we have no record of you, you'll have to phone in."

I walked out of the store without saying anything. What is wrong with people? I phoned the store a couple of days later and they identified me immediately and arranged a free repair straight away.

**

The train journey to Basingstoke became uneventful as Berkshire morphed imperceptibly into Hampshire, where I began to switch off a little and let the train cradle me into a pleasing state of relaxation. Just as I'd reached it, some low level murmurings began at the far end of the carriage about a bag being in the walkway, followed by some slightly louder murmuring about identifying the owner of the bag, then another question to someone else about whose bag this was, and a now a question to the carriage about who claimed ownership for the next suitcase and I realised that every bag on the train was being asked to be identified by its owner. Behind me was the luggage rack, and in the luggage rack was one of my bags. My rest was therefore disrupted by the slow but inescapable build-up as the train guard shuffled through the walkway rousing old ladies from their chat and causing younglings to pluck headphones from their ears. Finally it was my turn.

"Who's bag is this in the luggage rack?" I continued to recline with my eyes closed. "Who's bag is this in the luggage rack please?" (I know I've misspelt "whose" but I feel sure that if I'd asked the guard to write his words down, that's how he would have spelt it.)

"That's my bag. What's up?" Gary (he looked like a Gary) leant forward and stared at me before unblinkingly declaring that since there had been a terrorist incident that morning in continental Europe, they were taking precautions.

Now, I am nothing but grateful to all the Home Office employees who spend their days looking at their computer screens between parted fingers and their nights wide awake in rigid fear at the covert horrors plotted by evildoers in the world, but when there's a security breach on a different landmass, does that really compromise the safety of every commuter on a midmorning shuttle between Reading and Basingstoke?

**

Basingstoke presented itself to me in sunshine and it didn't look half bad. That said, it didn't look half good either, for it is not possible in central Basingstoke to escape the sense that the town is made of prefabricated buildings and exists not because it is at a water source or a river crossing or a gap between hills, but rather because civil servants had decided that this is where the people were going to live, like it or not.

The most curious thing about Basingstoke is that after leaving the train station, you are funnelled, whether you wish it or not, across the road and into the town's shopping centre. Not the main shopping high-street, you understand, but an actual commercial shopping mall with lockable glass doors and shiny tiled floors and air conditioning. Festival Place, it's called, though the festival clearly wasn't in place today. I began to take note of the shops as I passed them. Apart from all the usual chains, I was interested to see not one but two shops specialising in clothing for Britain's flourishing obesity market and three Greggs The Bakers. I wondered if the two were connected. I walked past a Poundland, and then a couple of minutes later another Poundland too.

We were in the run-up to Valentine's Day and whilst I had (let the record state) organised a lovely on-the-day surprise for my Debs, there was still the business of a physical present for me to attend to. I decided to buy her a new necklace, and browsing online that morning, the Accessorize website suggested something that would fit the bill was in store. As I looked for Accessorize, I walked past Marks and Spencer.

Let me say here and now that I have the utmost respect for and pride in Marks and Spencer. If I am ever made British Ambassador to a parallel country on Mars and am asked to do a show and tell on five things that are magnificently British, those five things will be Marks and Spencer, The Times, Radio 4, Stephen Fry, and The 2012 Olympic Opening Ceremony. But – and I'm really sorry to fill the most recent few minutes of your life with tales of poor customer service, but this is Marks and Spencer, and Marks and Spencer isn't meant to be as bad the train companies or the out of town furniture stores and I'm concerned that the infection is spreading.

I noticed a denim dress in the window on one of the mannequins and thought this to be just Debs's style. Coupling it with the silver jewellery seemed a capital idea and I popped inside. Marks and Spencer have chosen not to group together all the dresses in one place, all the suits in another, all the shoes elsewhere and so on, so when I entered Marks and Spencer, I was confronted with an array of recently-manufactured sub-brands that were meant to mean something to me, such as Per Una, Indigo, North Coast, Blue Harbour, Autograph, and so on. I wandered towards a bit of racking where I could see some jeans, but a brief search revealed no denim dress. I wandered towards the Indigo section where dark blue clothes should logically live. No denim dress. I wandered around a little bit more. No denim dress. In desperation, I rode the escalator up to the first floor and three quarters of the way up, walked back down the escalator for a few seconds in the style of Mr Bean to maintain a vantage point from where I could scan the whole shop floor. No denim dress. I came back down and found a shop assistant to whom I ventured that I'd seen a denim dress in the window that looked like a great Valentine's Day present and with the day itself not being very far away now, could she, you know, show me where it was? Well, I followed her wanderings much in the way a toddler follows its mother, but possibly with a lesser measure of faith in where she was heading. First of all we went to the jeans section (I sighed a little inside and weakly explained that I'd already had a look) then with a heavy heart, we trudged on to Indigo where no denim dress had in the intervening time teleported itself into existence and it was meekly explained to me that the window displays were changed every few days so she couldn't guarantee that the dress was anywhere in the store. How is this allowed to happen?

On to Accessorize to find the necklace, but simple jewellery didn't seem to be anywhere on sale. I passed a section specialising in the sort of Egyptian-themed jewellery that Cleopatra might have been buried in, some ostentatiously diamonique chokers, giant pairs of circles that were unclear if they were for the wrists or the ears, little sparkly owls that Accessorize clearly hoped a woman would pay to let perch on her breast, and a column of bikinis, anklets, toe rings, sarongs and flip flops, because it was winter. But could I see the necklace from the website? I could not. I shuffled back out into the street, feeling a double-whammy of disappointment, unable to buy either of the presents I had hoped. What now? Go to the pub, of course.

If the British high street is a faded force, then the pub has almost died out completely. In 1979, there were approximately 70,000 pubs in the UK. In 2015, that number was 50,000. But seemingly bucking this trend was Wetherspoons. If pubs back in 1979 were filled with a blueish haze of cigarette smoke, this pub today had been overtaken by pollution of a different kind. Several groups of young men in their 20s were just sitting there staring at their phones (not an activity I mind in itself) but – and here's the thing – they all had their volume turned up and were each trying to consume some sort of noisy content whilst sitting in each other's company. All of them, at the same time. Out loud. And in a confined public place too. I couldn't understand it.

I have a difference of opinion with myself on Wetherspoons. On the plus side, the food and drink is inexpensive and tasty, there's no muzak to interfere with conversation, no smoking, the lighting is just right and the pub is the right size to feel a sense of comfort and anonymity at the same time. Yet meanwhile, and I really don't mean to sound all hoity-toity here, Wetherspoons has a clientele from a particular walk of life which is not mine. I looked around; in the middle of a weekday, the place was three-quarters full, noisy and mainly populated by fraying, greying grandfathers recounting anecdotes that weren't funny when first told and hadn't aged well since. They were uniformly hunched over their pints and had eyes like – excuse my venture into dirty language but it is the best simile I have ever heard – piss-holes in the snow. The women were either older than me with body shapes that put me in mind of binbags half-filled with water or younger than me with a broad back and a cackling, shrieking manner that almost constituted a breach of the peace. The décor was plasticky and laminated, the staff were dressed all in black – very possibly paid for by themselves if Wetherspoon's employment practices were were anything to go by, and the beer was clearly a little too temptingly cheap for some – a rare example of a low price causing suffering for both supplier and customer. I'd hoped there'd be a football match on a screen to pass the time but Wetherspoons doesn't screen sport because it puts beer prices up, which I sort of respect. On the floor next to the adjacent table to mine, a champagne ice bucket had been employed to catch drips from a leaky roof – an apt metaphor. At that moment, a tray of glasses was dropped behind the bar. Everyone cheered like it was the best thing that would happen that day. Tiring of gulping beer, I located a menu – a giant laminated card, standing upright on my table like a gravestone - and started to work my way through it in search of a meal. It took me about twenty minutes. I have never been faced with such a bewildering array of choice. The menu was so large it overhung the edges of the circular table I was sitting at and passers-by kept clipping its corner as they brushed past. Special offers abounded, but certain ones only applied on certain days of the week and/or only at certain times of certain days. Certain meals could be embellished with avocado or sticky sauce or corn on the cob or melted blue cheese or scores of other items, many of which must, statistically be rarely ordered and therefore lurk in the fridge for as long as may be needed, perhaps even longer. The pricing structure depended on the combination of the food chosen and it was a genuine effort to calculate what was eligible for me to buy at this point in time and how much it would all ultimately cost, never mind what I wanted. Some food combinations included certain drinks in the meal deal. The drink I had already ordered complied with some offers, but not others. My appetite bewildered itself out of me and having nothing better to do while I drank, I counted the items on the menu. Including all combinations from starter to coffee, there were 173 choices. I dined only on delicious beer before going on somewhere else.

Minutes later, I was in a department store, idly fingering polo t-shirts. My eye was caught by a green and white checked shirt that sparked joy in me from the rack (this is my rule when it comes to buying clothes – I don't buy them, they have to buy me) and I wandered over and inspected it only to find that whilst I liked it, I still, on balance, preferred having £30 in my life to owning it, so I wandered on. Two minutes later, I saw an identical shirt hanging on a 50% off rail. But not in my size. There was only one thing to do.

I laid both shirts down at the till, gave the winning smile that had influenced Pauline at the train station earlier in the day and enquired of the lady behind the desk whether she would sell me the shirt in my size at the lower price? Shirley (let's call her) looked genuinely perplexed at this request and was lost for words, as if she had never conceived that this might happen. She repeated my question back to me so the enormity of what I was trying to achieve could have time to fully dawn on her.

"I'll do a price check on the till and see what it says," trilled Shirley with an uncertain face. The till beeped and the display read "Men's shirt. £6." Shirley's eyes bluescreened and she pressed a panic button under the till. A tall child called Ollie came over and put into words for me everything I had just experienced with all the vacant peppiness of a local radio DJ, before explaining that he was going to call Sarah over for help, thus making his role in the interaction redundant. Sarah was much more like it, so professional that I wondered if she was someone down from Head Office for the day because the CEO wanted everyone to spend some time reconnecting with the shop floor. Sarah breezed over with calm efficiency, glanced at the screen, wrinkled her nose and tilted her head to the side a couple of times as though trying to solve a puzzle before pressing a couple of buttons and stating an unfussy "all sorted sir, £6 please." I wondered how any department store could profitably operate when three employees were needed to sell a shirt for £6. The answer was in Monaco: This was British Home Stores.

**

Not long after this visit, Debs and I were at dinner with close friends Andrew and Ruth. As our four toddlers slept upstairs, we all concluded that we were now unarguably in life's middle generation and wondered what to do with this new status. I ventured the opinion that whilst I had nothing to legitimately complain about in life, I'd begun to notice a certain ennui creeping in to my leisure time. A brewing sense of having seen all this before and that I was beginning to bottom out on life's experiences. I'd sipped enough real ale to know what it tasted like. I'd hit enough golf balls for the pleasure to wear off. I'd watched enough football matches on television to understand that there'd be a winner and a loser in a couple of hours' time, whatever happened. I'd sat on plenty of beaches, I'd climbed plenty of hills. What else was there to do?

Shortly after this, Andrew and Ruth presented me with something totally unexpected and guaranteed to restore lost wonder. And it would happen in Basingstoke.

There is literally nothing I would like to do less in the world than jump out of an aeroplane, so the notion of a parachute jump has always been totally off limits to me, but Andrew and Ruth had offered me ten minutes in a parachute simulator – all of the thrill of parachuting without every fibre of your being screaming at you that this was it: Death was seconds away. On Youtube, it looked like a circus safety net had been strung across a large horizontal fan and the column above the fan fenced in, enabling the rider to hover in mid-air. It seemed like such a simple concept that I wondered why no-one had thought of making it available as an experience in a large provincial town until now. And here I was, about to – thanks to the consideration and no doubt considerable generosity of my friends – go and have a go myself.

But Andrew and Ruth are not just friends, they are the best friends that God puts in your life like a family that you chose for yourself. Not only had they given me a voucher, but they'd made it into a whole family double-date incorporating a couple of hours at a waterslide park as well. It was in this waterslide park that I began to notice something new. Stripped to my waist and surrounded by men and women similarly half undressed, I began to notice something. Most people were tattooed. Andrew, Ruth, Debs and I had come to be in the minority. I wasn't quite sure how this had happened. Were we the weird and unusual people because we had never thought it a good thing to subject ourselves to the pain of a blade cutting through our skin and leaving an ink blot that would remain on our skin until our coffins burned? The action of a tattooing needle is enough to put me off in itself. Think of a sewing machine repeatedly jabbing itself into your flesh 150 times a second. I can't think why anyone would ever choose to do it, or why the first person ever did it and what the world thought of him.

Tattoos have only been around for the last 100 years. They were initially a badge of honour for sailors, who upon some maritime achievement would have an emblem inscribed upon them in a suitably macho way, but at last count (2010, according to an article I read in The Guardian) one fifth of all British adults are now inked. Among 16 to 44 year olds, it's 29%. In America, 40% of those aged between 26 and 40 have gone under the needle. 14% of British teachers have them. Distinguished broadcaster David Dimbleby and refined actor Nigel Havers both have scorpions on their shoulders. At the dawn of the 21st century, there were 300 tattoo parlours in the UK. A decade later, there were 1500. 1500. In the leafy town of Wokingham recently, I saw a permanent sign outside a tattoo parlour there that said "WE WILL NOT TATTOO BABIES" How many people in a wealthy town on the Surrey/Berkshire border are requesting that their baby be tattooed so that a sign need be erected to address this problem? Call me an old fusty, but I simply can't understand this need to express oneself in such an irreversible way.

Snapping out of my daydream, quietly agog at all the fleshy smudges being paraded in front of me by Basingstoke's finest, Andrew and Ruth informed me that this waterslide park contained a feature the like of which I not only would never have seen before, but also never considered a possibility. I was informed that there was a waterslide that I should ride with no prior knowledge of what was to happen to me in it, but I was just to ride from start to finish and report on what happened. Now, if you know how hard it is to avoid spoilers in this internet-saturated life of ours, or even if you have tried to avoid finding out the football scores until *Match of the Day* comes on, then you have perhaps understood 10% of what it is like to be stood among excitable teenagers for twenty minutes queuing for a waterslide whilst at all costs trying to block out squealed tales of what the waterslide is like. About halfway through the 20 minutes of queueing, in swimming trunks, between tribes of excited 17 year old girls in swimsuits, I began to feel that I was too old now to be doing this sort of thing. But eventually, I arrived at the mouth of the chute, and with the slight sense of 'everyone's watching me because there's nothing else to watch', climbed into the rubber ring I was presented with and launched myself into oblivion. It was one of these waterslides that loops around outside the building for half a minute before returning you to the warmth of indoors, and as I descended the curves, I wondered what this unique experience was going to be. So far, so normal. But suddenly, it happened. Shortly after re-entering the building, I entered a level section and seemed to run out of momentum, my speed reducing to a crawl. Health and Safety signs ahead suddenly abounded, warning me to KEEP HANDS AND LEGS INSIDE AT ALL TIMES. I rounded a gentle bend, and, at a speed that bordered on the insignificant, without warning passed over strong jets of water that proceeded to launch me *uphill* to a new section of the slide. I had never considered that a waterslide might be contrived to power its rider up a slope. I laughed uncontrollably like a child and, at something approaching the speed of a car on a motorway, descended down a wide drop into the exit run-out. I declared to Andrew, Ruth and Debs that it was quite the best thing I had done in years and, my appetite whetted, went to ride another slide. This one was more predictable, but more profound also in its climax – if ever 'profound' has been an adjective employed to describe a waterslide. It had one of those 'black hole' finishes where you are slingshot into and around a giant bowl with a plughole in the bottom of it. It was both one of the most excruciating and prophetic experiences of my life; I was fired into the bowl at such a precise angle that I must have spent thirty seconds orbiting the pit. It's a long time when you're doing it, I can tell you. All the time, you are prepared for the drop through the drain, but the moment takes an eternity to arrive. I was reminded of the glorious medical abbreviation "CTD" used in British hospitals as part of doctors' official annotation – "circling the drain" meaning a patient clearly is on the point of death and it won't be long now. And here I was, circling the drain, unable to escape my fate and unable to look away from the vortex through which I'd disappear for a full half minute until, inescapably, I dropped shoulder-first through the hole to find myself diagonally upside down, comfortably out of my depth in a cylinder of what must have been three metres of water. It was the closest to the feeling of death I have ever come and I was reminded that no matter what I achieve in life or manage to distract myself with, I am always circling the drain. And so are you.

**

I am not alien to risk, but parachuting was always, and will always be, beyond me. I therefore thank Andrew and Ruth for giving me my kicks on the ground. My instructor was called Gareth, and he showed me and a group of strangers into a little room filled with lockers and TV screens, in which we were shown a short video which rather grandly informed us that what we were about to experience was not a ride, but a sporting discipline. This was not simply a one-off thrill, but our first entry into the competitive sporting world of base-flying, or whatever they called it, I wasn't writing anything down. We were told about the various shapes we could form in mid-air, with enough training (and lucrative repeat visits) – 'Spiderman', 'Double Eagles' etc. Then the video finished and Gavin came back into the room and ordered us to take off any jewellery and excess clothing before he furnished us with blue jumpsuits which were to be our defence against the updraught we were shortly to face. Gareth then furnished us with those wraparound plastic goggles you only see on parachutists and a pair of yellow foam earplugs, with instructions to remove neither once we were in the flight chamber. This is where the nerves started to build.

There was perhaps thirty feet of void under the floor mesh, and happily they'd concealed the fans around a bend in the tube so we could be spared the sight of whirling blades as we floated face down. The chamber was probably ten feet across, but the biggest surprise was the height above – there was maybe forty feet of chimney which immediately brought about the thought of what would happen if, when trying to arrange one's body into the Lying Leopard position, one accidentally found oneself splattering against the ceiling? It didn't bear thinking about, but the potential was there for all to see. Gareth walked me into the chamber and tossed me onto the wind. I spun around like a helicopter in distress before Gareth caught me and put his face in front of mine and then, with a knowing look and against the roar of the fans, extended a thumb and little finger from his fist. This was a hand signal from the safety video to keep my arms and legs out; how I wish I'd paid more attention to it. After a few false starts, I was eventually flying. Hovering on a cushion of air, suspended from nothing, and able to rotate my palms to deflect the wind and broadly steer myself over to a clutch of spectators from where my friends and family were waving at me. I had truly experienced the most white-knuckle experience of my life, and I'd done it in Basingstoke. My theory was correct. I didn't need to go far or be too deliberate to experience the joys of travel.

And that is my point. Between the summer of 2013 and 2017, I had – without really at any point ever intending to, socialised with monkeys on top of a mountain in the sea in Gibraltar, chatted naked with work colleagues in a Finnish sauna, ascended Seattle's Space Needle, climbed an ancient brick observatory in central Copenhagen, seen the birthplace of the Boy Scout movement in Poole Harbour, gazed at the Sistine Chapel ceiling in The Vatican, rubbed shoulders with millionaires in Monte Carlo, and seen dolphins in the wild in Wales. But my conclusion at the end of all this was that it hadn't been necessary to board a plane and cover thousands of miles to see exceptional things. Often, these exceptional things were closed, or out of order. It's nice to go, of course, but a visit to my nearest unvisited town showed me there is wonder to be had just outside our front doors too.

So, if there's a point to all of this, a nugget of truth that I can share, it's that all this unexpected travel has taught me that it isn't necessary to be deliberate about travel and seek out glamourous destinations – indeed it isn't even necessary to travel at all to find wonder in the world; it's everywhere.

Nick Procter

About the author:

Nick Procter grew up in Kingston upon Thames, was educated at Tiffin School, then the University of Warwick and has been making it up as he goes along ever since. The son of an airline employee, Nick had visited all five continents before becoming a teenager and has continued to travel obsessively at every possible opportunity since. Just before publishing, he unexpectedly went to Romania, heads to Canada next month and has Sweden on the radar too. So there might be a sequel, but he has a wife and two children under 11, a full-time job, he's actively involved in his local church on weeknights and on Sundays, coaches a children's football team on Friday nights and Saturday mornings and runs the @QuotesBryson account on Twitter. What you have just read took him three years to write.

Printed in Poland
by Amazon Fulfillment
Poland Sp. z o.o., Wrocław